CULTURES OF POPULAR MUSIC

Andy Bennett

OPEN UNIVERSITY PRESS
Buckingham · Philadelphia

Open University Press
Celtic Court
22 Ballmoor
Buckingham
MK18 1XW

email: enquiries@openup.co.uk
world wide web: www.openup.co.uk

and
325 Chestnut Street
Philadelphia, PA 19106, USA

First Published 2001

A catalogue record of this book is available from the British Library

ISBN 0 335 20250 0 (pb)   0 335 20251 9 (hb)

Library of Congress Cataloging-in-Publication Data
Bennett, Andy, 1963–
    Cultures of popular music/Andy Bennett.
        p.   cm. – (Issues in cultural and media studies)
    Includes bibliographical references (p.) and index.
    ISBN 0-335-20251-9 – ISBN 0-335-20250-0 (pbk.)
    1. Popular music – Social aspects.   2. Popular culture.   3. Music and youth.
    I. Title. II. Series.

ML3470.B448 2001
306.4′84–dc21   2001021422

Typeset by Type Study, Scarborough
Printed and bound by CPI Group (UK) Ltd, Croydon, CR0 4YY

This book is for Moni

CONTENTS

SERIES EDITOR'S FOREWORD

'Popular music' is one of those phrases that somehow manages to be both precise and elusive in its meaning at the same time. Everyone knows just what they mean when they say it, yet seldom find themselves in complete agreement with anyone else's preferred definition. Closer scrutiny reveals that the words 'popular' and 'music' both carry the burden of a troubled history, each of them having been made the subject of intense cultural conflict over time, space and place. Echoes of these conflicts continue to resonate throughout current debates in important ways, especially when questions are raised about who has the power to define 'what counts' as popular music today.

Andy Bennett's *Cultures of Popular Music* explores a diverse array of popular music styles in relation to their audiences, from 1950s rock 'n' roll to contemporary dance music. Beginning with an overview of the socio-economic circumstances which gave rise to the development of the post-war youth market, the discussion promptly proceeds to identify several key technological innovations which revolutionized the music industry in countries like Britain and the USA. At the same time, youth 'counter-culture' movements, especially in the 1960s, are similarly shown to have had a lasting influence on the formation of certain styles of popular music. In the chapters which follow, individual genres of popular music are analysed with the aim of discerning how they have been appropriated, re-worked and stylistically 'localized' in different cultural contexts around the globe. Heavy metal music is the first such genre to be examined, with Bennett then turning his attention to the punk phenomenon, reggae, rap and hip hop, bhangra, and dance music (especially house and techno) within club cultures. The latter portion of the book is then devoted to exploring the meaning and significance of music-making activities for young people, before concluding with an account of different media representations of contemporary youth (very much a contested category) and the importance of music in their daily lives. This is an exciting book, not only due to the sheer breadth and depth of its treatment, but also for the perceptiveness of its insights.

The Issues in Cultural and Media Studies series aims to facilitate a diverse range of critical investigations into pressing questions considered to be central to current thinking and research. In light of the remarkable speed at which the conceptual agendas of cultural and media studies are changing, the authors are committed to contributing to what is an ongoing process of re-evaluation and critique. Each of the books is intended to provide a lively, innovative and comprehensive introduction to a specific topical issue from a fresh perspective. The reader is offered a thorough grounding in the most salient debates indicative of the book's subject, as well as important insights into how new modes of enquiry may be established for future explorations. Taken as a whole, then, the series is designed to cover the core components of cultural and media studies courses in an imaginatively distinctive and engaging manner.

Stuart Allan

ACKNOWLEDGEMENTS

The inspiration for this book has come primarily from teaching under-graduate courses in popular music, youth culture and related areas and from attending various popular music related conferences since 1994. I would, therefore, like to express my thanks to those students at the universities of Durham, Glasgow, Kent and Surrey who have participated in lectures and seminars and to my colleagues in the field of popular music studies for their support.

INTRODUCTION

We fight our way through the massed and levelled collective taste of the Top 40, just looking for a little something we can call our own. But when we find it and jam the radio to hear it again it isn't just ours – it is a link to thousands of others who are sharing it with us. As a matter of a single song this might mean very little; as culture, as a way of life, you can't beat it.

(Marcus 1977: 115)

Without a doubt, **popular music** is a primary, if not *the* primary, leisure resource in late modern society. The sound of pop permeates people's lives in a variety of different ways. From nightclubs and live gigs, through cinemas and TV commercials, to what Japanese music theorist Hosokawa (1984) refers to as the 'autonomous and mobile' form of listening facilitated through the invention of the personal stereo; for a great many people, popular music is an omnipresent aspect of their day-to-day existence (Hosokawa 1984: 166). As Frith (1987: 139) observes: 'We absorb songs into our own lives and rhythms into our own bodies; they have a looseness of reference that makes them immediately accessible'.

Equally significant about popular music is the way in which it functions at a collective level. Every week in cities around the world people gather in clubs and venues to listen and dance to their favourite musics. The summer months bring festivals where music consumption is mixed with relaxation and socializing as people forge new friendships and associations based around common tastes in music, fashion and **lifestyle**. Popular music has also been linked with political issues and social change. In 1969 500,000 people gathered at a rural site near the town of **Woodstock** in upstate New York for the Woodstock Music and Art Fair, an event which, among other things, protested about the US's continuing involvement in the Vietnam war. During the 1980s, popular music became the focus for a series of globally broadcast mega-events (Garofalo 1992a), beginning with Bob Geldof's Live

Aid concerts in Britain and the US in aid of the famine in Ethiopia. Geldof later described the Live Aid event as a 'global joke box' to raise awareness about the famine. Although the political naiveté of Live Aid has been justi-fiably criticized (see, for example, Garofalo 1992b) the event's principal suc-cess was that it was able to focus, however briefly, people's attention on a world problem by utilizing a key element of their leisure and lifestyle.

Since the late 1960s, popular music has become a key focus in the related disciplines of cultural and media studies and sociology. Every era of post-Second World War popular music, and the cultural scenes this music has inspired, has been the subject of study in one or each of these disciplines at some level. The purpose of this book is to examine and evaluate, for the first time in a single volume, key studies of popular music styles and their audi-ences from 1950s rock 'n' roll to contemporary dance music. In addition, the book broadens the conventional Anglo-American scope of studies on popu-lar music and style. Seven of the chapters included here illustrate how Anglo-American popular musics and their attendant, primarily youth cultural, styles have been appropriated, reworked and effectively 'localized' in non-Anglo-American contexts.

The ten chapters in this book are developed from courses I have taught to undergraduate students in several UK universities. Each chapter is intended to give students a grounding in the subject matter presented while at the same time highlighting, via textual references, key studies for further read-ing. Through their investigation of different eras of post-war popular music and style, the chapters also provide contextual illustrations of the signifi-cance of current theoretical concepts such as **globalization**, 'localization', 'risk' (Beck 1992), **cultural reterritorialization** (Lull 1995) and 'new ethnic-ities' (Back 1996).

Chapter 1 begins by providing an overview of the socio-economic circum-stances which gave rise to the development of the post-war youth market, a centrally defining feature of the western consumer boom during the 1950s and early 1960s. The chapter also examines the technological innovations which revolutionized the music industry during this period and set the scene for the rapid worldwide appeal of rock 'n' roll, the first distinctive 'youth music'. The remainder of the chapter examines the cultural significance of rock 'n' roll music for young people around the world and critically evalu-ates sociological readings of the early style-based **youth cultures** to which rock 'n' roll and subsequent derivatives gave rise.

Chapter 2 focuses on the more political relationship between the youth **counter-culture** and popular music during the mid to late 1960s. The chap-ter begins by examining the shifting nature of popular music in the mid-1960s from three-minute commercial pop songs to longer pieces of music often relying on the improvisational skill of musicians and newly developed electronic sound effects. Such shifts in popular music aesthetics, it is illustrated, corresponded with a desire on the part of counter-cultural youth to experiment with alternative lifestyles based around the use of hallucinogenic drugs, eastern religion and the rejection of the western **technocracy** (Roszak 1969). The chapter then goes on to examine critically sociological and cultural studies readings of the term 'counter-culture' before looking at several of the individual movements which coalesced under the broader heading 'counter-culture', notably the anti-Vietnam war protest and the Black Power Movement.

Chapter 3 examines the significance of **heavy metal** music, a genre which, if until recently ignored by academic researchers, is unrivalled in terms of its longstanding popularity. Having looked at the development of heavy metal during the late 1960s, the chapter considers the periodic shifts in the heavy metal style, from the **soft** and **glam** metal of the 1980s to contemporary **extreme metal** styles. The chapter then focuses on the relationship between heavy metal music and its audience. This begins with an examination of how early heavy metal songs promoted traditional notions of patriarchy and male power to a male-dominated, white, working class, adolescent following. It then illustrates how metal's broadening appeal during the 1980s involved a shift towards a more ballad-based lyrical and musical style, typified by the 'soft metal' of bands such as Bon Jovi, which attracted a greater female metal audience than previous heavy metal styles. The chapter next examines how contemporary extreme metal forms shun many of the conventions established by earlier heavy metal styles, returning to a heavy guitar based sound and introducing a new range of song themes focusing on the risk and uncertainty (Beck 1992) that impacts on the lives of young people in postindustrial urban settings. The chapter concludes by examining official reactions to heavy metal, notably by parental interest groups and the courts, which stress the harmful effects of heavy metal on young audiences by linking it with teenage suicide, satanic rituals and other forms of antisocial behaviour.

Chapter 4 looks at the **punk** phenomenon. Beginning with an overview of the origins of punk in the US **garage band** and New York underground scenes, the chapter goes on to consider how the punk style was appropriated and developed in Britain during the mid-1970s by groups such as the Sex Pistols. This analysis of British punk is then developed through an examination of punk's relationship with the mass media and the way in which punk rock was used in the construction of a **moral panic** (Cohen 1987) by the British tabloid press and TV news programmes. The chapter then goes on to evaluate readings of the punk style, with particular reference to the work of

Hebdige (1979). Finally, the chapter looks at how aspects of British punk have been appropriated in other national and regional contexts where local circumstances have resulted in distinctive localized reworkings of the punk style and aesthetic.

Chapter 5 is the first of three chapters which examine the relationship between youth, style, music and ethnic identity beginning with a look at **reggae**. Having outlined the development of reggae music in Jamaica where, through the work of artists such as Bob Marley and Peter Tosh, it became associated with the Rastafarian movement, the chapter examines the cultural significance of reggae for African Caribbean youth in Britain. Consideration is then made of how, as a result of reggae artists' involvement in the British **Rock Against Racism** movement and the cross-cultural alliances formed between black and white youth in multi-ethnic areas of British cities, reggae music attracted a white youth audience in Britain. Finally the chapter looks at how reggae music has been rearticulated by Aboriginal youth in Australia as a means of protesting against racial exclusion and the exploitation of the Aboriginal people by the dominant white Australian population.

Chapter 6 focuses on **rap** music and **hip hop** culture. Beginning with a look at the origins of rap and hip hop in the South Bronx district of New York as a means of attempting to stem the tide of interracial violence, the chapter then considers the significance which rap assumed as a means for African American and Hispanic youth to address related social problems, such as poverty, racism and low self-esteem, which resulted from the urban ghettoization of these and other ethnic minorities. This is followed by a consideration of how rap and hip hop, despite their US origins and initial focus on a specific range of problems associated with urban life in inner-city ghettos, have become global forms characterized by localized reworkings in a range of urban settings across western Europe, Asia and Oceania.

Chapter 7 looks at the significance of **bhangra** and other forms of Asian dance music for Asian youth in contemporary Britain. Since the mid-1980s emergence of 'bhangra beat', Asian dance music has provided Asian youth in Britain with an important resource for exploring notions of identity and place in Britain. This chapter examines the development of bhangra beat from a traditional Punjabi folk music before going on to consider its significance for Asian youth in Britain during the 1980s. The chapter then illustrates how the appeal of bhangra subsequently declined during the 1990s as new Asian dance music styles emerged that drew upon developing club musics such as **house** and **techno**. Finally the chapter examines how these new Asian dance music styles have in their turn inspired new expressions of Asian youth identity, enabling young Asians to challenge popular stereotypes of Asians in Britain.

Chapter 8 focuses on contemporary dance music and **club cultures**. Having traced the stylistic development of two formative dance music styles, house and techno, the chapter goes on to examine how the arrival of contemporary dance music styles in British clubs during the late 1980s coincided with the increasing use of a new amphetamine-based stimulant **Ecstasy**, which, in conjunction with the **rave**, an illegally organized dance music event usually held in disused inner-city warehouses or remote rural areas, ensured that the dance music phenomenon became the centre of a new moral panic in Britain. The chapter then looks at recent research on dance music fans or 'club cultures' (Thornton 1995). Beginning with a consideration of how club cultures are held to challenge conventional subcultural theory, examination is made of the interactions between club culture and **new social movements** in Britain. Finally the chapter examines the relationship between club cultures, music and gender.

Chapter 9 examines the theme of youth and music-making. For many years, academic studies of the relationship between youth and popular music tended to focus on youth as consumers rather than makers of music. During the 1990s, however, an increasing number of studies have appeared that consider the significance of music-making for young people. This chapter examines the various claims which have been made for the meaning and significance of music-making activities in young people's lives. Beginning with a look at the processes of music-making itself, and the way in which the learning of songs, rehearsal and live performance give rise to micro-organizational practices which bond members of a group together, the chapter goes on to consider how the fact of being part of a pop or rock group provides young people with shared 'pathways' (Finnegan 1989) through which they are able to construct identities as musicians and/or artists, thus creating distance between themselves and more mundane everyday life institutions such as the family, school and work. Finally, consideration is made of the relationship between young people, music-making education and personal development.

Chapter 10 concludes the book by examining the ways in which the **retro-marketing** of popular music styles and associated memorabilia, particularly from the 1960s, has led to nostalgic representations of youth music and youth culture. As such, it is argued, youth has become a 'contested' category, the **babyboomer** generation continually reliving their memories of being young during the 1960s and comparing such memories of their own youth with the attitudes and sensibilities of contemporary youth. Drawing on studies which address this issue, it is illustrated how these comparisons have resulted in terms such as **Generation X** by babyboomer writers and journalists who claim that contemporary youth is apathetic and apolitical. The

chapter then considers some of the problems inherent in such representations of contemporary youth and illustrates how current youth cultures
and youth musics must be viewed in their relevant socio-economic contexts
if they are to be fully understood and objectively evaluated.

As this brief introduction illustrates, a primary aim of this book is to provide the reader with a knowledge of and insight into the key popular musics
and associated youth cultural styles that have characterized the post-Second
World War and subsequent eras. To a very large extent, the origins of post-
war popular music and youth style are rooted in socio-economic and technological changes that took place in the years directly following the end of the
Second World War. These changes and the shifts in youth leisure and entertainment to which they gave rise provide the focus for Chapter 1.

POST-WAR YOUTH AND
ROCK 'N' ROLL

Rock music has involved young people as no other pop or elite art has ever
done. In fact, it has involved young people as nothing else at all, aside from sex,
has done in generations. It has made poetry real to them . . . It has firmly
allied youth, bound them together with an invisible chain of sounds and a
network of verbal images in defense against the Elders.

(Gleason 1972: 143)

This chapter explores the socio-economic factors and attendant technological developments and innovations which gave rise to the transformation of
the term 'youth'. Between 1945 and 1955, youth changed from a taken-for-
granted and largely unacknowledged transitional stage between childhood
and adulthood to a cultural category marked by particular stylistic trends,
tastes in music and accompanying patterns of consumption. Instrumental in
this redefinition of youth was the development of the post-Second World
War youth market. Thus, as Shumway explains:

> the youth culture of the 1950s and later could not have happened with-
> out teenagers having become a significant market – that is, without their
> having significant disposable funds. Having that money and an
> increased independence from family, teenagers began to identify them-
> selves as a group.

(Shumway 1992: 119–20)

As I will presently consider, the desire among post-war youth for distinctive
forms of collective identity resulted in a number of visually striking images
and styles which a number of theorists (see for example, Hall and Jefferson
1976; Brake 1985) suggest were symbolic of structurally grounded
'subcultural' sensibilities. The post-Second World War period then is
crucial to our understanding of youth culture, both as an aspect of everyday life and an object of academic study. However, this is not to suggest

that consumption had played no part in the everyday lives of young people prior to the Second World War. Although direct comparisons between the consumption patterns of post-war and pre-war youth are difficult to make, largely due to the lack of published research on youth consumption prior to 1945, there is clear evidence of musically and/or stylistically distinct youth cultures and gangs in the years leading up to and during the Second World War. Thus, for example, Willett's study of the **Swing Jugend** ('Swing Kids') documents the widespread interest among young people in central Europe in the music of American jazz artists such as Duke Ellington, Benny Goodman, Glenn Miller and Artie Shaw during the late 1930s and early 1940s. When war broke out, the Swing Kid movement became a salient form of resistance to Nazi ideology both in occupied European countries and in Germany itself. Thus, as Willett explains:

> The orientation of the *Swing Jugend* was patently pro-American as some of their brash nicknames (Texas Jack, Alaska Bill) and the names of their clubs (the Harlem Klub, the OK gang Klub and the Cotton Klub) attested. Clubs existed in most German cities, including Stuttgart in the south and Dresden in the east.
>
> (Willett 1989: 160)

In a further study of pre-Second World War youth culture, Fowler (1992) identifies a series of locally situated and stylistically distinct youth gangs in the cities of inter-war Britain. Describing one particular gang, the Manchester-based Napoo, Fowler writes:

> The Napoo gang . . . which regularly met at a dancehall in Belle Vue immediately after World War One, wore a highly distinctive uniform borrowed from American gangster films. Each gang member wore a navy blue suit, a trilby and a pink neckerchief. The fear the gang aroused among the population of Ancoats, where its members lived and worked, suggests that the Napoo should be viewed as an essentially pre-Teddy boy youth cult.
>
> (Fowler 1992: 144)

Despite such evidence of a cultural relationship between youth, music and attendant forms of visual style prior to the Second World War, however, the appearance of music and style-driven youth cultures at a more widespread, and increasingly global, level began to occur only when youth became a distinct consumer group.

The development of the post-war youth market

The post-war youth market was the direct result of a series of socio-economic shifts which occurred after the Second World War. During the post-war period the west experienced an economic boom which in turn led to a growth in consumerism (see Leys 1983). Prior to the Second World War, consumerism had been an essentially middle class activity. Following the Second World War, however, increasing affluence and technological breakthroughs in mass production resulted in consumption becoming an accepted part of life for the working classes too (Chaney 1996). The new demand for consumer products was met by a rapid expansion in the types of commodities available. A whole range of items from cars to electrical household appliances, such as washing machines, food mixers, electric irons, televisions and record players, became much more widely available than they had been before the Second World War. New techniques of mass production also meant that such items were more cheaply available than they had been before the war.

The post-war period, then, saw consumerism become a way of life for many sections of society, including the young. The increased spending power of young people gave them new levels of independence from their families. As Bocock observes:

> The young had emerged as a new, major market in the 1950s in Britain and Western Europe, following the United States which had experienced less disruption in the 1940s than war-torn Europe. Young people were employed in relatively well-paid jobs in new industries.
>
> (Bocock 1993: 28)

Such independence was significantly enhanced by the burgeoning youth market. The consumer industries quickly realized that young people presented a highly viable and lucrative market and, consequently, a whole range of commodities designed specifically for them began to appear. These commodities included fashion clothes, cosmetics such as lipstick and mascara, as well as relatively new goods such as plastic 45 rpm (revolutions per minute) records, record players and transistor radios. Thus, in addition to financial independence, young people of the post-war generation had much greater control over their leisure time than previous generations of youth. Commodities and forms of leisure designated exclusively as aspects of a 'youth lifestyle' meant that young people became far less dependent on the family home and the leisure preferences of their parents. As Chambers (1985) points out in his study *Urban Rhythms*:

> Leisure was no longer simply a moment of rest and recuperation from work, the particular zone of family concerns and private edification. It was widened into a potential life-style made possible by consumerism. To buy a particular record, to choose a jacket or skirt cut to a particular fashion, to mediate carefully on the colour of your shoes is to open a door onto an actively constructed style of living.
>
> (Chambers 1985: 16)

Central to the new marketed youth identities, then, were items such as fashion clothing, magazines and music. While all of these commodities played their part in articulating the collective identity of youth, the most significant aspect of post-war youth culture was the music which effectively became its signature tune, rock 'n' roll (post-war technology also facilitated mass production of the electric guitar, the key rock 'n' roll instrument, see Chapter 9). As with other youth-orientated commodities, rock 'n' roll music was facilitated by the technological advances made during the immediate post-war years. Such advances in technology enabled new forms of production and distribution which were crucial to the impact that rock 'n' roll had on young people. Although, as Frith (1983) points out, the commercialization of music did not begin with rock 'n' roll, the cultural resonance that rock 'n' roll assumed was uniquely marked by the technological factors which gave rise to its emergence.

During the nineteenth century, commercial music had taken the form of sheet music, most households across Europe and the US possessing a piano (Frith 1983: 32). Thomas Edison's invention of the **phonograph** during the 1880s in the US marked a fundamental change in the way in which music was marketed and heard by people. The cylindrical shaped phonograph was the forerunner of the vinyl record and allowed for acoustic sounds to be recorded and reproduced electronically. In 1888 another US inventor, Emile Berliner, took this idea further with the development of the **gramophone**. The gramophone worked on the same principle as the phonograph but used discs instead of cylinders (Frith 1988a: 14). As with the phonograph, however, the gramophone was very expensive to produce. Moreover, during the actual recording process, the music had to be recorded straight onto disc and the results were not always satisfactory, with much of the sound quality being lost.

It was not until the late 1940s that a cheap but highly efficient alternative to disc recording was found. This alternative was audio tape, originally invented by German scientists during the Second World War for use in broadcasting. Its first commercial use was not by the music industry, but by radio stations as a low-cost method of prerecording interviews and advertising jingles. Tape recording was also used by film studios as a way of producing film soundtracks. However, the music industry soon began to realize the benefits of using tape in the recording process and by 1950 tape had completely replaced the disc. A major advantage of the switch from disc to tape was that recording costs dramatically decreased. Equally important was the new level of control which tape allowed over the recording process. As Frith points out:

> Tape was an intermediary in the recording process: the performance was recorded on tape; the tape was used to make the master disc. And it was what could be done during this intermediary stage, to the tape itself, that transformed pop music-making. Producers no longer had to take performances in their entirety. They could cut and splice, edit the best bits of performances together, cut out the mistakes, make records of ideal not real events.
>
> (Frith 1988a: 21–2)

At the same time, new techniques of mass production and the invention of the new, plastic 45 rpm record, meant that a far greater number of records could be produced. Thus, as Peterson explains:

> The 45 was important to the advent of rock primarily because it was (virtually) unbreakable. One of the great expenses of 78s was the extreme care that had to be taken in handling and shipping them, and each of the major record companies developed a national distribution system that was geared to handling its own delicate 78s . . . The smaller, lighter, virtually indestructible 45s made it much cheaper to ship records in bulk, making feasible the development of independent national distribution companies.
>
> (Peterson 1990: 101)

If technological innovations such as those described above were crucial to the development of rock 'n' roll music, equally important was its relatively instant popularity among teenagers. It is to the significance of rock 'n' roll as a distinctive 'youth music' that I now turn.

The cultural impact of rock 'n' roll

Half a century after it first appeared, it is easy to overlook the cultural impact of rock 'n' roll on its audience. Yet, this musical style changed forever the way in which popular music was produced and marketed and also the way in which it was socially received. As Middleton (1990) observes, prior to the arrival of rock 'n' roll, popular music had comprised 'a relatively narrow stylistic spread, bounded by theatre song on the one side, novelty items deriving from music hall and vaudeville on the other, with **Tin Pan Alley** song, Hollywood hits and crooners in between' (Middleton 1990: 14). When the first rock 'n' roll records appeared popular music became an altogether different type of cultural form. Thus, as Billig explains:

> [rock 'n' roll] sounded different from anything previous generations had listened to. The whine of the electric guitar, the crisp drumming, the echo effects, and, later, more complex mixtures of electric and acoustic instruments, all made rock 'n' roll a new sound . . . The generation that had lived through the hard times of the depression and the Second World War, preferred its music soft and romantic. Their children, growing up in safer, more affluent times, wanted to hear more dangerous music. They responded to simple chords, a jumping beat and loud electric guitars.
>
> (Billig 2000: 5, 19)

The roots of rock 'n' roll music lay in the rhythm and blues developed by African American musicians who, having migrated from the South of the US to northern cities such as Chicago, began to electrify the music of the original African American bluesmen (Chambers 1976). The term rock 'n' roll was first coined by Alan Freed, a radio disc jockey (DJ) from Cleveland, Ohio, following a visit to a local record store. As Gillett (1983) writes in his book *The Sound of the City*:

> Alan Freed . . . was invited, sometime in 1952, to visit a downtown record store by the owner, Leo Mintz. Mintz was intrigued by the musical taste of some of the white adolescents who bought records at his store, and Freed was amazed by it. He watched the excited reaction of the youths who danced energetically to music that Freed had previously considered alien to their culture – rhythm and blues.
>
> (Gillett 1983: 13)

While Freed championed the black roots of rock 'n' roll, regularly featuring the music of black artists such as Fats Domino and the Drifters in his shows, other DJs tended to play cover versions of rock 'n' roll songs by white artists. By the mid-1950s, if rock 'n' roll was starting to gain favour among young white audiences then it was a music which had been cleaned up for white consumption. As Gillett points out, the record industry attempted to 'knock the rough edges off rock 'n' roll [arguing] that people didn't want their music to be as brash, blatantly sexual, and spontaneous as the pure rock 'n' roll records were' (Gillett 1983: 41). The result was all-white groups such as Bill

Haley and his Comets, whose song 'Rock Around the Clock' was used as the title track of the first feature length film devoted to the new rock 'n' roll sound (see Denisoff and Romanowski 1991; Lewis 1992).

When *Rock Around the Clock* was first screened in Britain, shortly after its release in 1956, it resulted in a string of minor disturbances. Cinema seats were torn out and in several major cities youths were arrested and later fined for aggressive or insulting behaviour as they left cinemas (Street 1992: 304). Across Europe, reactions to *Rock Around the Clock* were even more extreme than in Britain. In the West German city of Hamburg cars were overturned and shop fronts and street signs vandalized by young people as police used water cannons in an attempt to quell the unrest (Krüger 1983). Similarly, in the Netherlands, where *Rock Around the Clock* was banned in several major cities, 'young people took to the streets to demonstrate for their right to see the film' (Mutsaers 1990: 307). Disturbances were also reported in Toronto, Sydney and in Auckland, New Zealand although, according to Shuker, apart from several minor incidents, the responses of young New Zealanders to *Rock Around the Clock* were 'generally restrained' (Shuker 1994: 257).

Rock 'n' roll in search of an idol

If the music of Bill Haley clearly generated a great deal of excitement among teenagers, the image of Haley and his group, the Comets, was decidedly out of step with the young audiences for which they performed. As Bradley (1992) explains, Haley's 'plump, energetic, affable, ageing' appearance could never hope to 'inspire much identification among boys or romantic adulation among girls' (Bradley 1992: 59). The rock 'n' roll phenomenon was still in need of an artist who could appeal to white audiences on a musical level while at the same time retaining the rawness, sexuality and excitement associated with black rock 'n' roll artists such as Little Richard. This role was to be assumed by Elvis Presley. Presley, who Beadle (1993) describes as 'the first pop star in the modern sense', was working as a truck driver when he was discovered by Sam Phillips, head of a small independent record label, Sun Records, based in Memphis, Tennessee (Beadle 1993: 5). Presley first visited Sun Records to record a song as a present for his mother's birthday. However, Sam Phillips was so impressed with Presley's voice that he invited him back to record some more material. In recalling these early sessions, Sam Phillips said of Elvis: 'I noticed a certain quality in Elvis' voice, and I guessed he had a feeling for black music. I thought his voice was unique, but I didn't know whether it was commercial' (Palmer 1976: 205).

When Elvis Presley began to record rock 'n' roll songs for Sun Records, he restored the rawness and emotion missing in the work of other white rock 'n' roll artists. Indeed, Spencer (1997) suggests that Presley was instrumental in what he terms the 'sexual seduction of whites into blackness' which ultimately gave rise to 'new and acceptable attitudes about sexuality' in white society (Spencer 1997: 114). Such seduction was further enhanced by Presley's image, which was quickly emulated by many white male teenagers, and his stage performances, which injected a source of spectacle into rock 'n' roll that was, up until this time, unknown to white audiences. According to O'Sullivan (1974) Elvis signalled the arrival of the new teenage pop idol, thus marking the end of the pop star of indeterminate age.

In keeping with the rise and appeal of rock 'n' roll generally, the importance of new technologies cannot be overlooked in attempting to chart the cultural impact of Elvis Presley on young audiences. Presley first reached a nationwide audience in the US through the medium of television. Indeed, in the case of young people outside the US, Presley remained an essentially 'mediated' star, television appearances and subsequent films rather than live performances being the way in which Presley was experienced on a global level (apart from several impromptu performances in Germany during his tour of duty there as a soldier in the US Army, Elvis never performed anywhere outside the US). Moreover, the spectacle of Elvis on TV created a moral panic among the parent culture which further endeared him to his young fans. The following account by Shumway (1992) provides a graphic illustration of the controversy surrounding Elvis's early television performances:

> What was most remarkable about Elvis on television was the dancing or gyrating that he did while he performed. His first TV appearances, on the *Dorsey Brothers' Show*, included some of his dancing, but, perhaps because the shows were seen by relatively small audiences or because Elvis's dancing was photographed from above, these appearances produced no significant reaction. In his first appearance on the *Milton Bearle Show*, however, Elvis's dancing was both more extreme and went on not only during the instrumental break but during the entire last half of the performance of 'Hound Dog'. The reaction of both professional critics and the self-appointed guardians of morality was swift and harsh. The public outcry nearly caused NBC to cancel Elvis's next scheduled TV appearance, on the *Steve Allen Show*. Rather than cancel the show, the network devised a plan to contain Elvis. Allen dressed him up in tails and had him sing 'Hound Dog' to a live basset hound. Later in the same year, Elvis was restrained by court order from

making any offensive gyrations on stage in Jacksonville, Florida. Early in 1957, in what was Elvis's third appearance on the *Ed Sullivan Show*, Sullivan insisted that Elvis be photographed from the waist up.

(Shumway 1992: 125–6)

However, it was not simply the visual representation of Elvis himself that endeared him to the fans. Elvis's early television appearances also included shots of the audience which, in turn, served as a frame of reference for other fans watching the show at home on television. These fans learned from the televised audience how to respond to Elvis. A further passage from Shumway's (1992) study illustrates this point:

> When Elvis is featured on national TV programmes, the audience becomes part of the show. In the Berle performance, the film cuts between shots of Elvis and shots of the audience, not as a large mass of indistinguishable faces, but of particular faces whose response tells us of the excitement the performer is generating . . . These pictures showed other fans how to respond appropriately . . . while at the same time . . . creat[ing] a new representation of male sexuality.
>
> (Shumway 1992: 127)

Ehrenreich *et al.* (1992) make a similar series of observations in relation to early Beatles' performances in the US during 1964. Thus, according to Ehrenreich *et al.* (1992), fans already knew how to respond to the Beatles having watched TV footage of the group performing in Britain, such footage being similarly intercut with scenes from the audience:

> When the Beatles arrived in the United States, which was still ostensibly sobered by the assassination of President Kennedy two months before, the fans knew what to do. Television had spread the word from England: The approach of the Beatles is a licence to riot. At least 4,000 girls (some estimates run as high as 10,000) greeted them at Kennedy Airport, and hundreds laid siege to the Plaza Hotel, keeping the stars virtual prisoners.
>
> (Ehrenreich *et al.* 1992: 86)

If mediated images of Elvis and the Beatles were instrumental in securing loyal and enthusiastic audiences for these artists, they were also ensured the popularity of Elvis and the Beatles on a global scale. If rock 'n' roll was the first musical form to exploit the potential of the global media, this in turn ensured it gained an audience which went far beyond the US and Britain. Similarly, the demand for rock 'n' roll music resulted in the appearance of 'home-grown' rock 'n' roll artists in many different countries throughout the world.

Rock 'n' roll as a 'global' music

As noted above, the first indications of the extent of rock 'n' roll's global appeal came as newspapers around the world reported on the response of local youth to screenings of the film *Rock Around the Clock*. However, it was not simply the consumption of rock 'n' roll sounds and images from the US and Britain which transformed rock 'n' roll into a youth music on a global scale. Equally important, if often overlooked, were local arrangements for the production and consumption of rock 'n' roll music.

In the Netherlands, for example, the local rock 'n' roll scene was dominated by **Indobands**. These were groups comprising Indonesian immigrants whose 'apparently natural musical abilities' and affinity with the guitar (which was used in traditional Indonesian music) gave them a distinct advantage over indigenous white musicians in emulating the sound of US and British rock 'n' roll artists (Mutsaers 1990: 308). Indeed, according to Mutsaers (1990: 310): 'White musicians are reported to have painted their hair black and darkened their faces in order to gain musical credibility'. The dominance of Indobands in the Dutch rock 'n' roll scene created special concerns for the Dutch authorities regarding the effects of rock 'n' roll on young people. In particular, there were concerns over reactions of audiences to the live shows of Indobands. At dance halls where the groups played there were often violent clashes between white Dutch boys and 'Indo' boys who, it was alleged, were 'stealing' the girlfriends of the white boys (Mutsaers 1990: 310). Indobands were also very popular with German audiences, one particular group, the Tielman Brothers, moving to Germany where they became 'the best-paid live act in the history of Indorock and at that time of Eurorock altogether' (Mutsaers 1990: 312).

The extent to which rock 'n' roll became a global phenomenon is further illustrated by Shuker (1994) in his account of the music's impact on youth in New Zealand:

> As with their overseas counterparts, by the mid-1950s New Zealand youth were more visible and more affluent. Contemporary press advertising reflected increased awareness of youth as a distinctive market, particularly for clothes and records. Dances and concerts catering for youth increased, with 10,000 people attending the Ballroom Astoria – 'New Zealand's Biggest Dance Attraction' – in a regional centre, Palmerston North. Youth clubs conducted rock 'n' roll dances, and the nationally broadcast Lever Hit Parade began in November 1955.
>
> (Shuker 1994: 256)

As in other countries, the appeal of rock 'n' roll among young New Zealanders also functioned as the catalyst for a local scene, one of the most famous home-grown rock 'n' roll artists being Johnny Devlin, 'a self-conscious Presley imitator [and] a natural singer and showman' (Shuker 1994: 258). Devlin enjoyed huge success in New Zealand, performing sell out shows and being regularly 'mobbed by screaming girls' (Shuker 1994: 258).

The iconic status of Elvis Presley also informed a rather less likely rock 'n' roll success story in the former Soviet Union. When rock 'n' roll records first began to filter into the USSR, initially in the form of gifts brought by western visitors, and subsequently as illegal imports intended for the black market (see Easton 1989), the Soviet authorities adopted an overtly negative attitude, claiming that rock 'n' roll 'was dirty bourgeois propaganda aimed at westernising the Soviet Union' (Bright 1986: 361). Despite such official opposition to rock 'n' roll, however, the USSR had its own rock 'n' roll scene. One of the biggest stars of this scene was Dean Reed, a US born singer-songwriter who Nadelson describes as the Elvis Presley of the Soviet Union, 'so famous his icon was for sale in shops alongside those of Yuri Gagarin and Joseph Stalin' (Nadelson 1991: 3).

Nadelson's biographical account of Dean Reed is significant not simply because of the alternative history of rock 'n' roll in the former USSR and wider Eastern Bloc which it portrays, but also because of its insights into the growing desire of Soviet youth for the products of the western popular culture industries during the Cold War years, even as such products were systematically barred by the authorities. Indeed, as Nadelson illustrates, Soviet youth's interest in western popular culture began not with rock 'n' roll but with 'the movies and the records which the Red Army captured in Berlin after the [Second World] war' (Nadelson 1991: 76). These included *Sun Valley Serenade*, a film whose Glenn Miller soundtrack included 'Chattanooga Choo Choo' which the *Stilyagi* (the Style Hunters), a local Moscow youth culture (see Pilkington 1994), adopted as 'their anthem' (Nadelson 1991: 76). As Chapters 2 and 4 will illustrate, this interest among Russian youth and the youth of other Eastern Bloc countries in western popular music and style continued throughout the years of Soviet rule despite the various attempts of government bodies to deter such interest.

As the above examples illustrate, far from being simply an Anglo-American phenomenon, rock 'n' roll music became popular throughout the world during the 1950s and 1960s. Similarly, the recognition of rock 'n' roll as a distinctive youth music was also acknowledged by young people on a global scale. An integral aspect of rock 'n' roll and subsequent post-war popular music styles were the styles and fashions of young fans. This was particularly noticeable in Britain where a succession of stylistically spectacular and highly distinctive youth cultural groups emerged during the post-war years.

Post-war youth culture and the CCCS

The first sustained attempt to make a sociological study of the post-war youth style in Britain was from theorists based at the Birmingham Centre for Contemporary Cultural Studies (**CCCS**) (see also Bennett 2000). Central to the work of the CCCS is the concept of **subculture** first developed by the American **Chicago School** of sociology during the 1920s and 1930s. The Chicago School theorists wanted to construct a sociological model of juvenile delinquency as an alternative to the individualist criminological accounts which argued that deviance was symptomatic of individual disorder (see Sapsford 1981). The Chicago School argued against this explanation of deviance, suggesting instead that deviance was a product of social problems such as unemployment and poverty. Furthermore, they argued, given that these problems were a common aspect of everyday life for many individuals, deviant behaviour, for example theft, violence and drug taking, could be seen as 'normalized' responses, particularly in relation to the young who would resort to deviance as means of empowering themselves.

The CCCS modified the original Chicago School model of subculture through the application of a structural Marxist perspective that focused on the collective style of post-war British youth 'subcultures' such as the Teddy boys, the mods and the skinheads. Hall and Jefferson's (1976) *Resistance through Rituals*, the centrepiece of the CCCS's work on post-war youth cultures, produced a new theory of subcultural style in response to the then widely endorsed 'embourgeoisement thesis' which argued that, with the increasing affluence of the post-war period, British society was becoming classless (see, for example, Butler and Rose 1960). The class struggle which had characterized the previous 150 years, it was argued, had ended as working class people became more middle class in their outlook due to their increased wealth (Leys 1983: 61). Such arguments were very easily applied to young people, the emergent youth market being seen by many as the single most important influence on post-war youth and the catalyst for a new unified youth culture as young people abandoned the class-based identities of the pre-war years and bought into new consumer lifestyles (Reimer 1995). The CCCS theorists rejected the view that the increased affluence of post-war working class youth had resulted in their assimilation into a unified teenage consumer culture. Instead they argued that the emergent youth styles, if indeed indicative of the newly acquired spending habits of working class youth, also symbolized a series of 'subcultural' responses on the part of working class youth to the socio-economic conditions of their class position.

According to the CCCS theorist, Phil Cohen (1972), youth subcultures were to be understood in terms of their facilitating a collective response to the break up of traditional working class communities. Cohen suggested that the urban redevelopment programmes in the East End of London during the 1950s, together with the relocation of families to 'new towns' and modern housing estates, culminated in an irreparable rupturing of traditional working class ways of life as these families struggled to come to terms with the loss of former working class communities and their various support structures, while at the same time attempting to integrate into a new environment and new patterns of existence. Subcultures, argues Cohen, were an attempt on the part of working class youth to bridge the gap between life on the new estates and the former patterns of traditional working class community life:

> It seems to me that the latent function of subculture is this – to express and resolve, albeit 'magically', the contradictions which remain hidden and unresolved in the parent culture . . . [each subculture attempts] to retrieve some of the socially cohesive elements destroyed in their parent culture.
>
> (Cohen 1972: 23)

From this point of view, subcultures are seen to form part of an ongoing struggle on the part of working class youth to reassert a sense of community. This reading of subcultural style informs several other CCCS studies. In his work on the 1950s Teddy boy style, Jefferson argues that

> the group life and intense loyalty of the Teds can be seen as a reaffirmation of traditional slum working class values and the 'strong sense of territory' as an attempt to retain, if only imaginatively, a hold on the territory which was being expropriated from them.
>
> (Jefferson 1976: 81)

Similarly, Clarke (1976: 99) argues that the subcultural style of the skinhead 'represents an attempt to re-create through the "mob" the traditional working class community as a substitution for the real decline of the latter'. The visual image of the skinhead, suggests Clarke (1976: 56), 'resonated with and articulated skinhead conceptions of masculinity, "hardness" and "working-classness"'. A somewhat different interpretation of working class youth style is put forward by Hebdige (1976a) in his study of mods. Thus, according to Hebdige (1976a), the mods' **fetishization** of expensive and highly desirable commodities, such as Italian sharp suits and designer sunglasses, symbolized an emphasis on leisure time, rather than physical territory, as a threatened space. Hebdige argues that the mods' collective antidote to their workaday existence as office boys and unskilled labourers was to take control of their night-time and weekend leisure through conspicuous consumption and a disregard for the structured time of the working week articulated through all-night clubbing and a steady stream of speed pills. Such collective sensibilities are clearly illustrated in Franc Roddam's 1979 film about mod culture *Quadrophenia* (re-released in 1997). Thus, as Lewis observes:

> [by day] we see Jimmy, the film's hero, at work as a mail boy at a posh advertising firm. Surrounded by images of inaccessible women and wealth, Jimmy finds the whole work scene debasing . . . [by night and at the weekend] Jimmy ably follows [the mod] fashion, embracing the hell-bent hedonism with a kind of desperate fervor.
>
> (Lewis 1992: 86–7)

The work of the CCCS has been criticised on a number of grounds. One of the most salient criticisms of subcultural theory has been made by McRobbie and Garber (1976), who point out the CCCS's failure to include in their work any account of girls' involvement in subcultures. In their study 'Girls and subcultures', McRobbie and Garber (1976) identify a strong teeny bopper culture among young girls. They argue that while this teeny bopper culture is an equally significant form of youth culture as the more male dominated subcultures, it is less visible because of the stricter parental control to which girls are subjected, such control forcing them to construct their teeny bopper culture around the territory available, the home and the bedroom (McRobbie and Garber 1976: 219). In subsequent work, McRobbie (1980) attributes the failure of the CCCS to acknowledge this home-centred teeny bopper culture to the selective bias of the CCCS researchers themselves. Thus, she argues,

> while the sociologies of deviance and youth were blooming in the early seventies the sociology of the family was everybody's least favourite option . . . few writers seemed interested in what happened when a mod went home after a week-end on speed. Only what happened out there on the streets mattered.
>
> (McRobbie 1980: 68–9)

A number of other writers have also criticised the sociological interpretation of post-war youth put forward by the CCCS. Frith (1983), for example, has argued that one of the central problems with the CCCS approach lies in the 'romantic' notions of resistance which it attaches to subcultures. Frith takes issue with notion of style as signifying 'the moment of symbolic refusal' in the 'act of symbolic creation', adding:

The problem is to reconcile adolescence and subculture. Most working-class teenagers pass through groups, change identities, play their leisure roles for fun; other differences between them – sex, occupation, family – are much more significant than distinctions of style. For every youth 'stylist' committed to a cult as a full-time creative task, there are hundreds of working-class kids who grow up in a loose membership of several groups and run with a variety of gangs. There's a distinction here between a vanguard and a mass, between uses of leisure *within* subcultures.

(Frith 1983: 219–20)

Such an argument is clearly critical of the CCCS's notion of tight coherent subcultures, suggesting alternatively that such groups may in fact be characterised by a series of floating memberships and fluid boundaries. A similar position is taken by Jenkins (1983) in his study *Lads, Citizens and Ordinary Kids*. Like Frith, Jenkins is critical of the fact that subcultural theory not only tends to overlook the essentially interconnected nature of so-called subcultures but also regards such groups as ideologically separated off from the wider society. Thus, he argues, 'the concept of subculture tends to exclude from consideration the large area of commonality between subcultures, however defined, and implies a determinate and often deviant relationship to a national dominant culture' (Jenkins 1983: 41).

In my own critique of the CCCS I take issue with the Centre's idea of working class resistance as a centrally defining aspect of post-war youth style. The concept of 'resistance', I argue, revolves around the very tentative argument that, despite the possibilities for visual creativity and experimentation with identity opened up by post-war youth fashions and other commodities, 'working-class youth were somehow driven back to the fact of class as a way of articulating their attachment to such commodities' (Bennett 1999a: 602). I further suggest that, rather than accentuating issues of class divisions, 'post-war consumerism offered young people the opportunity to break away from their traditional class-based identities [and adopt] new, self-constructed forms of identity' (Bennett 1999a: 602).

Finally, Thornton (1995) makes the point that, in focusing entirely upon conditions of class as a basis for both the origins and stylistic response of subcultures, the CCCS overlook the other influences upon the collective self-image of youth, in particular the role played by media representation. Thus, argues Thornton:

When [the CCCS] come to define 'subculture', they position the media and its associated processes outside, in opposition to and after the fact of subculture. In doing so, they omit precisely that which clearly

delineates a 'subculture', for labelling is crucial to the insiders' and outsiders' views of themselves.

(Thornton 1995: 119)

According to Thornton then, rather than emerging as fully formed, grassroots expressions of youth solidarity, subcultures are the product of youth's
dynamic and highly reflexive relationship with the mass media. The mass
media are responsible, argues Thornton, for providing youth with many of
the visual and ideological resources which they incorporate into collective
subcultural identities.

Conclusion

During the course of this chapter I examined the socio-economic factors
which gave rise to the post-Second World War youth market and the influence of this market on the spending patterns, tastes and collective awareness
of young people. I have shown how the ready availability of new youth commodities, notably fashion items, magazines, films and popular music, during
the post-war period, was instrumental in youth's realization of itself as a
'culture', that is to say as a separate social category marked off from the
parent culture and from childhood by a series of distinctive visual images
and accompanying sensibilities of style and taste. Central to youth's stylistic
revolution during the post-war period, I have illustrated, was rock 'n' roll,
the first genre of popular music that youth could claim as 'its own'. In the
final section, I considered some of the explanations put forward by theorists
from the Birmingham CCCS to interpret the significance of British post-war
youth style. As subsequent chapters will illustrate, although the CCCS has
been variously criticised, its work, particularly the concept of subculture,
has been highly influential in studies of a number of contemporary youth
music and styles from punk to rave.

Further reading

Bennett, A. (1999) Subcultures or neo-tribes? Rethinking the relationship between
     youth, style and musical taste, *Sociology*, 33(3): 599–617.
Bennett, A. (2000) *Popular Music and Youth Culture: Music, Identity and Place.*
     London: Macmillan (Chapter 1).
Bocock, R. (1993) *Consumption.* London: Routledge (Chapter 1).
Bradley, D. (1992) *Understanding Rock 'n' Roll: Popular Music in Britain
     1955–1964.* Buckingham: Open University Press.

Chambers, I. (1985) *Urban Rhythms: Pop Music and Popular Culture*. London: Macmillan (Chapter 1).

Frith, S. (1988) *Music for Pleasure: Essays in the Sociology of Pop*. Oxford: Polity Press (Part 1 pp 11–23)

Gillett, C. (1983) *The Sound of the City: The Rise of Rock and Roll*, 2nd edn. London: Souvenir Press (Part 1).

Hall, S. and Jefferson, T. (eds) (1976) *Resistance through Rituals: Youth Subcultures in Post-War Britain*. London: Hutchinson.

Shuker, R. (1994) *Understanding Popular Music*. London: Routledge (Chapters 2 and 9).

Shumway, D. (1992) Rock and roll as a cultural practice', in A. DeCurtis (ed.) *Present Tense: Rock and Roll and Culture*. Durham, NC: Duke University Press.

2 | SIXTIES ROCK, POLITICS AND THE COUNTER-CULTURE

San Francisco in the middle sixties was a very special time and place to be part of. Maybe it *meant something*. Maybe not, in the long run . . . but no explanation, no mix of words or music or memories can touch the sense of knowing that you were there and alive in that corner of time and the world. Whatever it meant . . . There was madness in any direction at any hour . . . You could strike sparks anywhere. There was a fantastic universal sense that whatever we were doing was *right*, that we were winning . . . that sense of inevitable victory over the forces of Old and Evil. Not in any mean or military sense; we didn't need that. Our energy would simply prevail . . . We had all the momentum; we were riding the crest of a high and beautiful wave.
(From the novel *Fear and Loathing in Las Vegas* by Hunter S. Thompson 1993)

While there is no question that . . . the forces arrayed in support of the existing hegemony are formidable, there are also numerous instances where mass culture – and in particular popular music – issues serious challenges to hegemonic power.

(Garofalo 1992b: 2)

If the 1950s marked the beginning of youth's long-term cultural investment in popular music and its attendant styles, the counter-cultural movement of the years 1965 to 1970, together with the politicized rock music that shaped many of its central ideas, represents a similarly significant period in post-war youth cultural history. Certainly, this was not the first time that music had been used as a platform for socio-political commentary. For much of the twentieth century folk music played a central role in left-wing politics in the US, while the folk 'revival' of the early 1960s created a more global aware-ness of the link forged by earlier singer-songwriters, such as Woody Guthrie, between folk music and political issues (see, for example, Denisoff 1972). But the period from the mid-1960s to the early 1970s represented the first time that popular music, a mass cultural form, had been used to political effect. Prior to the mid 1960s, popular music had been considered by folk fans and other musical 'purists' to be too firmly located in the yoke of capitalism, and thus too 'commercial', to lend integrity to the communication of socio-political ideas.

During the mid-1960s, however, it became clear that such a view of popular music and its relationship to the wider cultural industries of capitalism was oversimplistic – that there was scope for artistic control of musical and lyrical content and for the dissemination of values which, in some cases, were anti-hegemonic from the point of view of capitalist ideology. The shakedown which would end the association of popular music with the 'hit factory' mentality of Tin Pan Alley songwriters began around 1965 as young people's experimentation with hallucinogenic drugs, notably Lysergic Acid Diethylamide or **LSD**, and alternative lifestyles drew them to the experimental music of psychedelic rock groups, such as The Grateful Dead and Pink Floyd, in locations as far apart as San Francisco's **Haight-Ashbury** district and London's UFO (Unlimited Freak Out) club (see Whiteley 1992: 63). Equally important was the intellectualization of pop lyrics during the 1960s, 'the seeming triviality' of 1950s pop being replaced by a 'rock poetry' which 'express[ed] the more serious feelings of [the] new age' (Billig 2000: 114).

This chapter examines what is in many ways a unique relationship between popular music, youth and socio-political awareness as it manifested itself during the mid to late 1960s. In addition to looking at some of the main counter-cultural events which characterised these years, I will also examine several of the individual movements which coalesced under the counter-cultural banner – the anti-Vietnam war movement, the Civil Rights Movement and the emphasis on a new awareness of the world based on the hallucinogenic drugs and/or appropriation of religion and beliefs from India and the far East. These aspects of the counter-culture have been chosen as they most graphically illustrate the impact of counter-cultural ideology on young people and the part played by popular music in the communication of counter-cultural beliefs.

The counter-culture

If popular music became inextricably linked to the dissemination and appropriation of socio-political ideas during the mid to late 1960s then the cultural bedrock for this liaison between music and politics was the counter-cultural movement. The dominant sociological interpretation of the counter-culture suggests that it consisted of white middle class youth who were disillusioned with the way their parent culture 'controlled' society and had no desire to become caught up in the machinery of social power themselves. In *Resistance through Rituals* (Hall and Jefferson 1976), the seminal youth culture study by the Centre for Contemporary Cultural Studies (CCCS) in Birmingham, England (see Chapter 1), Clarke *et al.* (1976) apply this interpretation of the counter-culture to their class-based reading of youth cultures in post-war Britain. Thus, they argue, if working class subcultures presented a threat to middle class power from without, then the counter-culture posed a similar threat from within. According to Clarke *et al.* the counter-culture

> spearheaded a dissent from their own, dominant, 'parent' culture. Their disaffiliation was principally ideological and cultural. They directed their attack mainly against those institutions which reproduce the dominant cultural ideological relations – the family, education, the media, marriage, the sexual division of labour.
>
> (Clarke *et al.* 1976: 62)

Significantly, this interpretation of the counter-culture was not simply a feature of the cultural Marxism central to the CCCS and other British sociological research at the time.

In the US too, there was a common feeling among sociologists and other academic theorists that the counter-culture constituted a direct attack on the part of white middle class youth against the dominant ideological machinery set in place and maintained by its parent culture. Such a view is typified by Reich (1971) in his book *The Greening of America*. Thus, according to Reich:

> Parents have unintentionally contributed to their children's condemnation of existing society. Not by their words, but by their actions, attitudes and manner of living . . . With the unerring perceptiveness of a child, their children have read [the] messages from the lifeless lives of their 'successful' parents, have seen marriages break up because there was nothing left to hold them, have felt cynicism alienation and despair in the best-kept homes of America. And will have none of it.
>
> (Reich 1971: 187)

Reich's view is shared by Roszak (1969) who argues that the counter-culture was not simply opposed to the hegemonic power of its parent culture but also to the 'technocracy' which the parent culture had created. Roszak describes the technocracy as 'that social form in which an industrial society reaches the peak of its organizational integration. It is the ideal men usually have in mind when they speak of modernizing, up-dating, rationalizing, planning' (Roszak 1969: 5). From the point of view of the counter-culture, argues Roszak, the basic disregard of the technocracy for human emotion and creativity was completely unacceptable. The only solution, therefore, was for young people to reject it; to 'drop out' of the system and create a new way of life. Roszak describes the counter-culture as 'technocracy's children', disaffected middle-class youth who wished to break out of the bourgeois world of their parent culture. Thus writes Roszak:

> by way of a dialectic Marx could never have imagined, technocratic America produces a potentially revolutionary element among its own youth. The bourgeoisie, instead of discovering the class enemy in its factories, finds it across the breakfast table in the person of its own pampered children.
>
> (Roszak 1969: 34)

In the context of the late 1960s and early 1970s, such an interpretation of the counter-cultural movement allowed for a timely revision of the original Marxist model of social change in a way which illustrated the existence of not only working class but also middle class dissent within capitalist society. The consequent implication, according to theorists such as Clarke *et al.* (1976) and Roszak (1969), was that revolution and subsequent social change no longer turned on the success of a working class uprising, but could now be a two-pronged assault on the ruling class both from without and within. There are, however, two essential problems with such an interpretation of the counter-culture. First, there was a clear disjuncture between the types of political action engaged in by counter-cultural groups and that required for the type of large-scale social change envisaged by social theorists. Certainly there were a number of localised examples of radical political action, a notable example taking place in the streets of Paris during May 1968 when student protests concerning poor facilities at the university campus in Nanterre, an outer suburb of Paris, turned into a full-scale revolt involving factions of both the middle and working classes. As Halliday writes:

> What started as the action of small revolutionary groups swelled into the most significant mass contestation of the State since the Commune, arousing large numbers of the French working class [who] joined in huge demonstrations in solidarity with the students: a general strike was initiated, then, despite the reluctance of trade union leadership, it turned into factory occupations by nearly ten million workers . . . the militant students continued to play a key role during and after the insurrection they had ignited. Action groups were set up to help workers produce propaganda materials . . . Links between workers and students were formed which were to form the basis for future common actions.
>
> (Halliday 1969: 320)

Despite the occurrence of such organised, politically motivated cross-class actions, however, the counter-cultural movement was not uniformly politicized in the radical sense suggested by the Paris incident and similar pockets of protest across Europe and the US. Indeed, certain generational spokespersons to whom the counter-culture looked for inspiration actively warned against the exercise of brute force or aggression in the attempt to create a new way of life and a new society. Thus, for example, the Beatles song 'Revolution', released in 1968, reflected upon some of the more violent examples of the counter-cultural action occurring at that time in Europe and the US. According to Greil Marcus:

> The Beatles were giving orders and setting up rules, singing words that were perfectly intelligible, making sure nobody missed anything, singing a song that neatly caught the listener in a logical trap. No one takes sides with the "minds that hate" that the Beatles were singing about.
>
> (Marcus 1972: 130)

The second problem inherent in the Marxist interpretation applied to the counter-culture is its underlying assumption that the latter comprised wholly of white middle class youth. According to Clecak (1983), not only were people from a variety of social and cultural groups involved in the counter-culture but also the term counter-culture itself was, in reality, simply an umbrella term for an amorphous range of activities and ideologies which, for a brief period during the 1960s, found a common voice. The counter-culture, suggests Clecak (1983: 18), enabled a wide range of groups 'to find symbolic shapes for their social and spiritual discontents and hopes'. These groups included:

> (1) The civil-rights movement, beginning with blacks but quickly encompassing such other racial minorities as American Indians, Hispanic Americans, and Asian-Americans; (2) the young, especially college students and disaffected intellectuals; (3) the peace and anti-war movements; (4) the poor; (5) women; (6) the human-potential movement; (7) prisoners and other 'outcasts'; (8) gays and lesbians; (9) consumers; (10) environmentalists; (11) the old; and (12) the physically different (the disabled, the very fat, the very tall, the very short).
>
> (Clecak 1983: 18)

A similar point is made in a more recent study by Eyerman and Jamison (1998) who suggest that:

> During the 1960s youth not only gained self-consciousness, it became the model and set standards for the rest of society in many spheres of

culture, from the most superficial like clothing and hair-styles, to the most deeply rooted like the basic social interactions of men and women and blacks and whites.

(Eyerman and Jamison 1998: 113)

As with Clecak (1983), Eyerman and Jamison (1998) point to the essentially diverse, heterogeneous nature of both the individuals and socio-political and cultural ideals which merged together within, or took their lead from, the counter-cultural movement. Clearly then, there are fundamental problems with those attempts to theorize the counter-culture as an exclusively white middle-class phenomenon and the interpretation of the counter-culture as a catalyst for cross-class action on the scale needed to effect large-scale social change. The point remains, however, that the counter-culture did serve as a common point of reference for a number of loosely affiliated collective causes and in each case popular music functioned as a galvanizing force.

Music, drugs and the counter-culture

In a way which has not been repeated in the history of post-1945 popular culture, during the mid to late 1960s music became a centrally significant medium for the dissemination of a range of socio-political issues, from US involvement in the Vietnam war to the Civil Rights Movement, to the rejection of western political and cultural ideology. As Eyerman and Jamison (1998: 108) point out: 'Movement ideas, images, and feelings were disseminated in and through popular music and, at the same time, the movements of the times influenced developments, in both form and content, in popular music'.

Perhaps one of the most salient documents of this dialectical relationship between music and counter-cultural ideologies is the film *Easy Rider*. Released in 1969, the film stars Peter Fonda and Dennis Hopper as Wyatt and Billy, two **hippies** who use money acquired through drug trafficking to buy chopperized motorcycles and finance a road trip to Florida. The soundtrack for *Easy Rider*, a selection of popular songs of the day, including Steppenwolf, the Jimi Hendrix Experience, The Byrds, The Band and The Electric Prunes, is 'carefully [used] as a musical commentary throughout the picture' in a way intended to illustrate the close relationship between the sensibilities communicated by song lyrics and the knowledge, views and aspirations of those seeking out alternative ideologies and lifestyles across the US during the late 1960s (Denisoff and Romanowski 1991: 169).

The key to music's role in counter-cultural ideology was its power to convey a sense of 'community' among those who listened to it and understood its message. According to Frith (1983), in the context of the late 1960s *rock music* (the idiom formally used in much academic and journalistic writing to distinguish politically and artistically informed popular music from its chart-orientated counterpart)[1] functioned like folk music, in that it 'articulate[d] communal values [and] comment[ed] on shared social problems' (Frith 1981: 159). As Frith points out, such community building properties were not inherent to the music itself but rather resulted from the way in which it was perceived and responded to by audiences. Thus 'music (whether folk or pop or rock) is not made *by* a community, but provides particular sorts of communal *experience*' (Frith 1981: 164, original emphasis). This aspect of music and its particular bearing on rock in the late 1960s is further illustrated by Sardiello in a study of **Dead Heads**, a term given to fans of the leading 1960s psychedelic rock band the Grateful Dead, whose recording and touring career continued into the 1990s. According to Sardiello (1994: 115), Dead Heads 'construct and maintain a sense of unity and feeling of belonging which extends beyond the concert setting'.

The power of music to convey feelings of togetherness and community among members of the counter-culture in the ways described above was first witnessed at the 'Human Be-In', an event that took place in January 1967 in San Francisco's Golden Gate Park. Among the many rock bands who performed at the event was the Grateful Dead, at this time a relatively unknown local group from San Francisco's Haight-Ashbury district who performed long improvised sets characterised by spontaneous experimentation with sound, a style which would later become known as **acid rock** (Whiteley 1992). In the previous year the Grateful Dead had provided the music for a series of **happenings** – combinations of light shows, avant garde films, live music, **tape loops** and lurid poster art – held in hired bars and clubs around San Francisco (see Wolfe 1968). Organized by Ken Kesey (author of *One Flew Over the Cuckoo's Nest*) the happenings were used primarily as a way of promoting LSD, a synthetic hallucinogenic drug developed by Swiss chemist Dr Albert Hoffman during the 1930s (Edelstein 1985).

Also present at Golden Gate Park's Human Be-In was Timothy Leary, a former Harvard University professor. Sacked from Harvard because of his experiments with LSD, Leary 'went on the road as [a] full-time psychedelic salesm[a]n' (Edelstein 1985: 182). Attending hippie gatherings across the US, Leary communicated a simple message to the young people present – 'turn on, tune in and drop out'. In his study *The Hippies: An American Moment*, Stuart Hall (1968) examines both the literal and submerged aspects of Leary's message:

To 'tune in' means, literally, to 'attune' oneself to another way of life; but it is also a submerged metaphor from the mass media. There is, the phrase suggests, more than one channel of perception through which we experience the world . . . This idea is repeated in the second phrase – 'turn on'. Literally, this invites the hippy to switch to the use of mind expanding drugs and to turn on as many members of straight society as he can reach. But, again, metaphorically, it also means to switch to a more authentic mode of experience, to leave the routes of middle class society for more private, apocalyptic channels. 'Drop out' is perhaps the most complex message of all in its associative meaning. Again, it means, literally, that the hippy should reject [middle class values such as] work, power, status and consumption . . . But the phrase 'drop out' [also] has a more precise social and political reference . . . [Hippie] 'drop-outs' often stay within hailing distance of the university campus. They constitute part of the *informal* community of scholars.

(Hall 1968: 4–5)

According to Hall then, rather than representing an unstructured lifestyle of hedonism and self-gratification, drug use, as it featured in hippie culture, was about the subversion of the existing social order through the unlocking of alternative experiences which were not orientated towards educational success, status, money and power. Music was also regarded by the hippies as a crucial medium for attaining higher states of awareness. Arguably, the relationship between drugs and music during the 1960s has been exaggerated. Indeed, a famous case in point is the Beatles song 'Lucy in the Sky with Diamonds', claimed by many to be a direct reference to LSD but defended by John Lennon as a title he took from a painting by his son Julian (see Palmer 1976: 250; Whiteley 1992). Nevertheless, sociological research conducted during the late 1960s does suggest that particular aesthetics of drug use and music consumption were inscribed in the hippie lifestyle. Willis's (1976) research on the cultural meaning of drug use for hippies argued that there was a direct relationship between the use of mind-expanding drugs such as marijuana and LSD and particular ways of experiencing music.

From the point of view of the hippies interviewed by Willis (1978), careful use of drugs and music could enhance the senses and open up new ways of experiencing the world. At the same time, suggests Willis, the music itself was produced in such a way that particular patterns of consumption were demanded of the listener. Electronic effects, such as echo and **feedback** 'were used to give the impression of space and lateral extension' when listened to under the influence of drugs (Willis 1978: 167). Willis suggests that the relationship between music and drugs in the hippie lifestyle is *homological*,

homology representing 'the continuous play between the group and a particular item which produces specific styles, meanings, contents and forms of consciousness' (1978: 191). Thus, in relation to hippie culture, Willis argues that collective values and expectations are inscribed within drugs and music relating to their combined effects on perception. Willis further maintains that it is only through an appreciation of such cultural values, acquired via a total absorption in the hippie lifestyle, that the 'correct' use of drugs and music can be learned and practised.

In addition to experimentation with hallucinogenic drugs, many individuals involved in the counter-cultural movement also turned to eastern religions in an attempt to acquire new levels of consciousness. According to Glock and Bellah (1976) the heavily spiritual aspect of eastern religions such as Hinduism served to restore a meaningful pattern of personal and social existence to the counter-culture which was absent in the utilitarian individualism of the west. Other theorists take a more critical view of the counter-culture's appropriation of eastern religious belief. Hall (1968), for example, suggests that hippies took from eastern religion those ideas and doctrines which could be conveniently worked into the hippie lifestyle while simultaneously ignoring the more restrictive features of eastern belief such as the proscription of sex and drugs. The resulting pastiche of eastern belief and locally acquired counter-cultural ideology is effectively summed up in the following observation by Hall:

> The sacred books of Eastern religion and mysticism, the erotic code books, the figures of the Buddha and of Karma, fragments of eastern philosophy, the adoption of the kashdan, the simulated orientalism of Leary's ritual LSD 'performances', the music of Ravi Shankar, the zitar [sic], the looping and winding dances, the Buddhist chants of Allen Ginsberg – all of these are elements in the eclectic orientalism of Hippie life, representing a return to contemplation and mystical experience.
>
> (Hall 1968: 8)

Such was the fascination with the 'East' that during the late 1960s many young Hippies from the west made pilgrimages to eastern countries such as Turkey, Iran, Afghanistan and Pakistan. In May 1968, a Member of Parliament (MP), Philip Goodhart, suggested that: 'Hippies are . . . the major British contribution to the Afghan scene' (cited in Shearman 1983: 1396). Many hippies, unhappy with socio-political conditions in their own countries, tried to settle in eastern locations, often with little success. The young westerners failed to make sense of the native populations of eastern countries resulting in a disregard for local customs and feelings. The hippies' quest for spiritual knowledge in eastern locations represented a further misinterpretation of eastern philosophy as gurus pointed out that answers often lay in the journey itself rather than in reaching the destination.

The anti-Vietnam war campaign

In addition to forging new directions in youth lifestyles, such as experimentation with hallucinogenic drugs and eastern religion, the counter-culture also embraced several forms of organised protest against the dominant political **hegemony** in the west. One of the most significant protest movements to emerge from the counter-culture was the anti-Vietnam war campaign. Film footage of the peace march on the Pentagon building in Washington DC in October 1967 remains a poignant reminder of the counter-culture, as young hippies are seen inserting flowers down the barrels of rifles held by Pentagon guards. For demonstrators in the US, and in western Europe, the key issues were the senseless nature of the Vietnam war which, it was argued, had 'sunk into an apparently endless slough of mud and dead bodies' and the action of the US government, preventing the self-determination of smaller countries in defence of its own corporate interests (Snowman 1968: 149).

This anti-war feeling was shared by many popular musicians, who attempted to make their views known via anti-war songs. During the 1969 Woodstock festival, Country Joe MacDonald, in a performance that was immortalized through its inclusion in the documentary film *Woodstock* (see Young and Lang 1979), played a major role in popularizing the anti-war campaign with the 'Fixin' to Die Rag', a powerful anti-Vietnam war song that chimed perfectly with the mood of the 25,000 strong audience:

> And it's one, two three, what are we fighting for?
> Don't ask me I don't give a damn, the next stop is Vietnam . . .
> You can be the first ones on the block to have your boy come home in
>   a box

Gleason (1972: 139) writes of the 'Fixin' to Die Rag' that there was no 'comparable medium' for the counter-culture's anti-war message. It was direct, hard hitting and highly damning of the US government which, it was argued, was sending thousands of healthy young men to their deaths in a war which had only an economic rationale. Similarly, the promotional film to the Doors' anti-war song 'The Unknown Soldier' showed singer Jim Morrison being blindfolded and shot, a scene intended to parody the 'summary executions of . . . untried opponents' often featured in US media reports about the Vietnam war (Snowman 1984: 163). Other popular music artists also delivered powerful anti-war messages. For example, Joni Mitchell's song 'Woodstock', dedicated to the Woodstock Festival, contains the line:

I dreamt I saw the bombers turning into butterflies.

Similarly, Mitchell's contemporary, Joan Baez, visited children's hospitals in the North Vietnamese capitol Hanoi at a time when the city was being heavily bombed by US aircraft. Many observers suggest that the anti-Vietnam war campaign was largely ineffective in its efforts to end the war and that the eventual US withdrawal from Vietnam was not as a result of the campaign, nor the satirical attacks of musicians. Indeed, Buckman (1970) argues that the victory of the Vietcong in the 1968 Tet offensive and the escalating costs of US involvement in the war were much more instrumental in starting peace talks than a dozen marches on Washington, or a thousand protest songs. Nevertheless, the efforts of the anti-Vietnam war campaign resulted in some success. It could be argued that the campaign made it effectively impossible for the US administration to claim that the country was wholeheartedly behind the US's involvement in Vietnam.

The Civil Rights Movement

If the anti-Vietnam war movement marked one of the ways in which the emphasis of the counter-culture changed from passive to direct action during the late 1960s, so the reaction of African Americans to their treatment in the US became more radical. Throughout the 1960s a number of protest movements, some initiated by both blacks and whites, had fought to gain equality for African Americans. In 1960 four 'freshmen' from an all-Negro college 'sat-in' on a segregated lunch counter at F. W. Woolworth in Greensboro, North Carolina. This style of non-violent action spread to South Carolina and Virginia. Following the first arrests white students began to join in with the protest action, sometimes being jailed with black students. In October 1966, the Student Nonviolent Coordinating Committee (SNCC) was established to enable students to become organised in the battle for civil rights (see Buckman 1970: 134–5).

However, neither the SNCC nor President Kennedy's Civil Rights Bill, passed in 1964 after his assassination, did anything to alleviate the abject poverty and 'total political impotence' of African Americans (Buckman 1970: 135). Amidst increasing racial discrimination, harassment and the consequent onset of inner-city riots, the most violent examples being in New York's Harlem district and in the black quarters of Rochester, Philadelphia, the civil rights organizations were superseded by the Black Power Movement. Under the leadership of such figureheads as Malcolm X and Eldridge Cleaver, black militants began forming their own political and economic organizations and banding together in armed groups for their own self-defence. Embracing the basic tenets of the Muslim faith and its central figure Muhammad, the Black Power Movement was supplied with much of its political rationale by Stokely Carmichael, who Snowman (1984: 154) describes as the movement's 'most articulate and charismatic leader'. Interpreting the views of Carmichael, Snowman makes the following observation:

> All the other ethnic minorities in the United States . . . had achieved a measure of political and economic power only after a period in which they faced the rest of society with a united – and closed – front. Blacks, therefore, owed it to themselves to buy black, to sell black, to vote black – to think black.
>
> (Snowman 1984: 154–5)

Prominent in this new wave of direct action urged by the Black Power Movement was the Black Panther group. The Panthers demanded land, bread, housing, education, clothing, justice and peace as repayment for the murder and exploitation of black people.

Black music in the US also became more radical during the late 1960s. James Brown's 'Say It Loud, I'm Black and I'm Proud' and Aretha Franklin's 'Respect', for example, summed up perfectly the mood and feeling of the Black Power Movement with their expressions of **black pride**. As Billig (2000: 110) notes: 'With black pride, there was an increasing feeling that African Americans should support and protect their own culture. Music had to be specifically black to appeal to black audiences'. Another significant black American artist of the late 1960s was guitarist and songwriter Jimi Hendrix. Born in Seattle, Washington State, Hendrix was one of only a few musicians from the US's ethnic minorities to gain acceptance in the white mainstream rock industry. By the late 1960s Hendrix had 'become passionately involved in the gangs of Harlem [and] in the growth of the Black Muslim Church' (Palmer 1976: 253). Moreover, Hendrix's decision in 1969 to form an all-black group, the Band of Gypsies, was clearly influenced by the Black Power Movement. Eric Burden of British rhythm and blues group The Animals said of Hendrix:

> If you want to see what an American black is going through today, where his mind is at, go and see Hendrix . . . and you'll realise why there are race riots in America and why the country is so close to civil war. He's a wizard on the guitar, but his music is so disturbed and so explosive. He is exorcising generations of anger.
>
> (Burdon cited in Palmer 1976: 253)

Some white musicians also expressed solidarity with the Civil Rights and Black Power movements. The Young Rascals, for example, publicly announced that they had no interest in performing on the *Ed Sullivan Show*, which they considered to be a bastion of conservative white America, and that they were not prepared to 'appear on a concert bill unless there [were] also black artists presented' (Gleason 1972: 145).

Counter-cultural ideology and non-western youth

As much of the work examined in this chapter serves to illustrate, the counter-culture is typically represented as a western phenomenon driven by a disaffected youth's rejection of western capitalism, **cultural imperialism** and the foreign policy of particular western governments. However, more recent socio-historical research has begun to illustrate that the impact of the counter-culture was more widely felt during the late 1960s and early 1970s. In the final part of this chapter I want to consider expressions of counter-cultural ideology in two settings outside the western world – the former Soviet Union and Mexico. As noted in Chapter 1, although the Soviet authorities imposed severe sanctions on young people who embraced aspects of western popular culture this did little to deter the interest of Soviet youth in popular music and its attendant stylistic sensibilities. The vast size of the Soviet Union and limited media and communication in more rural areas meant that such interest in popular music was confined to the larger cities, such as Moscow and Leningrad, in European regions of the country. While demand for western popular music had been steadily grow-ing in these Soviet cities since the late 1950s such demand increased dramatically during 'the late 1960s when the Beatles entered their hippy/ Buddhist stage' (Easton 1989: 47). Thus, as Pond states:

> The majority of Russian youth was set alight by the mixture of anarchy and collectivism which they felt the Beatles represented . . . They became for the Soviets not only musical but spiritual leaders.
> (Pond 1987; cited in Easton 1989: 47)

The Soviet authorities continued in their attempts to control, or at best sup-press, the interest among Soviet youth in western popular music. Partly, this was done on the grounds of maintaining public order but also in the inter-ests of keeping Soviet society free of any potentially corrupting influences from the west. However, as Easton (1989) points out, if western popular music was seen as a bourgeois, decadent genre that represented the decay in capitalist countries [this] thesis conveniently ignored the fact that much of the Western rock movement revolved around protest at this very decay.

(Easton 1989: 49)

Moreover, the Soviet authorities remained blatantly indifferent to the onset of social decay and disillusionment in their own nation. By the late 1960s there were clear signs that communism as it had been realized in the Soviet Union was falling far short of people's expectations. In particular, the stagnation and corruption of the Brezhnev era had caused much bitterness, especially among the young. The gulf between the official interpretations of Soviet society and the reality of the situation in Russia meant that many young people could no longer hold onto the hopes and dreams which had inspired the generation which their parents belonged to.

In effect during the late 1960s sections of youth on both sides of the 'iron curtain' simultaneously lost faith in the political ideologies of their respective governments and the wider social beliefs which such ideologies had engendered. Alternative discourses were found in the lyrics and expressed ideas of rock musicians. For Soviet youth, however, the political value of rock music was only fully realized when local expressions of the rock community began to take form. If western rock and popular music became a source of hope and inspiration, the precise meanings of the rock discourse were not properly understood by Soviet youth whose knowledge of English was, by and large, very limited. The response to this was the formation of a local rock scene comprising of groups who sang in Russian and focussing on issues which were particular to Soviet society and intimately understood by the youth of the nation.

One of the most well known and enduring of the Soviet rock groups formed during the late 1960s was Aquarium. The leader of Aquarium, Boris Grebenshchikov, became a cultural and spiritual leader for the disillusioned Russian youth. Like many rock artists in the west, Boris Grebenshchikov has achieved cult status among young people in Russia who acknowledge their respect for him through **graffiti** messages written on the walls of the building where he lives. As Easton observes:

Boris's communal apartment . . . in Leningrad bears witness to the kind of emotions inspired by these 'custodians' of the popular conscience. The stairwell leading up to his flat on the eighth floor is literally covered with graffiti. 'Boris, you are life'. 'We cannot live without you'. 'Aquarium – the mind and conscience of the Soviet youth' (a parody of a famous Lenin poster).

(Easton 1989: 50)

As Easton (1989) explains, in addition to singing about themes which are common to popular music in any language – themes such as 'love and estrangement [and] disappointed expectations', Grebenshchikov also focuses on issues which are more specific to Russian life and society. Thus, writes Easton (1989: 50): 'Boris is also concerned at the loss of individuality in Soviet society: "Our lyrics are spiritually orientated. Who am I in relation to power? Do I want to be guided? Who guides me? Who controls me?" '.

In certain respects, the arrival of the counter-cultural consciousness in Mexico is comparable with its manifestation in the Soviet Union. Like Soviet youth, young people in Mexico had difficulty in gaining access to western recordings and relied instead upon performances by 'local bands that, by necessity and default, emerged as the interpreters of a countercultural consciousness exploding around the world' (Zolov 1999: 97–8). Similarly, the growing interest among sections of Mexican youth in counter-cultural music and values led to considerable concern on the part of the authorities and parents who felt that such an interest 'not only distracted political energies but also reinforced subservience to foreign values' (Zolov 1999: 111). However, such criticisms of the Mexican counter-culture overlooked the extent to which it drew on aspects of local culture, notably 'indigenous dress, and hand crafted jewellery' (Zolov 1999: 111). Moreover, as Zolov observes, such a

revalorization of the indigenous culture . . . opened up an important psychic space for dissent. This opening offered Mexican youth a vehicle that was both modern and culturally relevant. It allowed youth to invent new ways of being Mexican, ways that ran counter to the dominant ideology of state sponsored nationalism.

(Zolov 1999: 111)

As in the US and western Europe, much of the more militant counter-cultural activity witnessed in Mexico took place during the year 1968. While this was due in part to 'the reverberations of the Paris uprising' and the **Prague Spring** (the latter referring to May 1968 when Russian tanks took control of the city of Prague in the former Czechoslovakia) (Zolov 1999: 119), direct action by the Mexican counter-culture was also precipitated by more local issues.

During 1968 Mexico City was the host for the Olympic Games. The Mexican media represented this as evidence of the transformation of Mexico 'from a bandit-ridden, agrarian economy into a modern, industrialised nation' (Zolov 1999: 119). However, from the point of view of students and political activists, such a representation of Mexico was hypocritical given the country's history of police oppression and the dictatorial nature of the governing regime. As global media attention focused on the Olympics, students in Mexico City used the opportunity to mount an organised protest movement which called for an end to police brutality and oppression and justice for victims of repression. The focus for the student movement was the Universidad Nacional Autónoma de México (UNAM). As Zolov observes:

> At the UNAM, gatherings organized around folk-music performances, political theater, poetry readings, and collective mural paintings all formed an integral aspect of student-movement culture. The raising of political consciousness associated with the student movement reinforced the place of Latin American folk music over rock, which was still more strongly identified with youthful diversion than with serious political struggle. But foreign rock's close associations with the avant-garde and ties to student-movement culture elsewhere in the world kept it from being condemned as imperialist, except by the most radical elements.
>
> (Zolov 1999: 123)

As in other parts of the world then, the counter-culture in Mexico encompassed a range of youth protest movements designed to proactively engage with the dominant hegemonic power. Similarly, as with the US and western Europe, popular music became centrally involved in Mexican counter-cultural activity as a communicator of alternative socio-political ideologies.

Conclusion

In this chapter I have examined the relationship between popular music and counter-cultural ideology during the mid to late 1960s. Focusing upon several of the most significant movements to emerge from the counter-culture, I have examined the ways in which music informed a range of alternative lifestyles and perceptions of the world which involved a rejection of western political and cultural hegemony. I have also illustrated how, rather than being confined to the youth of western nations, counter-cultural ideas spread to other parts of the world where they were operationalized in localised forms of youth. While it would be incorrect to suggest that the counter-culture changed the world in any significant way, the legacy of counter-culture continues to be felt in a range of proactive movements, many of which derive directly from the alternative ideologies first expressed by groups and movements associated with the counter-culture.

The growing support for human rights and the work of such organizations as Amnesty International clearly owes something to the progressive socio-political discourse of the counter-culture. Similarly, the turn towards organic farming and the increasing reliance upon alternative herbal medicines can also be rooted back to the counter-culture. While many of the original hippie **communes** soon foundered, several have survived and become self-sufficient communities. The current **neo-Greenism**, the road-building protests and New Age **Travellers** also clearly owe something to counter-cultural ideology. Indeed, McKay (1996) goes so far as to suggest that all the forms of youth protest which have followed the counter-culture have their roots in its political and cultural ideologies. Thus, he argues:

> There are connections, surprising ones maybe that belie a straightforward generational reading of events over the past three decades: individual activists like Penny Rimbaud or Fraser Clark move through from one moment to another – hippy to punk, hippy to rave; the space of the free festival is re-energized by punk, is transformed by rave culture; the lifestyles of New Age travellers are co-opted and politicized by peace campaigners or road protesters.
>
> (McKay 1996: 7)

Note

1 In a critique of this rock/pop distinction, Harker (1992) argues that the emphasis on the authenticity of 'rock' – a form which, it is claimed, appealed largely to a middle class, intellectual audience during the 1960s – serves to marginalize 'the musical practices and tastes' of working class people, for whom, according to Harker, more obviously 'commercial' music, such as chart records, disco music and Christmas albums, would have been the preferred choice (Harker 1992: 251).

Further reading

Clarke, J., Hall, S., Jefferson, T. and Roberts, B. (1976) Subcultures, cultures and class: a theoretical overview, in S. Hall and T. Jefferson (eds) *Resistance through Rituals: Youth Subcultures in Post-War Britain*. London: Hutchinson (pp. 57–71).

Easton, P. (1989) The rock music community, in J. Riordan (ed.) *Soviet Youth Culture*. Bloomington, IN: Indiana University Press.

Eyerman, R. and Jamison, A. (1998) *Music and Social Movements: Mobilizing Traditions in the Twentieth Century*. Cambridge: Cambridge University Press (Chapter 5).

Frith, S. (1981) The magic that can set you free: the ideology of folk and the myth of rock, *Popular Music*, 1: 159–68.

Hall, S. (1968) *The Hippies: An American 'Moment'*. Birmingham: Centre for Contemporary Cultural Studies, University of Birmingham.

Halliday, F. (1969) Students of the world unite, in A. Cockburn and R. Blackburn (eds) *Student Power: Problems, Diagnosis, Action*. Harmondsworth: Penguin.

Harker, D. (1992) Still crazy after all these years: what *was* popular music in the 1960s?, in B. Moore-Gilbert and J. Seed (eds) *Cultural Revolution? The Challenge of the Arts in the 1960s*. London: Routledge.

Reich, C.A. (1971) *The Greening of America*. London: Allen Lane.

Roszak, T. (1969) *The Making of a Counter Culture: Reflections on the Technocratic Society and its Youthful Opposition*. London: Faber and Faber.

Zolov, E. (1999) *Refried Elvis: The Rise of the Mexican Counterculture*. London: University of California Press.

3 | HEAVY METAL

It was just after 11.00 pm on Friday night, and I was looking for a club called Rebels. 'A club for extraverts' [*sic*] said the owner, Steve, on the phone. 'A club for headbangers', said everyone else. You know the kind of guys with long limp hair, circa 1969, playing imaginary guitars, and girls, well I wasn't sure about the girls. But I knew they were still into Led Zeppelin, sorry Led Zep, and Deep Purple, twenty years on. Youth cults come and go, but this one has endured, or the pause button has got jammed, one or the other.

(Beattie 1990: 53)

Until the beginning of the 1990s, heavy metal music and its audience received very little serious attention from academic researchers. Such indifference on the part of academics was significant, given the longevity of heavy metal's appeal in a sphere of popular culture notable for fads and fashions. Moreover, heavy metal had generated, and continues to generate, such appeal despite receiving virtually no airplay on terrestrial TV channels and commercial radio stations (Kotarba 1994) and being generally shunned by music critics (Shuker 1994: 147–8).

This chapter examines the phenomenon of heavy metal, from the heavily amplified blues-rock of Led Zeppelin which, according to some observers, initially defined the heavy metal style (Christgau 1981; Waksman 1999) to the complex and infinite array of subgenres comprising the current 'metal' scene (Friesen and Epstein 1994; Harris 2000). In addition to looking at some of the musical and performative traits associated with heavy metal, I will also be concerned with the ways in which heavy metal is appropriated and experienced by fans of the genre. Studies of heavy metal invariably link the preference for heavy metal music among adolescents and people in their early twenties with issues such as low socio-economic position (Straw 1983), unsettled family life (Arnett 1991, 1996) and postindustrial risk and anomie (Locher 1998). Moreover, it is argued, the factors influencing a

preference for heavy metal make for a ready association on the part of disempowered and disaffected young people with what Harrell (1994) terms
the poetics of destruction in heavy metal lyrics, the latter frequently focusing on issues such as death, mutilation (Gross 1990; Harrell 1994), physical
violence and misogyny (Walser 1993; Sloat 1998). Indeed, the content of
heavy metal lyrics and its alleged effects upon young fans has been the subject of much debate, especially in the US where the music has been blamed
for a series of teenage suicides (Weinstein 1991; Shuker 1994).

The origins of heavy metal

The origins of the heavy metal sound can be traced back to the decline in
popularity of psychedelic music at the end of the 1960s. As Straw (1983)
notes, when psychedelia began to fade, rock music developed in three main
directions, country rock (typified by groups such as the Eagles), progressive
rock (pioneered by British groups such as Genesis, Yes, and Emerson, Lake
and Palmer) and heavy metal. In many ways, heavy metal represented a
return to the more gritty aesthetic of rock 'n' roll while at the same time
'retaining from psychedelia an emphasis on technological effect and instrumental virtuosity' (Straw 1983: 97). Chambers, in a rather more negative
assessment of heavy metal's blending of 1960s psychedelic music with the
basic chord structures of the blues, describes heavy metal as a 'mutant
offspring' that took psychedelic rock's 'largely guitar based aesthetic [and]
successfully transformed it into a loud and direct populism' (Chambers
1985: 123).

If there is a general consensus among theorists as to the origins of the
heavy metal sound, then the geographical origins of heavy metal remain dis-
puted. Thus, as Gross notes:

> Some music historians prefer to credit [US] band Steppenwolf with the
> invention of the heavy metal music form. In 1967 they recorded 'Born
> to be Wild', a tune that not only features many criteria that fit the
> modern day definition of heavy metal, but the words 'heavy metal thun-
> der' actually appear in the second verse of the song.
>
> (Gross 1990: 120)

Other writers, such as Breen (1991), argue that the heavy metal sound originated in Britain with the release of Led Zeppelin's eponymously titled debut
album in 1968, while Robert Walser (1993) suggests: 'If metal could be said
to have gotten started in a single place, it would have to be Birmingham,
England, the industrial city whose working class spawned Ozzy Osbourne,

Black Sabbath, and Judas Priest in the late 1960s and early 1970s' (Walser 1993: x). During the 1970s heavy metal became more globally prominent through the huge commercial success of groups such as Led Zeppelin, Deep Purple, Uriah Heep and US group Kiss, this success effectively 'consolidat[ing] heavy metal as a market force' and establishing a heavy metal youth scene (Shuker 1994: 149).

The longevity of heavy metal is undoubtedly due, to a very large extent, to the immense dedication and loyalty of the young fans who regularly attend heavy metal concerts and buy records, compact discs (**CDs**) and videos (Breen 1991: 200; Shuker 1994: 152). Studies of heavy metal audiences suggest a relationship between preference for heavy metal, ethnicity, gender and socio-economic status, a common description of the heavy metal audience being that it is predominantly white, male and working class (Shuker 1994: 150). In the context of Britain such claims have been easily made given that, initially at least, heavy metal musicians and fans emerged from the manual working classes as compared, for example, with progressive rock whose musicians and fans were generally middle class, university educated people (see Murdock and McCron 1976; Willis 1978; Macan 1997: 144–66). Placing such findings in a more global context, Breen (1991) makes similar claims regarding the socio-economic composition of the heavy metal audience in other parts of the world. Thus, argues Breen:

> Its intense popularity in working-class cities of Scandinavia and the contemporary experience of metal in the Australian context, suggests that heavy-metal, as a genre, draws its potent audience power from working-class youth.
>
> (Breen 1991: 194)

Such arguments become more problematic in the case of North America where, even in its formative years, heavy metal attracted a more middle class, suburban following. Nevertheless, early studies conducted in Canada and the US did suggest a relationship between preference for heavy metal, low educational achievement, socio-economic status and the combined impact of these factors on life chances. Thus, as Straw notes

> the [North American] heavy metal audience, by the early 1980s, consisted to a significant extent of suburban males who did not acquire a postsecondary education and who increasingly found that their socioeconomic prospects were not as great as those of their parents.
>
> (Straw 1983: 107)

As the 1980s progressed, however, such class and gender dimensions of heavy metal audiences became less pronounced as the audience base for heavy metal diversified and crossed over into pop. To a large extent, the 'popularization' of heavy metal that took place during the second half of the 1980s was due to the arrival of new 'soft metal' groups, such as Bon Jovi, who successfully combined the established heavy metal guitar-based sound with the keyboard and string textures of mainstream pop, thus widening the appeal of heavy metal considerably. Thus, as Walser explains:

> The 1980s was the decade of heavy metal's emergence as a massively popular musical style, as it burgeoned in both commercial success and stylistic variety. The heavy metal audience became increasingly gender-balanced and middle-class, and its age range expanded to include significant numbers of preteens people and people in their late twenties. By 1989, heavy metal accounted for as much as 40 percent of all sound recordings sold in the United States, and Rolling Stone announced that heavy metal now constituted 'the mainstream of rock and roll'.
>
> (Walser 1993: 3)

The impact of the new soft metal sound was immediately apparent, not only in the changing nature of the heavy metal audience but also in the new array of fashions, particularly styled leather jackets and spandex trousers in a variety of colours, and 'ornately cut, moussed and blow-dried' hairstyles (Weinstein 1991: 43), which largely replaced the faded denim and long, limp-haired look associated with heavy metal fans during the 1970s. In addition to its promotion of a new heavy metal 'look', the lyrical content of soft metal songs was also important in attracting a wider audience and, in particular, creating a female market for heavy metal. Commenting on Bon Jovi's change of musical direction for their 1986 release *Slippery When Wet*, the album which effectively defined the subgenre of soft metal, Walser makes the following observations:

> The most obvious change was in the lyrics: abandoning heavy metal gloom and doom, and creepy mysticism [Bon Jovi] began cultivating a positive, upbeat outlook, where the only mystical element was bourgeois love. Writing songs about romantic love and personal relationships, they tempered their heavy metal sound and image and pitched their product to appeal as well to a new, female market.
>
> (Walser 1993: 120)

However, if soft metal was something of an instant commercial success during the mid-1980s, then such success was relatively short-lived.

During the early 1990s heavy metal underwent another significant change in direction, both musically and aesthetically, the soft metal sounds of the 1980s losing their appeal in a seemingly 'overnight' fashion as a new range of metal subgenres, collectively categorized as 'Extreme Metal' (Harris 2000), began to gain in popularity. Extreme metal signalled a return to a more guitar-based metal sound which was less influenced by blues than earlier heavy metal styles and rhythmically more intricate (Denski and Sholle 1992: 43). Another distinguishing feature of extreme metal was its shunning of the showbusiness trappings, such as elaborate stagewear, lightshows and special effects, which had been a central feature of not only 1980s soft metal but also the large-scale **stadium rock** shows of 1970s heavy metal bands such as Led Zeppelin, Black Sabbath and Kiss (Denski and Sholle 1992: 43). Arguably, the more basic image and live performance format of extreme metal band was influenced in part by the Seattle-based grunge scene (whose best known groups included Nirvana and Pearl Jam) which rejected 'the glam aesthetic of eighties heavy metal and the slick elegance of techno pop' in favour of a more basic, **post-punk** musical and visual aesthetic (Santiago-Lucerna 1998). This said, however, the origins of the extreme metal scene can be traced back to the early 1980s and the formation of groups such as Metallica. Metallica's openly expressed antipathy towards 1980s soft metal (Denski and Sholle 1992: 43; Crocker 1993) and the group's crafting of an aggressive guitar-based musical style, which fans believed to remain true to the roots of metal, earned Metallica a form of underground status during the 1980s, illustrated by the fact that the group's 1989 album *And Justice for All* sold over 1 million copies despite receiving very little airplay by radio stations (Kotarba 1994: 141).

A significant aspect of extreme metal is that it is, like punk and rap, at least in their early years (see Chapters 4 and 6), an essentially 'hands on' musical style whose popularity owes much to the small-scale, localised nature of its production and performance. Commenting on the production and performance of heavy metal during the early 1970s, Straw has noted that:

> Heavy metal culture may be characterized in part by the absence of a strong middle stratum between the listener and the fully professional group. Only in rare cases in the early 1970s could there be found an echelon of local heavy metal bands performing their own material in local venues.
>
> (Straw 1983: 102)

This situation, which continued and indeed intensified during the 1980s with the increasing professionalization of heavy metal production and performance due to the commercial success of soft metal, is in stark contrast to the current extreme metal scene. Thus, as Harris observes:

> Whilst the Extreme Metal scene is characterised by a far greater level of decentralisation than Heavy Metal, local scenes have also been important in its development. Local scenes have been particularly important in pioneering new styles that have gone on to be popular throughout the global scene. In the 1980s, the San Francisco 'Bay Area' scene was crucial in the development of Thrash (involving bands such as Exodus and Metallica). In the late 1980s and early 1990s Death Metal was popularised via strong local scenes in Stockholm (involving bands such as Dismember and Entombed) and Tampa, Florida (involving bands such as Obituary and Deicide). In the mid-1990s Black Metal was popularised through the Norwegian scene (involving bands such as Burzum and Emperor).
>
> (Harris 2000: 16)

If the small-scale, local scene based character of extreme metal offers opportunities for creative involvement in a way that was largely missing from earlier heavy metal scenes, then equally important in accounting for extreme metal's appeal is the relationship between group and audience. The use of small venues and the proximity of the stage to the dance floor reduces the division between performer and audience giving rise to the same expressions of community and solidarity noted by Laing (1985) in relation to punk (see Chapter 4). This is expressed most visually through the act of **stagediving** where individual members of the audience climb up on to the stage while the band is performing and throw themselves off into the crowd below. Although appearing on the surface to be an individual act of daring or exhibitionism, stagediving relies both upon the willingness of the group performing to allow members of the audience up onto the stage and coordination between stagediver and crowd. As Arnett (1996: 92) observes, 'the act [of stagediving] demands trust in the swaying mass below to soften the landing'. Arnett's point is corroborated by Breen (1991: 200) who observes that 'significant bonding occurs when [heavy metal fans] stage or pit dive onto the hands and heads of the audience beneath them. Despite the risks they are always caught'.

Thus far, I have discussed the development of the heavy metal genre from its origins during the late 1960s through to the contemporary extreme metal scene. I want now to focus on more specific aspects of the relationship between heavy metal music and its audience as these have been taken up and discussed in academic studies of heavy metal.

Heavy metal and gender

The predominantly male nature of the heavy metal audience during the 1970s and early 1980s, and the almost exclusively male composition of bands (Whiteley 2000: 14), focused sociological attention on the gendered aspects of heavy metal. Frith and McRobbie's (1978: 373) treatment of this theme takes the male-centred character of heavy metal's 'control and production' as its starting point, subsequently using this assertion as a means for examining the construction of male sexuality by heavy metal groups and artists:

> Not only do we find men occupying every important style in the rock industry and in effect being responsible for the creation and construction of suitable female images, we also witness in rock the presentation and marketing of masculine styles.
>
> (Frith and McRobbie 1978: 374)

Frith and McRobbie introduce the term **cock rock** as a means of exploring the machoistic image presented by heavy metal artists:

> By 'cock rock' we mean music making in which performance is an explicit, crude and sometimes aggressive expression of male sexuality . . . Cock rock performers are aggressive, dominating and boastful, and they constantly seek to remind the audience of their prowess, their control. Their stance is obvious in live shows; male bodies on display, plunging shirts and tight trousers, a visual emphasis on chest hair and genitals.
>
> (Frith and McRobbie 1978: 374)

According to Frith and McRobbie, heavy metal performances become spaces for displays of male sexuality and male bonding between bands and their predominantly male audiences. This is promoted on-stage by the musicians' treatment of microphones and guitars as phallic symbols, a style of music that is 'rhythmically insistent [and] lyrics [that] are assertive and arrogant' (Frith and McRobbie 1978: 374).

In her study of the portrayal of women and female sexuality in heavy metal lyrics, Sloat (1998) argues that the majority of references to women involve forms of sexual subversion, typically through the use of words such as 'whore' and 'bitch', or by describing women as in need of, or craving, male sexual dominance. Sloat suggests that such lyrical traditions in heavy metal music are rooted in the patriarchal nature of contemporary capitalist societies and serve as an outlet for young adolescent males to deal with anxieties concerning their lack of social, physical and economic status:

Existing, as it does, in a culture of capitalistic and patriarchal values, and played primarily by and for young, white males who lack social, physical, and economic power, but are continually beset by messages promoting these types of power, heavy metal attempts to combat insecurities in the listeners by guaranteeing their place within the male dominated power structure . . . This is achieved by providing the adolescent males in the listening audience with an outlet for demonstrating their own power: women. Women become powerless victims in order to keep young males from feeling victims themselves.

(Sloat 1998: 295–6)

In a further analysis of female representation in heavy metal music, Walser (1993) broadens the focus of study beyond song lyrics to include other aspects of metal iconography, notably the art work of album covers and videos made to promote heavy metal artists. In doing so, Walser illustrates how the added dimension of the visual, especially in relation to video, is utilized in the construction of a further series of female images that again seek to represent women as a 'threat' to patriarchal power and authority:

Women are presented as essentially mysterious and dangerous; they harm simply by being, for their attractiveness threatens to disrupt both male self-control and the collective strength of male bonding.

(Walser 1993: 118)

At the same time, suggests Walser, the enhanced visual iconography made available to heavy metal artists through video has enabled the use of another strategy for dealing with the 'threat' posed by women, **female exscription**. Exscription involves the visual creation of scenes and gatherings from which women are absent. At the most basic level, this might take the form of a live or simulated live performance caught on video in which the all-male group performs for an all-male audience, the latter being by now a conventional heavy metal video format which, according to Walser (1993: 115), 'stresses the value of male bonding for creating close social ties while excluding the threat of the feminine'.

As Walser goes on to illustrate, however, such are the creative possibilities offered by video, that heavy metal artists need not necessarily resort to the performance video format in order to achieve female exscription. Thus: 'Even in nonperformance metal videos, where narratives and images are placed not on a stage but elsewhere, the point is the same: to represent and reproduce spectacles that depend for their appeal on the exscription of women' (Walser 1993: 115). Walser cites as an example of this the promotional video for Judas Priest's 1981 hit 'Heading Out to the Highway' which centres around drag racing, a predominantly male activity, on the open highway, the visual images presented in the video corresponding with the song's theme of 'freedom and adventure' (Walser 1993: 115). A further example of female exscription in heavy metal music can be seen in the work of British groups such as Black Sabbath and Iron Maiden, whose album covers, song themes and, occasionally, videos portray fantasy worlds inhabited by superhuman beings and monsters and 'evoking images of armoured, metalized male bodies' (Walser 1993: 116).

With the increasing popularity of soft metal during the mid-1980s, the machismo, misogyny, and female exscription associated with heavy metal was to some extent interrupted as metal periodically crossed over into the teenybop style. Teenybop is identified by Frith and McRobbie (1978) as the opposite of heavy metal's 'cock rock' image: 'If cock rock plays on conventional concepts of male sexuality as rampant, animalistic, superficial, and just for the moment, teenybop plays on notions of female sexuality as serious, diffuse, and implying total emotional commitment' (Frith and McRobbie 1978: 375). There are clear parallels between the male teenybop image described by Frith and McRobbie and the following account by Walser of soft metal group Bon Jovi's lead singer, Jon Bon Jovi:

> Though Bon Jovi offered typical experiences of the heavy metal dialectic of absolute control and transcendent freedom in a performative context of male bonding, lead singer Jon Bon Jovi also projected a kind of sincerity, and romantic vulnerability that had enormous appeal for female fans.
>
> (Walser 1993: 120)

The heavy metal scene of the mid-1980s also produced other gender representations in the form of **androgyny**. As Kaplan (1987) notes, androgyny involves an 'undertak[ing] of multiple identifications' which results in a 'blurring of clear lines between gender' (Kaplan 1987: 90). One of the first popular music artists successfully to confuse gender divisions in this way was David Bowie during his Ziggy Stardust phase of the early 1970s. As Hebdige (1979: 61) points out, 'Bowie was responsible for opening up questions of sexual identity which had previously been repressed, ignored or merely hinted at in rock and youth culture'. Using heavy make-up, hair-dye and an array of ornate stage costumes, Bowie's Ziggy Stardust character became 'the perfect pop androgyne, a chimera who bridge[d] the gap between masculine and feminine' (Zanetta and Edwards 1986: 116). According to Walser (1993), however, there are significant differences between the androgyny of David Bowie and 1980s 'glam metal' groups such as Mötley Crüe and Poison. Most notably, argues Walser (1983: 124), 'glam metal' lacks Bowie's 'ironic distance'. Indeed, according to Denski and

Scholle (1992), the androgynous image of glam metal is simply another way of asserting power over women, thus aligning it firmly with the patriarchal sensibilities evident in earlier forms of metal:

> the glam-styled body is seductive, but seduction is used to seduce the female and control her desire. For the male audience, the feminization of the body marks out a quite different discourse – one that overcomes fear of the feminine by incorporating it.
>
> (Denski and Scholle 1992: 52)

With the increasing popularity of extreme metal during the 1990s, the image of heavy metal groups became far more low key, eschewing make-up, costumes and jewellery associated with glam and soft metal and opting instead for more casual everyday clothes worn by young people, typically black jeans and T-shirts. Indeed, as Weinstein (1991: 52) notes, 'fans and performers, given the youthfulness of the band members and their fashion, are indistinguishable from one another'. In terms of gender composition, the metal audience again became predominantly male; likewise concert venues once again became scenes of male bonding rituals between band and audience. However, with the rise of extreme metal, the underlying rationale for such expressions of male bonding altered significantly, largely due to the lyrical content of extreme metal songs which no longer centred around themes of male sexuality and/or heroism but focused instead on issues of loneliness, despair and frustration in what Harrell (1994: 91) has called an 'unofficial expression of industrialism's emotional isolation and violence'.

Extreme metal, youth and postindustrial society

> At approximately 5.00 pm, Metallica came onstage . . . I was in a spot to observe a distinct change in the temperament and flow of the crowd. To this point the kids had been very much in a party mood, enjoying the music, the event, and the excitement. When Metallica began their set, bodies ceased to move and everyone's attention seemed to shift to the stories being told. Thousands of fourteen-, fifteen-, sixteen-year old kids, mostly boys, almost all attired in appropriate black T-shirt, did not so much sing along with Metallica as they *spoke* along. Song after song, the kids moved their lips in sync as they collectively tuned into another reality. This reality was not predicated by drugs, alcohol, or sensuality but by the ability of the narrative to collectively conceptualize individual experiences of growing up.
>
> (Kotarba 1994: 143, original emphasis)

As previously noted, the most apparent aspect of extreme metal lyrics is their engagement with contemporary social problems, particularly those confronting youth, such themes being largely ignored by earlier forms of metal music which, observes Harrell (1994: 92), were more concerned with 'the glorification of "sex, drugs and rock-n-roll" '. Such 'classic' heavy metal themes are absent from the lyrics of extreme metal songs – when drug and alcohol references are made this is generally in a negative context intended to emphasize their harmful effects (Harrell 1994: 92). Epstein *et al.* (1990) suggest that, from the point of view of the fans, the importance attached to a given genre of rock or pop music 'depends primarily on the extent to which it functions within their lives as a method of granting definition to experiences' (Epstein *et al.* 1990: 285). In this respect, it is possible to see how frequently explored themes of extreme metal songs, such as destruction, decay and disease, disillusion, corruption through power, confusion and isolation (Harrell 1994: 93) resonate in varying degrees with the experienced problems, and resulting outlook, of growing numbers of young people in contemporary society. A similar point is made by Berger, who in conducting interviews with death metal musicians and fans notes their stress on the importance 'of people coming together to listen to heavy music and using it to face the difficulties in their lives' (Berger 1999: 275).

The growth in appeal of extreme metal during the 1990s coincides with an increasing awareness among social theorists of how the socio-economic dislocation created by postindustrialization is leading to the creation of what is termed a **risk society**. First used by Beck (1992), the concept of risk society has significant implications for the life experiences of the young. In particular, increasing youth unemployment has resulted in a collapse of the division between work and leisure and its replacement by indefinite periods of unstructured free time (Furlong and Cartmel 1997). The acceptance of risk and uncertainty in everyday life is also argued to have produced an apolitical and disaffected stance on the part of many young people (a stance shared by members of many extreme metal bands: see Harrall 1994: 100). Taking into account such aspects of contemporary youth experience, Harrell suggests that one aspect of extreme metal's appeal for young people is its significance as a source of empowerment. Using the example of death metal, one of the many subgenres which collectively comprise extreme metal, Harrell makes the following observation:

> One of the most significant ways that death metal empowers its listeners is through the inversion of power. Power is after all largely a matter of positioning. And the way that rock music in general, and death metal in particular, places the group, the fan and the ideology in opposition to

the entrenched values of society – the 'we' vs. 'they' mentality . . . serves
to elevate the metalhead to a position of moral superiority.

(Harrell 1994: 101)

Combined with this is, arguably, a collective judgement among young fans
that extreme metal is more honest about the problems facing the world –
environmental, social and otherwise, that it shares the fans' own concerns
about such problems and is thus more authentic than 'commercial' forms of
music. Thus, as Weinstein argues:

> The sense of impending doom, ecological, economic, political, edu-
> cational, and social, has replaced a sense of progress and of hope for a
> future world that is better than the current state of affairs. Much of the
> distinctively youth-based music, especially thrash metal, cogently and
> emotionally articulates this view. Against commercial music's message
> of 'Don't Worry, Be Happy', young people . . . worry a lot.
>
> (Weinstein 1994: 81)

Heavy metal, Satanism and teenage suicide

During its 30-year history, heavy metal has been the subject of a number of
moral panics due to its alleged threat to the moral and physical well being
of young fans. Significantly, such moral panics have not extended to
Extreme Metal which, as Harris (2000: 15–16) notes, 'is virtually invisible
to non-scene members [and thus] "insulat[ed]" from these sorts of processes'. The most sustained campaign against heavy metal occurred during
the mid-1980s when it became the subject of censorship and legal action. At
the centre of such action was the Washington DC based **PMRC** (Parents
Music Resource Center), formed in May 1985 by the wives of government
administrators and members of Congress (see Martin and Segrave 1993).
Founded on the premise that popular music lyrics increasingly promoted
sex, drugs and violence, the PMRC began a censorship campaign which
sought to ban from the airwaves songs by artists as diverse as Prince, Sheena
Easton and Judas Priest (Martin and Segrave 1993: 292).

In the case of heavy metal, the concern expressed by the PMRC, and other
moral guardians, such as church ministers and psychiatric doctors (Weinstein 1994: 81), was particularly pronounced due to the references to
Satanism and black magic often present in heavy metal lyrics and the
imagery used on album covers, videos and promotional material (Richardson 1991: 210; Hinds 1992: 156; Walser 1993: 141–4). While some

observers, for example Carlson *et al.* (1989), argue that such imagery is latched onto and used by young heavy metal audiences purely as a form of shock tactics against the parent culture, this has done little to deter those parties who believe that the Satanic images presented in heavy metal are the root cause of antisocial behaviour in teenagers. Thus, as Richardson points out:

> What musicians and producers may be using as a marketing tool to increase sales to rebellious teenagers, others view as thorough-going evangelism for an international satanic conspiracy. This latter view sets the stage for legal actions in which heavy metal is blamed for anti-social acts.
>
> (Richardson 1991: 211)

During the 1980s, legal action mounted against heavy metal artists and their record companies. In 1985 representatives of the PMRC and another parental interest group, the Parent–Teacher Association, testified against heavy metal at US Senate Hearings held to examine the contention that heavy metal was harmful to teenage listeners (Weinstein 1994: 81). The same year a high profile court case took place in the US against British heavy metal artist Ozzy Osbourne. During the case, which inspired 'pickets, record burning' and demonstrations by Christian groups (Gaines 1991: 207), it was alleged that Obsourne's song 'Suicide Solution' had been responsible for the suicide of a 19-year-old fan and was also linked to other teenage suicides (Walser 1993: 147; Gaines 1991: 206). The case was subsequently dropped 'on the grounds that [it] violat[ed] constitutional protections of freedom of speech' (Richardson 1991: 211). However, as Walser notes, the suicide incident continued to be used by the PMRC as 'an example of the evil effects of heavy metal' (Walser 1993: 147).

Five years later, in a similar case brought against heavy metal group Judas Priest, it was alleged that music on the group's 1978 album 'Stained Glass' had motivated the suicide of one Nevada teenager and the attempted suicide of his friend (Walser 1993: 145; Black 1998). On this occasion it was claimed that subliminal messages on the record, achieved by 'backwards recording' were to blame for the incident. As Hinds (1992) points out, rumours of **back-masking** on heavy metal records date back to Led Zeppelin's 'Stairway to Heaven' which is alleged by some to contain the statement ' "I worship you, my Satan", backward throughout the song' (Hinds 1992: 156). In legal terms, however, the allegation of subliminal messages caused through back-masking was something of a novelty. Moreover, the claim prevented the case from being thrown out of court due to its infringement of the right to freedom of speech, the argument put forward by the prosecution being that such constitutional protection was intended only for 'supraliminal speech' (Richardson 1991: 212). Thus, as Richardson observes:

> [The] claim of immunity from First Amendment attack was based on a simplistic psychological theory about how such messages effect the human mind. Supposedly, such messages enter the mind without the subject's awareness, but can then 'surface' later, as ideas that the person thinks are his or her own, and therefore may be more prone to act on. Such invasion of a person's mind is viewed as a major violation of personal privacy that should be disallowed. In short, the constitutional protection for privacy overcomes the constitutional protection afforded for speech, if that speech is subliminal in character, because subliminal speech is assumed to be invasive by definition. Those who embedded the alleged subliminal messages should be liable for damages, especially if the embedding was done deliberately . . . However, they might even be found liable even if unaware of the possible impact of such messages, or if they placed messages inadvertently.
>
> (Richardson 1991: 212)

The case was finally dropped because of lack of evidence against Judas Priest. As Walser (1993: 80) observes: 'There seemed no credible motive for the subliminal crimes of which the band was accused'. Presiding Judge Jerry Carr Whitehead felt that there may have been subliminal messages contained on the 'Stained Glass' album but was not convinced of their deliberate insertion. More important, however, was Judge Whitehead's ruling that the case against Judas Priest had not provided evidence of effects, negative or otherwise, of subliminal messages on behaviour although, as Richardson (1991: 213) points out, the Judge 'explicitly left the door open for further scientific research on the issue'.

A less publicized but equally felt moral concern over the effects of heavy metal on young fans occurred in Norway during the early 1990s with the rise of Black Metal which, as Harris (2000: 20) notes, incorporated 'ideas of pagan, Viking, and anti-Christian heritage' into a discourse of nationhood 'that often crossed into overt racism'. Indeed, two members of Norwegian black metal groups were given 14 and 21 year jail sentences for racist murders (Vestel 1999: 10). Such radical forms of action were, and remain, untypical among followers of metal subgenres who, despite their critical view of contemporary society, are generally passive. In the case of Norway, however, the fascination among black metal fans with pre-Christian imagery and Viking symbolism resulted in a locally articulated form of neo-facism. Thus, as Vestel observes:

Black metal suddenly infused with a strange kind of nationalism that, for example, is reflected in the fans of the band Satyricon wearing T-shirts with 'Norway' written on their backs in types [*sic*] that hark to prehistoric runes. As a consequence of this nationalistic ideology, many fans in this period expressed racist views, saying they wanted Norway to be for true Norwegians, that is white, strong and Aryan – and of course non-Christian.

(Vestel 1999: 11)

A further cause for concern over black metal in Norway during the first half of the 1990s was church burning. A number of churches were burned down in Norway by black metal fans resulting in some of the offenders receiving jail sentences (Vestel 1999: 10). According to Vestel, the reasons given by black metal fans for engaging in this activity vary. Thus, some 'have explained the burning of churches as a way of spreading fear and cleansing [Norway] of Christian influence' (Vestel 1999: 11). Other church burners draw upon discourses borrowed from black magic in explaining their reasons for carrying out the act. Thus black metal fan Kristian Vikernes, now serving a prison sentence for murder, is stated in a newspaper report as saying that 'by burning down, old churches especially, [*sic*] the power of the building accumulated by age would be transmitted to him' (Vestel 1999: 12). As Vestel points out, however, irrespective of the personal reasons given by individual black metal fans for the burning down of churches, this action, like the discourse of nationalism in Norwegian black metal, clearly results from the way in which the music has been appropriated and inscribed with myth, fantasy and ideology, rather than any inherent qualities in black metal itself. In this respect, moral panics which may emerge in Norway concerning the effects of black metal music on the behaviour of young fans are, in essence, as ideologically biased as the moral panics in the US concerning heavy metal during the 1980s.

Conclusion

In this chapter I have examined the heavy metal phenomenon from its origins at the end of the 1960s through to the contemporary metal scene. Having presented a brief overview of heavy metal's musical and stylistic development, I went on to present an analysis of the relationship between heavy metal and its audience. I began by examining the representation of gender in heavy metal music and illustrated how, during the 1980s, this shifted from 'conventional' images of masculinity, predicated on notions of patriarchy and the sexual subversion of women, to forms of female exscription, the latter being enhanced through the advanced visual imagery enabled by the video. It was subsequently shown how, during the 1990s, emergent subgenres of heavy metal, collectively referred to as extreme metal, despite their essential male centredness, largely abandoned the gendered themes of earlier metal styles, focusing instead on issues of alienation and isolation. In the final section, I examined 'official' responses to heavy metal by the courts and organisations such as the PMRC, the latter being at the centre of an ongoing campaign against heavy metal, and other contemporary youth musics such as rap (see Chapter 6), which, it is claimed, produce harmful effects on young listeners.

Further reading

Arnett, J.J. (1995) *Metal Heads: Heavy Metal Music and Adolescent Alienation.* Oxford: Westview.

Berger, H.M. (1999) *Metal, Rock and Jazz: Perception and the Phenomenology of Musical Experience.* Hanover, NH: Wesleyan University Press.

Frith, S. and McRobbie, A. (1978) Rock and sexuality, in S. Frith and A. Goodwin (eds) (1990) *On Record: Rock, Pop and the Written Word.* London: Routledge.

Harris, K. (2000) 'Roots?' The relationship between the global and the local within the Extreme Metal scene, *Popular Music*, 19(1): 13–30.

Kotarba, J.A. (1994) The postmodernization of rock 'n' roll music: the case of Metallica, in J.S. Epstein (ed.) *Adolescents and their Music: If It's Too Loud You're Too Old.* New York and London: Garland.

Sloat, L.J. (1998) Incubus: male songwriters' portrayal of women's sexuality in pop metal music, in J.S. Epstein (ed.) *Youth Culture: Identity in a Postmodern World.* Oxford: Blackwell.

Straw, W. (1983) 'Characterizing rock music culture: the case of heavy metal, in S. Frith and A. Goodwin (eds) (1990) *On Record: Rock Pop and the Written Word.* London: Routledge.

Vestal, V. (1999) Breakdance, red eyed penguins, Vikings, grunge and straight rock 'n' roll: the construction of place in musical discourse in Rudenga, East Side Oslo, *Young: Nordic Journal of Youth Research*, 7(2): 4–24.

Walser, R. (1993) *Running with the Devil: Power, Gender and Madness in Heavy Metal Music.* London: Wesleyan University Press.

Weinstein, D. (1991) *Heavy Metal: A Cultural Sociology.* New York: Lexington.

4 | PUNK AND PUNK ROCK

Between the autumn of 1976 and the summer of 1977, a particular music, a
highly visible subcultural style, and an increasingly public crisis momentarily
fused together. Punk burst upon an unsuspecting London and quickly acquired
the propensity to act as a new folk devil . . . [the] punk's pallid body perforated
by safety pins, draped in pvc and locked in a dog collar; those glassy,
amphetamine blocked eyes staring out from beneath shocks of garishly dyed
hair. These were the signs that briefly captured the horrified fascination of the
outside world.

(Chambers 1985: 175–6)

In the popular imagination, punk is often regarded as a phenomenon which
began and ended in Britain. Many observers saw punk as a response both
to the oft stated blandness of chart music and increasing elitism of 'stadium
rock' during the 1970s and to the economic decline of Britain at this time.
Such a view of punk has been enhanced through its treatment in academic
texts which have, until quite recently, also emphasized the British-
centredness of punk and punk rock. During the course of this chapter, I
want to examine punk not as a localised British phenomenon but rather as
a global youth culture with roots in the US garage band scene of the mid-
1960s. Having considered the origins of the term punk and the punk ethic
as part of the New York underground scene of the mid-1970s, I will look
at how punk was subsequently adopted and adapted by British punk bands
such as the Sex Pistols. I will further suggest that the British punk image,
style and music became a model for its wider appropriation in western and
eastern Europe, where it again became intertwined with local cultural and
political sensibilities. Finally, I will consider the continuing relevance of
punk and punk rock in the context of particular locally situated youth
cultures.

The origins of punk

Punk's roots can be traced back to the US garage band scene of 1965 to 1968, described by Logan and Woffinden (1976: 405) as 'a transitional period in the development of American Rock 'n' Roll, the years between [the] Beatles/[Rolling] Stones-led invasion and [the] San Francisco-based rock renaissance'. Possessing very little in the way of conventional musical skill and performing experience, garage bands applied their rudimentary knowledge of guitar, bass, drums and, occasionally, electronic organ in copying the style of British bands of the time. Garage bands typically played at high school dances and 'Battle of the Bands' competitions, recording at most one or two singles before disbanding. Some of the best known examples of garage bands include The Kingsmen (who had a hit with 'Louie Louie'), The Standells, Swingin' Medallions and the Electric Prunes (Logan and Woffinden 1976: 405).

During the late 1960s interest in garage bands declined as US youth became drawn to the more politically orientated rock music of the counter-culture (see Chapter 2) and subsequently to the early 1970s progressive 'stadium' rock acts such as Genesis, Pink Floyd and Emerson, Lake and Palmer. With its emphasis on increasingly ambitious, large-scale stage sets and the use of state-of-the-art amplification systems (see, for example, Lull 1992; Macan 1997; Martin 1998) stadium rock dominated the music scene during the first half of 1970s. However, in the mid-1970s the garage band ethic was revived by New York-based musicians such as Patti Smith, Richard Hell and the Voidoids and the Talking Heads. Although the term punk had been loosely used in the garage band scene, the connotations of the term in US English – 'good for nothing' lazy, arrogant, antisocial – were embraced by the burgeoning New York scene which also took inspiration from the leading New York underground group Velvet Underground, who had become notorious for 'stunn[ing] audiences with harsh vocals and droning electronic music' (Cagle 1995: 81). Most significantly, the mid-1970s punk scene in New York represented a rejection of the stadium rock ethos. It was small-club music, played in a straightforward, musically uncomplex fashion. Thus, as Lenny Kaye, guitarist with the Patti Smith group, explains:

> in the early 70s . . . rock 'n' roll had gotten very complicated. Progressive rock, a sense that rock was an 'adult' medium . . . a sense that complexity and song cycles and . . . instrumental prowess and musicianship were the driving force. The fact that you could play three chords and get up on stage within a week was being lost.
> (Kaye cited in the BBC TV series *Dancing in the Street*, broadcast in July 1995)

Similarly, David Bryne, leader of the group Talking Heads, who played their early gigs in **CBGBs**, the now legendary New York punk venue, makes the following observation:

> Punk wasn't a musical style, or at least it shouldn't have been . . . It was more a kind of 'do it yourself – anyone can do it' attitude. If you can only play two notes on the guitar you can figure out a way to make a song out of that.
>
> (Bryne cited in the BBC TV series *Dancing in the Street*, broadcast in July 1995)

It was this strongly pronounced 'do it yourself' ethic of the New York punk scene that appealed to British fashion entrepreneur Malcolm McLaren when he visited the city in 1974. Together with his partner, fashion designer Vivienne Westwood (whose innovative designs were to define the punk image in Britain), McLaren, a former art school student, ran an alternative clothes shop named 'Sex' situated on the Kings Road in London (see Harron 1988). As part of the advertising campaign for his shop, but also because he was genuinely excited by the subversive potential of punk rock, McLaren decided to put together his own punk group which he named the 'Sex Pistols'. The line up of the Sex Pistols consisted of four regular customers in McLaren's shop: John Lydon (alias Johnny Rotten) the group's vocalist, guitarist Steve Jones, drummer Paul Cook and bassist Glen Matlock (subsequently replaced by Sid Vicious) (see Savage 1992). A further inspiration for British punk was the London-based **pub rock** scene. Indeed, as Friedlander (1996: 251) points out: 'Some band members, such as Joe Strummer of the 101ers [subsequently guitarist and vocalist with the Clash], simply stepped over the line from pub to punk'. In the same way that the New York punk scene had taken its inspiration from the US garage band scene a decade earlier, the London pub bands' emphasis on the importance of small 'pub' venues was inspired by the live music scene in Britain as this had existed prior to the arrival of progressive rock during the **Merseybeat** and blues boom periods. Thus, as Laing explains:

> the virtue of smallness was taken by pub bands from their memory of the Merseybeat and British R&B era. The size of the bar-room allowed for, even insisted upon, the intimacy between musicians and audience they believed was somehow essential for meaningful music. Pub rock's stance implied that things went wrong for bands when they became superstars and 'lost touch' with their original audiences.
>
> (Laing 1985: 8)

In both the US and Britain then, at a musical and performance level punk came to represent a rejection of the large-scale and increasingly grandiose nature of stadium rock. Inherent in this rejection was a staunchly ingrained opposition to the complexity and perceived self-indulgence of stadium rock music.

Anarchy in the UK

If the concept of punk rock was borrowed from New York, then the way in which it manifested itself in Britain was wholly different from the New York scene. British punk rock music had a much more aggressive image and sound than its US counterpart and the lyrical content too was often much more provocative in its tone. Also significant in the case of British punk was its relationship with the media. In his study of the media's treatment of the clashes between mods and rockers at seaside towns on England's south-east coast during the early 1960s, Stanley Cohen (1987) notes how the primary function of media reporting was to single out mods and rockers as **folk devils**. According to Cohen (1987: 10), folk devils constitute 'the gallery of types that society erects to show its members which roles should be avoided'. Because of its wide reach, the media's ability to use folk devils as a way of maintaining social order is particularly effective. Via the media, folk devils are, as Cohen illustrates, no longer publicized 'just in oral-tradition and face to face contact but to much larger audiences and with much greater dramatic resources' (Cohen 1987: 17).

Such moral entrepreneurship on the part of the media was instrumental in the construction of punk as a social menace in Britain. In December 1976 the Sex Pistols were invited to appear on Thames Television's news magazine show *Today*, a live broadcast at peak family viewing time. As Laing (1985: 36) points out, in the space of a 1 minute, 40 second interview, *Today* presenter Bill Grundy 'managed to sketch in the popular stereotype of punk'. By asking a series of rhetorical questions in quickfire succession, and urging the Sex Pistols to swear on TV, Grundy cemented into place the developing public image of punks as lazy, foul mouthed degenerates. The following morning a British tabloid the *Daily Mirror* reported a wave of public outcry and disgust at the behaviour of the Sex Pistols and the other punks present during the Grundy interview. As Harron (1988: 199) notes, the media and by definition the general public 'diagnosed [punk] not as a new music style but as a social problem'.

What set this particular example of 'folk devilization' apart from previous instances, however, was Malcolm McLaren's reflexive awareness and consequent exploitation of the moral panic which the media had set in motion with the Sex Pistols. Thus, as Harron points out:

> Even with hindsight . . . it is difficult to know whether McLaren was operating on a chaotic series of intuitions or according to an orchestrated plan, but what is clear is that he was the first rock manager to use the subversive possibilities of hype.
>
> (Harron 1988: 201)

McLaren's exploitation of the scandal and moral panic created by the Sex Pistols via the media continued with what was perhaps the most controversial Sex Pistols' song, 'God Save the Queen', released in June 1977 at the height of the national celebrations to mark the Silver Jubilee of Queen Elizabeth II's reign. The song, which contains the lines 'God save the Queen, She ain't no human being' immediately established itself as an anti-national anthem (Laing 1985: 38).

As a result many high street record shops in Britain refused to stock the record. 'God Save the Queen' was also banned from *Top of the Pops* and blacklisted by radio stations in Britain. Several publications refused to print an advertisement for the single, the sleeve of which featured a picture of the Queen with her eyes masked out by the song title and her mouth covered by the name 'The Sex Pistols'. The effect of all this negative publicity was that 'God Save the Queen' went to number one in the British charts and remained there for several weeks. As Laing (1985: 38) explains: 'This "inaudible" yet widely heard record sold an estimated 250 000 copies which, thanks to the censorship and the boycott, were listened to in an unusually attentive way'. Laing goes on to argue that by banning 'God Save the Queen', the music industry's institutions simply served to increase the controversy surrounding the song. In effect, such institutions 'virtually instructed anyone with access to ['God Save the Queen'] that its effects on them would be totally different from the leisure pleasure provided by the context of daytime radio or *Top of the Pops*' (Laing 1985: 38).

The punk style

While punk rock served to alert the media to the arrival of punk and to set the former's moral panic making machinery in motion, equally important in confirming punk as 'public enemy number one' was the punk style. In his book *Subculture: The Meaning of Style*, Hebdige (1979) argues that the cultural significance of the punk style must be read in the context of the social decay of Britain during the late 1970s – the dismantling of the welfare state, the rising level of unemployment, the race riots in Britain's inner cities and the increasing frustration of young people. In an earlier reading of youth style Willis (1978) argues that its cultural meaning resides in the *homological* relationship of given items to the value systems of certain subcultural groups (see Chapter 2). Thus, for example, according to Willis the studded leather jacket of the biker resonated with the biker's intended image of toughness and ruggedness. In Hebdige's (1979) view the homological method of interpreting subcultural style as an embedded set of collective sensibilities, determined in part by the structural conditions of class, is unworkable in the case of punk. Arguing that the meaning of punk was its essential 'lack' of meaning, Hebdige refers to an article on punk in *Time Out* magazine in December 1977 where a female punk is asked why she wears a swastika and answers: 'Punks just like to be hated' (Hebdige 1979: 177). Hebdige then offers an alternative, 'polysemic' reading of punk style based around the concept of **bricolage**, borrowed from the surrealistic artwork of Dadaist painters of the early 1900s. Bricolage involves the depiction of familiar everyday objects in new and unusual contexts in which they acquire surrealistic meanings. Hebdige suggests that the punk scene also engaged in a process of bricolage, taking familiar objects and reassembling them in new ways. Thus, he notes:

> Objects borrowed from the most sordid of contexts found a place in the punks' ensembles: lavatory chains were draped in graceful arcs across chests encased in plastic bin-liners. Safety pins were taken out of their domestic 'utility' context and worn as gruesome ornaments through the cheek, ear or lip . . . Hair was obviously dyed (hay yellow, jet black, or bright orange with tufts of green or bleached in question marks), and T-shirts and trousers told the story of their own construction with multiple zips and outside zips clearly displayed.
>
> (Hebdige 1979: 107)

According to Hebdige, all of these images and objects, including swastikas, were exploited by punks as empty signifiers. The central value of each object, from the point of view of the punk scene, was 'the communicated absence of any such identifiable values' (Hebdige 1979: 117).

One might reasonably assume on the strength of Hebdige's initial reading of the punk style that it was nothing more than a bizarre form of street corner society, an image turned 'non-image'. However, having discussed punk in terms of its anti-meaning, Hebdige then goes on to make very definite connections between the punk style and the socio-economic situation in Britain during the mid to late 1970s. The fragmented and chaotic image of punk was, according to Hebdige, synonymous with the malaise of British society during the latter half of the 1970s. The image and general style of the punk, Hebdige suggests, responded to socio-economic changes which were beginning to take hold of Britain at this time – the increasing joblessness, changing moral standards, the rediscovery of poverty and the onset of economic depression. Thus, argues Hebdige, the punks were essentially '*dramatizing*' Britain's decline by

> appropriat[ing] the rhetoric of crisis which had filled the airwaves throughout the [late 1970s] and translat[ing] it into tangible (and visible) terms . . . In the gloomy, apocalyptic ambience of the late 1970s – with massive unemployment, with the ominous violence of the Notting Hill Carnival, Grunwick, Lewisham and Ladywood – it was fitting that the punks should present themselves as 'de-generates'; as signs of the highly publicized decay which perfectly represented the atrophied condition of Great Britain. The various stylistic ensembles adopted by the punks were undoubtedly expressive of genuine aggression, frustration and anxiety.
>
> (Hebdige 1979: 87)

A number of salient criticisms have been directed against Hebdige's reading of punk style. Cohen (1987) identifies problems with Hebdige's use of **polysemy** as a means of interpreting the cultural significance of punk style. Thus, argues Cohen, polysemy 'may work for art, but not equally well for life. The danger is of getting lost in the forest of symbols' (Cohen 1987: xvi). Using the example of Hebdige's polysemic reading of the swastika's significance for punk, Cohen makes the following observation:

> Displaying a swastika shows how symbols are stripped from their natural context, exploited for empty effect, displayed through mockery, distancing, irony, parody, inversion . . . But how are we to know this? We are never told much about the 'thing': when, how, where, by whom or in what context it is worn. We do not know what, if any, difference exists between indigenous and sociological explanations.
>
> (Cohen 1987: xvii)

A further criticism is offered by Clarke (1981), who is critical of what he regards as the 'metropolitan centeredness [*sic*]' of Hebdige's reading of punk which, according to Clarke (1981: 86), 'begins with a heat wave in Oxford Street and ends in a Kings Road boutique'. Indeed, Hebdige's failure to consider how and why youth ' "in the sticks" ' adopted the punk style is further problematized by his notion of 'incorporation'. Thus, according to Hebdige, youth style can function as an object of 'authentic' expression only as long as it remains 'undiscovered' by the market. When a subcultural style becomes incorporated into the market it is simultaneously stripped of its cultural message and becomes simply another meaningless object of mass consumption (Hebdige 1979: 96). To begin with, such a contention involves a fabricated distinction between stylistic innovation and the youth market, the two being regarded by Hebdige as mutually exclusive despite his own observation that, in punk's case, 'the media's sighting of punk style virtually coincided with the discovery or invention of punk deviance' (1979: 93). Moreover, and perhaps more importantly, given that certain styles do originate at 'street level', Hebdige's contention that the market's incorporation of a style renders it culturally meaningless automatically closes off any consideration of the regional variations and local levels of significance which such styles acquire once they become more widely available as commercial products.

A further problem with Hebdige's study is its emphasis on punk as a working class subculture. Indeed, Hebdige's insistence on the working class origins of punk is central to his argument that punk symbolized, through the style politics of youth, the socio-economic decline of Britain. In such circumstances, working class youth, along with the youth of ethnic minorities would be the first to feel the effects. In this respect, it is significant that Hebdige refers to the Notting Hill Carnival and the race riots in Grunwick, Lewisham and Ladywood and their resonance with the anger of punk. The implication here is that during the late 1970s the youth of the white working classes and those of Britain's ethnic minorities were collectively displaying their anger at what was happening to them as the country's economy ran down and mass unemployment became the norm. Similarly, Hebdige's observations regarding punks' interest in Jamaican reggae music and his assertion that the rasta look of many young African Caribbeans in Britain during the late 1970s 'resonated with punk's adopted values – "anarchy", "surrender" and "decline" ' is clearly intended to lend credence to his assertion that punk was a primarily working class youth culture. The disempowered position of white working class youth, suggests Hebdige (1979: 64), enabled them to understand the frustration expressed through African Caribbean youth's appropriation of reggae music and the rasta look (see also Chapter 5). Indeed, it is clear that there was an element of unison between punks and the British rasta movement during the late 1970s, Rock Against Racism events often featuring punk and reggae acts on the same bill (Frith and Street 1992).

Nevertheless, according to Clarke (1981), Hebdige's reading of punk's social significance is thwarted by the fact that punk was not an exclusively working class phenomenon. Indeed, as Clarke goes on to illustrate, in its formative stages at least, punk was anything but working class. Thus, he contends, most of the punk creations discussed by Hebdige 'were developed among the art-school avant garde rather than emanating "from the dance halls and housing estates"' (Clarke 1981: 86). There is much to support Clarke's argument that punk, far from beginning life as a working class form of subcultural resistance, was the product of middle class artists and fashion designers. Neither Malcolm McLaren nor Vivienne Westwood could be described as working class, nor was the type of subversion which they planned through punk aimed particularly at a working class audience. Thus, as Shank (1994) observes, the Sex Pistols' early performances were in colleges in an attempt 'to attract an educated audience who would observe the spectacle of the Sex Pistols . . . and seize the possibilities for action thereby created' (Shank 1994: 93). Indeed, it is significant in this respect that an early group of punk fans, the so-called 'Bromley Contingent', which spurned several important punk groups including Siouxsie and the Banshees, were middle class art students who used their punk style and self-conscious antisocial mannerisms as a way of shocking the residents of the quiet suburban area where they lived (Shank 1994: 93–4). A similar point is made by Frith:

> The left argument was that punk was a stage in the movement from class consciousness to class political consciousness: this depended on a description of punk as rank and file music, the direct expression of the way things were – a kind of realism. But even in terms of reflection theory, punk as spontaneous expression, the argument did not make a lot of sense. The pioneering punk rockers themselves were a self-conscious, artful lot with a good understanding of both rock tradition and populist cliché; the music no more reflected directly back onto conditions in the dole queue than it emerged spontaneously from them.
>
> (Frith 1980: 167)

An alternative reading of punk is offered by Chambers (1985) in his book *Urban Rhythms*. Certainly there are several points on which Chambers and Hebdige agree. Thus, both writers emphasize the discontinuities present in the punk image – the signs and images stripped from their original meanings and juxtaposed in new and seemingly meaningless relations, for example, the swastika worn in conjunction with a Karl Marx T-shirt and the safety pin worn through the cheek or the lip. Similarly, like Hebdige, Chambers argues that punk's main weapon of resistance was its total negativity. Thus argues Chambers:

> Punk's infuriating 'dumbness', those 'blank' faces frozen in the press shot, removed it from available referents. Punk could only be defined

negatively, as an absence, a perverse void; its internal semantics remained unknown.

(Chambers 1985: 176)

However, Chambers contests the notion that punk was an essentially working class subculture. Instead, argues Chambers, the appeal of punk cut right across class divisions. It was not simply a form of protest by working class youth at the worsening conditions of their class existence. Rather, punk served as rallying call to bored and frustrated teenagers and twenty-somethings from a whole range of backgrounds who saw, on the one hand, their life chances eroding while the dominant society refused to acknowledge the severe socio-economic problems engulfing the nation. Punk's visual and sonic attack on the sensibilities of the British public then, was in a sense, instructing them to 'wake up' and take stock. 'There is no future, in England's dreaming' sang Johnny Rotten of the Sex Pistols and, according to Chambers, this very much summed up the feelings of the punk scene as a whole:

Through their music and stylistic commitment, [the punks] suggested and enlarged the spaces for subversive cultural 'play' . . . Punk proclaimed the necessity of violating the quiet, everyday script of common sense. It proposed a macabre parody of the underlying idealism of 'Englishness' – that dour pragmatism that sees no future beyond the present, and no present except that inherited, apparently unmodified, from the past.

(Chambers 1985: 185)

Despite punk's allegedly antisocial and anarchic tendencies, its spectacular affront on the moral sensibilities of the British public was relatively short-lived. This is illustrated clearly by virtue of the fact that, in the context of Britain, punk and punk rock are now firmly associated with a specific time, the late 1970s, and a convergence of socio-economic and musical and stylistic sensibilities as unique as that which prefigured the rise of rock 'n' roll in the early 1950s. The temporality of punk and punk rock in Britain is played out in a variety of homages to punk from Savage's (1992) *England's Dreaming* to Hebdige's (1988) essay 'Mistaken identities: why John Paul Ritchie didn't do it his way' which 'mark[s] the passing not only of Sid [Vicious] and Nancy [Spungeon, Vicious's girlfriend with whose murder the former Sex Pistol was charged before he himself died of a heroin overdose in February, 1979 (see Savage 1992)] but also the "moment" of the punk "subculture" ' (Hebdige 1988: 8). Similarly, Rimmer (1985: 4), in writing about the British New Romantic scene of the early 1980s, suggests that it was as if 'punk never happened'.

Punk in a global context

While the British punk scene had all but disappeared by the beginning of the 1980s, elsewhere in the world punk grew in popularity, often becoming a coherently politicized movement combining aspects of the British punk style and ethic with an outlook framed by local issues and concerns. An effective illustration of how punk was adapted and reworked in a local context is given in Szemere's (1992) study of the punk scene in Hungary during the early 1980s. According to Szemere, the Hungarian punk scene borrowed from the ideology of marginalization central to British punk but added new, more locally significant, dimensions to this ideology. What young Hungarians brought to their reworking of punk was, Szemere (1992: 95) suggests, 'a particular view and experience of history'. During the early 1980s there was a widespread economic recession in Hungary coupled with a growing sense of insecurity. Hungarian youth were particularly affected by this. There was a commonly shared feeling among young people that the socialist system had let them down. For many, the punk scene represented a way in which they could begin to negotiate the situation of anomie which arose from Hungary's socio-economic decline. Initially, the Hungarian authorities played down the punk scene as right wing and fascist, a feature which, they argued, was inevitable given punk's western origins. However, the Hungarian punk scene quickly developed its own avant-garde, the latter possessing, as Szemere points out, 'the intellectual and political resources to challenge the official representations of the Western punk movement as fascistic [*sic*]' (1992: 99).

A further account of punk's engagement with local circumstances in the former Eastern Bloc is provided by Pilkington (1994) in her research on the punk scene in Russia. As with Hungarian punk, punk in Russia remained an essentially underground scene as both political and economic forces prevented it from entering the mainstream. Moreover, while part of the appeal of British punk, from the point of view of young punks themselves, had been the subversion of everyday meanings, this was more difficult in Russia where there was a basic lack of the commodities needed to effect such subversion. Thus, as Pilkington (1994: 228) explains, 'there can . . . be no social base for a movement subverting consumerist lifestyles in a society where a safety pin or a dustbin bag is an article of deficit, not abundance'. Indeed, the upshot of this situation was that some of the most articulate examples of punk protest in Russia centred upon the lack of items such as 'condoms, hairspray and cigarettes which prevented the punks from living the kind of lifestyle they wished to' (Pilkington 1994: 229).

In western Europe, articulations of punk culture have also drawn upon the musical and visual style of the British punk scene inscribing the latter with knowledges and sensibilities framed by local issues. In Germany, for example, German-language punk rock groups such as Die Toten Hosen regularly perform at **Rock gegen Rechts** (Rock Against Racism) concerts. Another important event in the German punk's calendar is 'Die **Chaos Tage**' ('the chaos days'), an unofficial annual punk gathering in Hannover during the first weekend in August (see Geiling 1995, 1996). According to Geiling (1995), the coincidence of Die Chaos Tage with the chain stores' 'end-of-summer' sale and the Maschseefest (a local outdoor festival) provides the perfect setting for German punks to protest against what they consider to be the obsessive consumerism of the dominant society. Since it began in 1982, the Chaos Tage gathering has met with increasing opposition from the local police, while its representation in the media has given the event an almost mythical quality as a scene of extreme social unrest (a further example of the way in which local media have transformed punk into a moral panic). Geiling identifies a further aspect of the German punk scene's militant stance in relation to particular local issues through his analysis of punk's involvement in the **Berlin Hausbesetzer-Szene** (squatting scene). According to Geiling since its initial involvement in the Berlin scene during the early 1980s, the spectacular style of the punk image together with the lyrically and musically aggressive tone of the music has performed an important role in marking out the cultural space of German squatting movements and articulating their collective cause at a national level.

Other studies of the German punk scene, for example by Müller-Wiegand (1990) and Hafeneger *et al.* (1993), have served to illustrate how the social and cultural significance attached to punk can take on substantially different meanings even within the same country. In their comparative research on the punk scene in Frankfurt am Main and Fulda, Hafeneger *et al.* (1993) illustrate the differing forms of cultural significance which being a punk assumes in each of these settings. In Frankfurt, one of Germany's principal cities and the country's banking and financial centre, punks are considered by non-punks to be 'old fashioned' not only stylistically but also ideologically (Hafeneger *et al.* 1993: 26). Frankfurt punks react to such accusations through a total commitment to the punk style. Collective emphasis is placed on the need to both behave and look like an 'authentic' punk as defined by the British punk image of the late 1970s. The experience of punks in Fulda, a small city approximately 50 miles to the north-east of Frankfurt, is considerably different. While punks in Fulda are similarly ostracized, this is not because they are considered out of step with current fashions and youth sensibilities but because they are deemed to be socially deviant. Thus, the local punk scene must deal with a rather different set of social circumstances which casts punks as 'outsiders' who must keep their distance and are not to be trusted (Hafeneger *et al.* 1993: 69). Hafeneger *et al.*'s (1993) research contributes an important overview of the contrast between of the experience between urban and rural punks, a contrast which, as Clarke (1981) notes, is missing from British research on punk style.

The music and image of British punk has also made a considerable impact on local punk scenes in the US. Interestingly, a view often expressed by musicians, writers and others who were involved in the British punk scene maintains that the strong economic position of the US during the 1970s acted as a cultural barrier towards a general understanding and appreciation of punk among the nation's youth. Thus as John Lydon comments:

> You have to bear in mind that they'd just come out of the Vietnam war and the whole situation ... was very, very different. Economically [America] was in a much better position than it is now, and it's funny that now that things are beginning to crumble and fall apart and their economy's going down the toilet they're turning a definite eye towards punk. Now they get it.
>
> (Lydon cited in the BBC TV series *Dancing in the Street*, broadcast in July 1995)

Nevertheless, there is clear evidence not only of British punk's relatively instant appeal for sections of US youth but also of its reworking in ways designed to address or negotiate local circumstances. In his study of the local music scene in Austin, Texas, Shank reflects on the impact made by a Sex Pistol's performance at a local venue:

> On January 8, 1978, the Sex Pistols played at a renovated bowling alley in San Antonio called Randy's Rodeo ... Every member of Austin's fledgling punk scene drove down Interstate 35 to San Antonio that night, even those who had prior engagements.
>
> (Shank 1994: 100)

Shank subsequently illustrates how this single performance by the Sex Pistols served as a galvanizing element in the development of the local punk rock scene in Austin. Moreover, in the same way that the Sex Pistols, through song titles such as 'Anarchy in the UK' and 'God Save the Queen', focused on issues and concerns acquired through experience of everyday life in Britain during the mid to late 1970s, local Austin punk rock bands drew lyrical inspiration from their everyday life experience as young Texans. In particular Austin punk bands engaged in satirical attacks against what they perceived as the ultra-conservative, red neck attitudes that dominate small-town Texan life. Shank offers an example of this with the song 'Glad He's

Dead' by local Austin punk band 'The Huns' which is intended as a searing commentary on local attitudes towards assassinated US President John F. Kennedy:

> The Huns' 'Glad He's Dead' was performed at their first show and became part of their repertoire. They released it on their own label, God Records, in 1979. The recording displays the stylistic debt the Huns owed to the Sex Pistols, and in many ways this song is the 'God Save the Queen' of the Raul's era . . .[1] After three verses attack John Kennedy for his Catholicism, the Cuban missile crisis, the death of Marilyn, Viet Nam, as well as the Bay of Pigs and integration of southern schools, the final verse describes the assassination scene and declares, 'Lee Harvey Oswald, America's friend'.
>
> (Shank 1994: 111–12)

Elsewhere in the US, punk meanings were similarly reworked in ways which addressed locally experienced social problems. In her work on youth homelessness in Hollywood, Ruddick (1998: 345) notes how during the late 1970s 'punk' squatters used their image as a way of 'develop[ing] a social identity which confronted their stigma'. Recasting punk's spectacular resistance as a means of reterritorializing run down, uninhabited buildings in Hollywood, the punk squatters were able to assume 'a strategic control of space' (Ruddick 1998: 346). Ruddick's work adds an important dimension to other research into the relationship between youth, music, collective identity and the micro-social spaces of late modern, postindustrial urban settings (see, for example, Skelton and Valentine 1998; Bennett 2000). Taking as its starting point the 'multiple enunciations of . . . space' (Keith and Pile 1993: 6) that characterize late modern urban life, this research focuses on the ways in which collective sensibilities of youth style, derived from aspects of fashion/retro-fashion and music, combine with locally acquired knowledges in the appropriation and 'marking out' of urban space. Using this analytical framework to explore the unique relationship between punk culture, squatting and the urban decay in sections of Hollywood during the late 1970s Ruddick makes the following observation:

> That the squatting punk sub-culture was able to sustain itself for so long in Hollywood was partly due to the ready availability of condemned buildings for use and, initially, clubs to play in. But the erosion of the quality of marginal space and the transformation of the subculture went hand in hand . . . in the early stages nobody cared if punks squatted in a condemned building – they would hang out as long as possible until somebody came to knock the thing down. These places

were trashed both as an expression of the sub-culture and also at times
to make them (strategically) habitable.

(Ruddick 1998: 349)

Punk's longevity in the US, together with its stylistic and aesthetic matura-
tion, is effectively captured in Andes' work on punk 'careers'. According to
Andes (1998), an individual's identification with punk can no longer be
effected through simple stylistic affiliation but is rather achieved through a
form of punk literacy; an immersion not only in the music of punk but also
in 'books about punk music, books of poetry by punk "celebrities", music
magazines, and punk fanzines' (Andes 1998: 217). As Andes' work illustrates, this form of punk literacy is often a more important signifier of one's
identification with and dedication to punk than visual image. Thus, from the
point of view of Andes' research respondents, many of those who opted for
the punk style were simply 'poseurs' who used the image as a means of drawing attention to themselves but had 'no deeper understanding of punk values'
(Andes 1998: 218). This study also demonstrates how those with an achieved
punk status will sometimes find ways of developing their punk careers by
'becoming involved at a more organizational or creative level [as] musicians,
promoters, fanzine writers, artists etc.' (Andes 1998: 218). Indeed, through
branching out into such activities, devotees can maintain an identification
with punk 'into their late twenties and beyond' (Andes 1998: 218).

Conclusion

In this chapter I have examined the phenomenon of punk from its origins in
the US garage band scene of the mid-1960s, through its appropriation and
stylistic reworking in Britain, to a globally situated youth culture whose
musical and stylistic shock tactics have become bound up with highly particularized local conditions and circumstances. During my analysis of punk
I have considered some of the key claims made by cultural and sociological
theorists in relation to punk's social significance and also illustrated a
number of salient criticisms of cultural studies and sociological treatments
of punk and punk rock. The point remains, however, that whatever claims
have been made for the importance of punk during particular periods in its
30-year history, it remains highly relevant for our understanding of contemporary youth. In addition to the continued currency of punk for youth in a
number of different urban locations around the globe, the legacy of punk
has inspired a range of contemporary youth musics including grunge and
hardcore. Thus, as Santiago-Lucerna (1998) states in reference to the

current 'alternative rock' scene in the US, many of these bands owe a musical debt to punk and to their own fledgling careers as punk bands: 'While some variations from their earlier days are clear . . . some of the basics of punk are very much present' (Santiago-Lucerna 1998: 190).

Note

1 Raul's was an alternative music venue in Austin during the late 1970s where many of the local Austin punk bands performed (see Shank 1994: 105).

Further reading

Andes, L. (1998) Growing up punk: meaning and commitment careers in a contemporary youth subculture, in J.S. Epstein (ed.) *Youth Culture: Identity in a Postmodern World*. Oxford: Blackwell.

Chambers, I. (1985) *Urban Rhythms: Pop Music and Popular Culture*. London: Macmillan (Chapter 7).

Friedlander, P. (1996) *Rock and Roll: A Social History*. Boulder, CO: Westview (Chapter 17).

Frith, S. (1980) Formalism, realism and leisure: the case of punk, in K. Gelder and S. Thornton (eds) (1997) *The Subcultures Reader*. London: Routledge.

Hebdige, D. (1979) *Subculture: The Meaning of Style*. London: Routledge.

Laing, D. (1985) *One Chord Wonders: Power and Meaning in Punk Rock*. Milton Keynes: Open University Press.

Ruddick, S. (1998) How 'Homeless' youth sub-cultures make a difference, in T. Skelton and G. Valentine (eds) *Cool Places: Geographies of Youth Culture*. London: Routledge.

Savage, J. (1992) *England's Dreaming: Sex Pistols and Punk Rock*. London: Faber and Faber.

Shank, B. (1994) *Dissonant Identities: The Rock 'n' Roll Scene in Austin, Texas*. London: Wesleyan University Press (Chapter 5).

Szemere, A. (1992) The politics of marginality: a rock musical subculture in socialist Hungary in the early 1980s, in R. Garofalo (ed.) *Rockin' the Boat: Mass Music and Mass Movements*. Boston, MA: South End Press.

5 | REGGAE AND RASTA CULTURE

> Reggae addresses a community in transit through a series of retrospective frames (the Rastafarian movement . . ., the Back to Africa theme) which reverse the historical sequence of migrations (Africa–Jamaica–Great Britain). It is the record of a people's journey – of the passage from slavery to servitude – and that journey can be mapped along the lines of reggae's unique structure.
>
> (Hebdige 1979: 31)

If punk rock did much to redefine the significance of popular music as a form of youth expression during the late 1970s, a similarly significant musical style to emerge during this period was reggae. Promoted globally through the work of artists such as Bob Marley and Peter Tosh, reggae combined highly distinctive musical and visual styles with a form of cultural politics that emphasized the importance of Africa as a spiritual homeland for African diasporic populations around the world. This chapter examines the cultural impact of reggae and the attendant Rastafarian or 'Rasta' style adopted by reggae artists and appropriated by followers of the music. Beginning with an overview of the origins of reggae, I will then consider reggae's significance as a central resource for the 'reconstruction' of the black identity. During this section of the chapter I will pay close attention to reggae's reception by African Caribbean youth in Britain, for whom reggae music and its attendant Rasta style provided a significant resource in the negotiation of socio-economic austerity and the mounting racism and racial exclusion that characterized Britain during the 1970s. I will then examine the impact of reggae on white British youth. In the final section, I consider local reworking of reggae music and Rastafarian style in Australia where Aboriginal appropriations of reggae have led to the music's use in protest over land rights and issues of racism and racial exclusion.

The origins of reggae

The cultural roots of reggae can be traced back to the Caribbean island of Jamaica. During the 1950s and early 1960s, the Jamaican music scene was heavily influenced by African American R&B (rhythm and blues), an amplified version of the original acoustic blues music performed by African Americans (see Chambers 1976). The proximity of Jamaica to the south-east coast of the US meant that Jamaicans were able to listen in to US radio stations which regularly featured R&B music on their shows. Similarly, migrant West Indians working in the US often brought back R&B records on return visits to Jamaica (Logan and Woffinden 1976: 413). Just as white rock 'n' roll artists in the US appropriated and reworked the R&B sound to create rock 'n' roll (see Chapter 1), Jamaican musicians also reinterpreted this sound in a locally distinctive fashion. Thus, as Logan and Woffinden (1976: 413) explain, the striding off-beat and rhythmic brass patterns of New Orleans R&B artists, such as Fats Domino and Amos Milburn, were taken over and imitated by the Jamaican musicians who accentuated the off-beat and modified the brass playing style.

This new R&B inspired sound became known as **ska**. Popular ska artists of the early 1960s included Byron Lee, Owen Gray, Laurel Aitken and Prince Buster (whose song 'Bring Back the Prince' was covered by white London-based group Madness during the British ska revival of the early 1980s: see Hebdige 1987). Chambers suggests that:

> 'Ska' represented a musical cross-breed between a fiery, indigenous culture and a black US music. Coming out of the occasional radio in the shacks and 'dungles' of West Kingston's Trench Town, Back O'Wall and Greenwich Farm.
>
> (Chambers 1985: 154)

By the summer of 1966 the ska style had begun to change. The music was becoming increasingly reliant on electrified instruments and had taken on a more relaxed feel, while the simple off/on beat was becoming increasingly more complex. The emphasis changed from horns to a heavy electric bass sound and cutting rhythms provided by electric guitars with high treble settings. This new, slower style of music found an appeal among West Kingston street gangs referred to locally as **rude boys**, a term which also become synonymous with the music. As Hebdige explains, rude boys

> were mostly unemployed and had taken to carrying German ratchet knives and handguns. They could be anything from fourteen to twenty-five years old and came from all over West Kingston. And above all, the

rude boys were *angry*. Conditions in West Kingston had hardly improved with the passing years. Rather than buckle under to a life spent doing menial work or no work at all, the rude boys took to the streets and to crime.

(Hebdige 1987: 72)

If 'rude boy' became the soundtrack for the aggrieved street gangs of West Kingston from which it took its name, then the emergence of reggae, a further development of rude boy sound, had an equally significant impact on young Jamaicans. The cultural significance of reggae is firmly rooted in the history of Jamaica as a British colony. The initial population of colonial Jamaica comprised mainly of slaves brought over from Africa to work on sugar plantations (see Hebdige 1987: 23–8) and white British settlers. Some white settlers – engineers, doctors and lawyers – were there to administer and maintain the colony, while others had been more or less forced into migration, notably Scottish crofters whose Highland homes had been seized by English landowners (Chambers 1985: 152). The events surrounding Jamaica's history as a British colony remain ingrained in its language, music, religion and everyday life. It is within this interplay of cultures, together with the influence of African American musical styles, that the roots of reggae are located. Thus, as Hebdige observes:

> reggae is transmogrified American 'soul' music with an overlay of salvaged African rhythms, and an undercurrent of pure Jamaican rebellion. Reggae is transplanted Pentecostal. Reggae is the Rasta hymnal, the heart cry of the Kingston Rude Boy, as well as the nativised national anthem of the new Jamaican government.
>
> (Hebdige 1976b: 140–1)

As this brief overview of reggae illustrates, the reggae style is largely an amalgamation of musical sounds from the African **diaspora**, a feature of reggae which has undoubtedly enhanced its global appeal. Equally important in charting reggae's cultural impact in a global context, however, is the music's association with Rastafarianism.

Reggae and Rastafarianism

If reggae began in Jamaica, its sound, style and underlying ethos bringing together a range of previously opposed and conflicting cultural strands bound up with the social history of the island, then it is as a global music that reggae has made its most recognizable impact. Thus, as Gilroy (1993) argues, reggae quickly ceased 'to signify an exclusively ethnic, Jamaican style and derived a different kind of cultural legitimacy both from a new global status and from its expression of what might be termed a pan-Caribbean culture' (Gilroy 1993: 82). A factor which contributed to reggae's transformation in this respect was its association with Rastafarianism, argued by some observers to have been there from the beginning, but considerably more noticeable from the early 1970s onwards. Like reggae, Rastafarianism has its roots in the colonialism and slavery of Jamaica's past. Colonialism was in part justified from the point of view of white European colonial rulers through their reading of the Biblical scriptures (Hebdige 1979: 32). The dualism of the biblical rhetoric, and in particular its reference to the 'Black Satan' and 'the snow-white Lamb of God', was interpreted as an instruction to the colonial authorities to enslave the native Africans and transform them into servants (Hebdige 1979: 32). However, through slavery, the African peoples grew familiar with aspects of European culture, including religion, and began to look for reflections of themselves in the texts of the Bible using 'the openness of [its] religious metaphors' to create their own reading and interpretation (Hebdige 1979: 33). As Hebdige points out, in the text of the Bible the slaves found their own solution and salvation in the form of

> an 'Africa' which lay dormant and forgotten inside the language of the white Master. Read between the lines the Text could be made to deliver up this Africa, to free it, and restore it to the 'righteous sufferer'.
>
> (Hebdige 1979: 33)

It is from this interpretation of the Bible that Rastafarianism originates. Central to Rastafarianism is the belief that Haile Selassie's accession to the throne of Ethiopia in 1930 represented the fulfilment of the biblical prophecies relating to the downfall of 'Babylon' (interpreted as the white colonial powers), and the deliverance of the black races (Hebdige 1979: 32; see also Lewis 1993). Up until the late 1960s, the Rastafarians of Jamaica had been systematically persecuted because they accentuated the racial, class and religious differences among the island's population that the newly independent government of Jamaica claimed no longer existed. Thus, as Lewis notes:

> the Rastas played out a kind of existential absurdity in Jamaican society. They defiled the sacred image of the white Jesus as liberator through their own theology of Haile Selassie, and yet they also offended the spiritualist churches, which supported Jamaica's poor, by shunning the practice of possession trances. The Rasta call for repatriation to

Ethiopia was a rejection of political involvement in their own society. Their refusal to imitate English mannerisms – the undisputed sign of respectability in Jamaican society – showed a disregard for convention. They viewed marijuana – a drug popular among the working poor as a palliative to help them endure labor in the fields – as a tool of illumination to make one aware of the bourgeois world. These traits marked the Rastas as a challenge and a threat.

(Lewis 1993: 9)

During the 1970s, however, the Manley regime initiated a shift in the industrial and ideological development of Jamaica away from Europe and the US and more towards Cuba and the third world (Hebdige 1979: 35). In this new political climate, the Rastafarians became more accepted in Jamaica. Manley's electoral campaign had 'favored Rastafarai symbolism' and he expressed such support for the movement that in 1977 the early Rasta leader, Archibald Dunkley, wrote in the Rastafari publication *The Ethiopian World* that 'Michael [Manley] has come to do the will of God for the Rastafarians' (cited in Lewis 1993: 69). The changing political climate in Jamaica coincided with the development of the local popular culture industry. The burgeoning reggae movement at the hub of this industry proved to be the perfect vehicle for the communication of the Rastafarian message at a global level. Reggae music and its Rastafarian message became, to use Gilroy's (1993: 82) description, a central medium 'in facilitating the transition of diverse settlers to a distinct mode of lived blackness'. Reggae singer Linton Kwesi Johnson further defined the relationship between reggae and Rastafarianism in an interview with British cultural theorist Stuart Hall during 1979. Thus explained Johnson:

I'm not a religious person myself, but Rastafarianism is the most important positive cultural movement that we have experienced in Jamaica and whose impact has been much wider than Jamaica in fact. What the Rasta have succeeded in doing is to correct the imbalance of colonial brain-whitening – as some people would call it – brainwashing. Rasta made Jamaicans proud of their history, their culture, their African heritage and their roots. As a spiritual force, it has brought a tremendous amount of creativity into reggae music. And it has contributed to the popular language of the people. A lot of people who are not even Rastas use Rasta words.

(Johnson cited in Lipsitz 1994a: 109)

At the centre of reggae's cultural collaboration with Rastafarianism was the Jamaican singer-songwriter Bob Marley. Born in 1945, Marley was the son of an English army captain and a Jamaican woman. In his late teens Marley became involved in the Jamaican music scene (see Logan and Woffinden 1976: 320–2; Hebdige 1987: 78–81). By the early 1970s, Marley, like many of his contemporaries, was becoming heavily influenced by Rastafarian beliefs, the second album by Marley and his group the Wailers being titled Rasta Revolution (Logan and Woffinden 1976: 322). Much of Bob Marley and the Wailers' work was concerned to convey the Rastafarian message as is clearly evidenced in the following extract from the group's 1977 hit 'Get Up Stand Up (For Your Rights)':

> Preacher man say Great God come down from the sky,
> Make every body feel happy, make everybody feel high,
> But if you know what life is worth,
> You will look for yours on earth,
> So now I seen the light,
> I'm gonna stand up for me rights,
>
> (cited in Hebdige 1976b: 140)

There are clear references in the above lyric extract to the central beliefs of the Rastafarian faith. At a broader level, through the lyric Marley is addressing issues 'of oppression and tyranny that [have] plagued the history of Jamaica since 1655' when the island became a colony (Sion 1998: 293). Marley is not the only Jamaican reggae artist to have addressed such issues which, according to Jones (1988: 26), 'often form the raw material for reggae lyricism'. For example, fellow reggae artist Peter Tosh, originally a member of the Wailers and co-writer of 'Get Up Stand Up (For Your Rights)', was similarly proactive against the oppression felt by many to be a continuing feature of everyday life in Jamaica (see Hebdige 1987: 22).

Reggae in Britain

During the 1970s reggae had a significant impact on African Caribbean youth in Britain who quickly identified both with the message of reggae music and with the Rasta style of its leading artists. Back (1993) has suggested that the notion of ethnic identity, as with other forms of social identity, can no longer be regarded as ' "real" or "essential" ' but rather needs to be seen as a 'multi-faceted phenomenon which may vary through time and place' (Back 1993: 128). In many respects, the appropriation of reggae and its attendant Rasta image by young people of African Caribbean origin in Britain serves as a telling illustration of the socio-temporal characteristics of ethnic identities suggested by Back. The cultural significance of reggae and the 'Rasta' look for young African Caribbeans in Britain is inextricably linked with the socio-economic situation of African Caribbean communities during the 1970s as well as with the discrimination and intolerance to which African Caribbeans were subjected by the dominant white population.

The first group of immigrants from Jamaica and the neighbouring island of Trinidad arrived in Britain on 21 June 1948 on board the ship *Empire Windrush*. They comprised mainly 'skilled' and 'semi-skilled' men who had come to Britain 'at the government's behest to help rebuild a country ravaged by war' (Wilmer 1998: 54). Anticipating a higher standard of living in Britain, better jobs, better homes, respectability and a place in which their families could settle down, African Caribbean immigrants attempted to integrate into British society (Foner 1978; Byron 1998). Initially accepting their low social position in the expectation that their children would fare better, the African Caribbean immigrants typically aspired to 'the same goals, and sought the same diversions (a pint of beer, a game of darts, a dance on Saturday night) . . . [as] their white working class neighbours' (Hebdige 1979: 40). As the 1960s progressed, however, it became obvious that the life chances of African Caribbeans in Britain were not becoming equal to those of whites. African Caribbeans found themselves ghettoized in decaying inner-city districts. Moreover, if unemployment among young people in Britain was increasing, then the ones who fared worst in the labour market were the children of the African Caribbean immigrants.

At this point, a fundamental change began to take place in the style and attitude of African Caribbean youth. Hebdige describes this transition thus:

> as the immigrants began to congregate in the decaying inner-city rings of Britain's larger cities, a new West Indian style began to emerge. This style was less painfully hemmed in by Britishness, less torn between sobriety and 'colour', and behind it there lay the suggestion (unwelcome to white eyes) that yet another immigration had taken place, that Britain had failed to supply the promised goods, and that the disaffected immigrants had psychologically moved out.
>
> (Hebdige 1979: 42)

The first noticeable changes in the stylistic sensibilities of many African Caribbean youth was a move towards wearing short-brimmed hats (later to become known as **pork pie hats**) with dark glasses and Italian style sharp suits. Hebdige describes this image and the style of walking and argot that accompanied it as 'a West Indian equivalent of the U.S. "soul-brother" look; tight-fitting, loose-limbed, black and yet urbane' (Hebdige 1979: 42). This image, which appropriated the name 'rude boy' from the West Kingston street gangs, was intended to mark out African Caribbean youth from white youth. Despite this, however, the style was quickly emulated by sections of white youth in Britain. Thus, the white British 'mod' style (see Chapter 1) appropriated both the sharp suits and ska music from African Caribbean youth while, as illustrated in the seminal film about the mod era *Quadrophenia* (see Lewis 1992: 86–7), remaining at the same time highly racist and parochial in its outlook. Similarly, white skinhead culture was also closely modelled on the rude boy image, the short-cropped hair of the rude boys being appropriated by the skinheads, who also attempted to mimic their loose-limbed style of walking (Hebdige 1976b). Focusing on the lyrical content of rude boy and other black musical styles, Chambers (1976) argues that the values of opposition and resistance which they expressed could be easily related to by white working class youth and resulted, for example, in 'Skinheads rewriting "black pride" lyrics as "white pride"' lyrics (Chambers 1976: 165).

The arrival of reggae music in Britain during the late 1970s significantly altered the way in which notions of 'blackness' and black identity were expressed. According to Price (1981: 134), from the point of view of the young African Caribbean, reggae 'helped to inject a much needed sense of ideological and cultural solidarity'. Particularly significant for African Caribbean youth in Britain was the Rasta image of reggae artists such as Bob Marley. The resulting rasta image in Britain, however, was an essentially adapted form which drew upon the Rastafarian aesthetic, learned and borrowed from the covers and sleeve notes of imported Jamaican reggae albums. This was subsequently reworked in a way that suited the needs of second-generation African Caribbean immigrants living in Britain. The religious aspects of Rastafarianism became less important to African Caribbean youth in Britain than its significance as a form of cultural resistance. Here was a style which African Caribbean youth could call its own; a style that was removed from white British culture and which white youth initially found hard to understand. Rastafarianism became a piece of cultural territory which was impenetrable from the outside; a localised reworking of the Jamaican Rasta style that stressed its essential 'blackness' in the face of a dominant white society whose racism was becoming increasingly institutionalized. As Hebdige points out, Rastafarianism in Britain

was a Rastafarianism at more than one remove, stripped of nearly all its original religious meanings: a distillation, a highly selective appropriation of all those elements of Rastafarianism which stressed the importance of resistance and black identity . . . The difference around which the whole Rasta style revolved was literally inscribed on the skin of black people and it was through appearance that this difference was to be extended, elaborated upon, realized.

(Hebdige 1979: 43)

Rastas in Britain began to fashion an image which was, in keeping with the reggae artists whose music they listened and danced to, more 'African'. The pork pie hat was replaced by the **tam**, a roughly woven, loose fitting hat. The sharp suits, which were manufactured from synthetic materials such as mohair and terylene, were replaced by more casual clothes made out of natural fibres such as wool and cotton. And, perhaps most characteristically, the short-cropped hair was allowed to grow out and plaited in 'knots' or 'dreadlocks'. According to Cashmore, **dreadlocks**

> were an element in redefining the black man to himself; to demonstrate that Rastas were prepared to go against the ideological grain and respond to white definitions with counter-definitions . . . The appearance of locks celebrated blackness: made its quality and possession esteemed and positively valued.
>
> (Cashmore 1983: 158–9)

Similarly, Mercer (1987: 424) notes how 'once "locks" were popularized on a mass scale – via the increasing militancy of reggae, especially – their dread logic inscribed a beautification of blackness'. Although the material conditions of African Caribbean youth remained unchanged, their ability to negotiate such circumstances was significantly transformed through the new cultural space which the Rasta image and reggae music created. According to Price (1981: 134), 'the entire identity of the [African Caribbean] youth revolve[d] around the ethnic style and symbolism of the music'.

White British youth and reggae

As previously noted, both reggae music and its accompanying Rasta look were so inextricably tied to the fact of being black that they did not easily translate for white youth in Britain who, up until this point, had appropriated black musics and style in a relatively unproblematic fashion, even if they continued to employ a deeply racist discourse. Hebdige's (1976b) views on the impenetrability of reggae and the Rasta style culture for white British youth are summed up effectively by his reading of the skinheads' failure to connect with this radical turn in the style of African Caribbean youth from rude boy to the Rasta look at the end of the 1960s. Thus, states Hebdige, even if he [the skinhead] could make that sympathetic passage from Notting Hill to Addis Ababa, from a whiteness which wasn't worth much anyway, to a blackness which just might mean something more, he only found himself trapped further in an irresolvable contradiction. For the rude boys had come of age and the skins were sentenced to perpetual adolescence.

(Hebdige 1976b: 150)

Nevertheless, both reggae, and to some extent the Rasta look, have been variously appropriated by sections of white British youth. Indeed, as Hebdige himself concedes, the increasing popularity of reggae in Britain during the late 1970s was largely due to the rise of punk. In the early days of punk there were no punk records, the ethos of the early punk groups being that music should be 'live'. At punk gigs, therefore, it was common to play reggae music over the **sound system** before and after a band's appearance on stage. Similarly, the handful of London-based punk clubs at this time featured reggae music. Hebdige also claims that there was a degree of affinity between the punk and Rasta movements due to their similarly oppositional stances against the dominant British society. Thus, according to Hebdige (1979: 64), from the point of view of the punk movement, Rasta culture was 'an alien essence, a foreign body which implicitly threatened mainstream British culture from within and as such it resonated with punk's adopted values'.

Another way in which punk was instrumental in securing a white audience for reggae music was the involvement of punk and reggae artists in Rock Against Racism concerts during the late 1970s. Thus, as Marks explains:

The alliance of punk and reggae groups in the late 1970s for Rock Against Racism concerts prompted a surge of interest in reggae, as well as a heady optimism engendered by the sense of working for a common aim. Many British reggae groups, formerly struggling with small record labels, were able to sign up to major companies . . . New Jamaican groups, like Black Uhuru and Third World, became very popular among punks and new wave fans; as a result there was renewed interest too in the work of longer-established musicians – like Culture, I-Roy, and Prince Far-I – who had hitherto been little known in Britain outside the West Indian community.

(Marks 1990: 111–12)

According to Marks, then, punk and reggae's allegiance at Rock Against Racism events initially galvanized a white following for reggae who empathized with the fundamental politics of its sound and lyrical content.

However, Marks also suggests that the subsequent appropriation of the reggae style by white post-punk artists, such as The Police, 'distracted chart audiences' from the political issues associated with reggae (Marks 1990: 112).

While the political motivation of reggae became one avenue for white youth's involvement in the British reggae scene, shared local experiences and the 'cross-racial affiliations' they engendered were another (Jones 1988: xiv). In an ethnographic study of white appropriations of reggae and other aspects of African Caribbean style in Birmingham, a multi-ethnic city in the English Midlands with a large African Caribbean population, Jones (1988: 128) suggests that in certain districts 'the cultural lives of both black and white communities have become harmonised around the shared spaces and cross-cutting loyalties of street, pub and neighbourhood'. Jones further suggests that the result of such harmonization, particularly as this relates to young people, is that racial distinctions become far less important, these being replaced by a shared feeling of community between black and white residents.

Using data generated via interviews and observations, Jones illustrates how one of the ways in which this shared feeling of community manifests itself is through common tastes in music and style. In particular, observes Jones, white youth are seen to adopt the reggae music and attendant Rasta look of their black peers. Thus, in this particular case, community rather than race becomes a key factor in the construction of identity. The key to understanding how this process works is Back's (1996) concept of **community discourse**. Back argues that community discourse allows for the construction of a given community and those living within it in specifically 'local' terms. Thus the existence of interracial tolerance in a particular area or community might be explained in terms of the fact that people have lived together there for a long time, know each other well and get on with each other. In illustrating this, Back uses as an example an area of London which he refers to as Southgate. According to Back, in Southgate community discourse 'acts as a resource that banishes "racial things" from everyday experience' (Back 1996: 112). At the same time, however, such tolerance is not extended to those groups living outside the area, the types of discourse being used in relation to the latter relying much more on media representations and stereotypes.

A further example of white appropriation of reggae in Britain is provided in Sion's (1998) study of Welsh singer-songwriter Geraint Jarman. According to Sion, Jarman's album *Fflamau'r Ddraig* (Dragon's Fire) released in 1980 was significant both in terms of its understanding and interpretation of reggae music and lyrical themes and for reworking the latter in ways that gave them 'potency and immediacy of expression in a local context' (Sion 1998: 291). The title track of the album focuses on a local socio-political issue current at the time of the album's release, the deliberate burning down of English holiday homes by Meibion Glynawr (The Sons of Glyndwr), a Welsh nationalist group. The song also comments on the reaction of the local police who arrested a number of suspects 'without any corroborating evidence' (Sion 1998: 294). As with Jamaican reggae, these themes are not directly addressed by Jarman but couched within a discourse that draws upon metaphysical images. Thus, the symbol of the dragon is used as a simultaneous metaphor for Welsh national identity (the dragon being the symbol of the Welsh national flag), fire and a wider, unseen form of power of which the acts of the arsonists was simply one manifestation:

> 'Dragon's Flames' [sic] . . . represents the voices of resistance that are not directly involved with the actions of the campaigners . . . Apart from being the most obvious symbolic representation of 'Welshness' the dragon is also a creature whose true realization is beyond our own experience and comprehension. In this sense, the arsonists become the anthropomorphic manifestations of the dragon: unseen, mysterious, breathing fire, and associated with the discourse of myth and fantasy.
>
> (Sion 1998: 295)

Sion's work begins to illustrate how reggae music, in addition to its significance as a form of cultural dialogue between the youth of African diasporic communities, has been appropriated by youth outside of such communities. Evidence of such non-African diasporic workings of reggae music can also be found elsewhere in the world.

Reggae and Australian Aboriginal youth

Recent research on the cultural impact of reggae in a global context provides further illustrations of the way in which reggae music and the Rasta style have been culturally reterritorialized (Lull 1995). A case in point is Davies' (1993) work on the significance of reggae for Aboriginal youth in Australia. Davies argues that there are a number of socio-historical similarities which connect Aboriginal and African Caribbean peoples. Both were subjected to white oppression and transported from their cultural homelands to be used as slaves. Such felt affinity on the part of young Aborigines with African Caribbean culture is, according to Davies, one of the primary reasons why reggae music was initially embraced by Aboriginal youth. Indeed, two of the leading Aborigine reggae bands, No Fixed Address and Us Mob, were formed at Adelaide's Centre for Aboriginal Studies in Music following Bob Marley's 1979 tour of Australia. At the same time, however, the appropriation of reggae music and the Rasta look by young Aborigines is also intended to articulate issues which are particular to the socio-cultural experience of the Aborigine people in Australia.

From the point of view of young Aborigines, the significance of reggae music is linked with the attempt to recover their cultural homelands from white landowners. As Davies (1993: 253) explains: 'Cultural survival for the Aboriginal Australians is tied to land rights, to origins, to a cultural integrity beyond contemporary industrial arrangements'. Thus, the appropriation of reggae music by Aboriginal youth is symbolic of their discontent with their place in Australian society. Since Australia was colonized, Aborigines choosing to move to the modern cities have had to live in very poor conditions, either in tin shanties on the city outskirts or in inner-city slum areas. Likewise, those Aborigines who continue to pursue a traditional tribal existence have been forced to live on reservations. According to Davies, the use of reggae music by Aborigine bands such as No Fixed Address and Us Mob to campaign for land rights must be seen in terms of two types of what Davies refers to as 'empowering practices'. First, he suggests, the music represents a form of empowerment through its 'reversal and decentring of colonial social relations' (Davies 1993: 256). Second, when the music of Aboriginal bands is distributed through mainstream TV and radio channels, the usually marginalized Aborigine community is given the opportunity to voice its discontent through a central and highly strategic medium and to take advantage of the widespread coverage which this offers.

Conclusion

During this chapter I have considered the development and cultural impact of reggae music. Beginning with a brief look at the origins of reggae in Jamaica, I then examined how the music's links with Rastafarian belief assured its wider cultural significance both for young Jamaicans and the youth of other ethnic minority communities of African descent around the world. I then focused upon the specific case of Britain, noting how, by appropriating aspects of the Rastafarian culture, young second-generation African Caribbean immigrants were able to effect their own form of resistance against the dominant white British culture. Subsequently, I considered some of the ways in which reggae music, despite its cultural association with Rastafarianism, has been adopted by white youth in Britain. In some cases such white borrowings of reggae have been motivated by a desire to forge political associations between black and white youth in Britain, while in other cases they have occurred at the level of everyday cultural exchange between the youth of multi-ethnic communities. In the final part of the chapter I looked at the wider global significance of reggae music through an examination of its appropriation by Aboriginal youth in Australia. In doing so I illustrated how, as in Britain, reggae music has once again enabled a marginalized ethnic minority to challenge issues of oppression, exclusion and exploitation by the dominant white society.

Further reading

Chambers, I. (1985) *Urban Rhythms: Pop Music and Popular Culture*. London: Macmillan (Chapter 6).

Davies, C.L. (1993) Aboriginal rock music: space and place, in T. Bennett, S. Frith, L. Grossberg, J. Shepherd and G. Turner (eds) *Rock and Popular Music: Politics, Policies, Institutions*. London: Routledge.

Hebdige, D. (1976b) Reggae, Rastas and Rudies, in S. Hall and T. Jefferson (eds) *Resistance through Rituals: Youth Subcultures in Post-War Britain*. London: Hutchinson.

Hebdige, D. (1979) *Subculture: The Meaning of Style*. London: Routledge (Chapter 3).

Hebdige, D. (1987) *Cut 'n' Mix: Culture, Identity and Caribbean Music*. London: Routledge.

Jones, S. (1988) *Black Culture, White Youth: The Reggae Tradition from JA to UK*. London: Macmillan.

Marks, A. (1990) Young, gifted and black: Afro-American and Afro-Caribbean music in Britain 1963–88, in P. Oliver (ed.) *Black Music in Britain: Essays on the Afro-Asian Contribution to Popular Music*. Buckingham: Open University Press.

Mercer, K. (1987) Black hair/style politics, in K. Gelder and S. Thornton (eds) (1997) *The Subcultures Reader*. London: Routledge.

Price, K. (1981) Black identity and the role of reggae, in D. Potter (ed.) *Society and the Social Sciences: An Introduction*. London: Routledge and Open University Press.

Sion, P.A. (1998) Voices of resistance: Geraint Jarman and the roots of reggae in Welsh popular music, in T. Hautamäki and H. Järviluoma (eds) *Music on Show: Issues of Performance*. Tampere, Finland: Department of Folk Tradition, University of Tampere. Conference Proceedings of Eighth International Association for the Study of Popular Music International Conference, University of Strathclyde, 1–6 July 1995.

6 | RAP MUSIC AND HIP HOP CULTURE

There may be nothing at this moment in pop music more exhilarating than a great new rap record – the street-smart immediacy, the juxtaposition of the beat and funky-fresh politics. Even if you don't like the stuff, you can sense that it matters.

(Gold 1995: 66)

While gangsta rap takes the heat for a range of social maladies from urban violence to sexual misconduct, the roots of our racial misery remain buried beneath moralizing discourse that is confused and sometimes dishonest.

(Dyson 1996: 178)

It is an indisputable truism that rap music has been more readily associated with the incidence of youth crime and violence, and thus more rigorously censored, than any other contemporary youth music. Media images of rap routinely fixate on its allegedly violent and misogynistic characteristics to the extent that any other representation of the music and its social significance are largely prevented from entering into the sphere of public perception (Epstein *et al.* 1990; Dyson 1996). Similarly, since its inception in May 1985, the Washington DC based Parents Music Resource Center (see also Chapter 3) has regularly sought to ban rap recordings due to their alleged 'glamoriz[ation of] graphic sex, violence and drug use' (Epstein *et al.* 1990: 382; see also Martin and Segrave 1993).

By the same token, however, the continuing popularity of rap, which first became a mainstream form of popular culture during the mid-1980s, makes it one of the most commercially successful musical styles of the late twentieth and early twenty-first centuries. Furthermore, research on rap music by sociologists and cultural theorists suggests that the music's increasingly global appeal (Mitchell 1996; Bennett 2000) cannot be attributed only to the 'shock' value which some observers link with the music's appeal for young people; rather, it is argued, the longevity of rap's appeal for young people is firmly linked with the way in which rap can be used as a means of engaging with and expressing dissatisfaction at the more restrictive features of everyday life in globally diffuse social settings. This chapter examines the origins of rap, and the wider hip hop culture from the which the music emerged, as a form of African American street culture and its subsequent development as a global form of contemporary youth culture.

The origins of rap and hip hop

According to Lipsitz (1994a), hip hop can be traced back to the Bronx district of New York during the early 1970s. Aware of the tensions that were being created as a consequence of urban renewal programmes and economic recession, an African American street gang member who called himself Afrika Bambaataa formed 'The Zulu Nation' in an attempt to 'channel the anger of young people in the South Bronx away from gang fighting and into music, dance, and graffiti' (Lipsitz 1994a: 26). While each of the elements in hip hop assumed significance as a form of expression for young people living in the Bronx, rap became particularly important as a community-wide means of addressing and negotiating the extreme socio-economic circumstances which characterised everyday life in the Bronx. In particular, the absence of a need for musical *skill*, in the more conventional sense of being able to play a musical instrument, gave rap an essentially 'hands-on' quality, making it an ideal medium through which young people could spontaneously express their views or simply vent frustration regarding issues such as interracial violence, poverty and unemployment – issues that were all exacerbated due to the ghettoization of the Bronx district and its labelling as a 'no-go' area. Thus, as Lipsitz explains:

> Bambaataa and his Zulu nation used their knowledge as consumers of popular music to become skilled producers of it . . . Hemmed in by urban renewal, crime and police surveillance, and silenced by neglect from the culture industry, the school system, and city government, they found a way to declare themselves through music.
>
> (Lipsitz 1994a: 26)

Rap is a narrative form of vocal delivery which is spoken in a rhythmic patois over a continuous 'breakbeat'. Keyes has suggested that the distinctive vocal technique employed in rapping 'can be traced from African bardic traditions to rural southern-based expressions of African Americans – toasts, tales, sermons, blues, game songs, and allied forms – all of which are recited in a chanted rhyme or poetic fashion' (Keyes 1991: 40). The beat in rap music is provided via a method of 'mixing' vinyl records together by utilising both turntables on a dual record-player deck. As Back observes:

> [Rap] music is dependent on the rearranging of musical fragments inter-mixed by the DJ. This is called break-beat music. The DJ is close to what Lévi-Strauss (1976) called a 'bricoleur' or craftsperson who makes use – in this case – of musical fragments in order to create new music. Here a beat or passage is identified by the DJ and, using two copies of the record, it is intermixed, enabling the seamless repetition of a percussive section of a particular record.
>
> (Back 1996: 192)

The concept of *bricolage*, a French term referring to the cultural transform-ation of the meaning of objects and symbols, first acquired a currency in youth cultural studies through the work of Hebdige (1979) who emphasized the bricoleurist quality of the British punk scene (see Chapter 4). Thus, according to Hebdige (1979: 26): 'Punk reproduced the entire sartorial his-tory of post-war working-class youth cultures subcultures in "cut up" form, combining elements which had originally belonged to completely different epochs'. In his description of the creative work of the rap DJ, Back (1996) suggests that a similar form of bricoleurist 'cut and mix' is achieved in musi-cal terms as fragments of music and lyrics from a range of genres are taken from their original contexts and recombined to make new pieces of music. This observed quality in rap has led some theorists to claim that this is a postmodern music whose reassembling of songs and soundbites from differ-ent eras, genres and 'cultures' of music corresponds with the blurring of styl-istic boundaries now occurring across a range of cultural and artistic concerns. Applying a more political interpretation to this alleged postmodern aspect of rap, Potter (1995) suggests that rap and hip hop are both logical and timely innovations in African American culture. Thus, argues Potter:

> If postmodernist art can be said to be haunted by a sense of belatedness, a sense of living in the ruins of the abandoned structures of modernism, then it should come as no surprise that African-American art in general – and hip hop in particular – has come into its own at this juncture of history . . . For many African-Americans in the United States, the dis-appointment of the political and economic dreams of the civil rights movement of the 1960s, along with the worsening economic situation of the inner cities have combined to bring about a similar sense of life on the edge.
>
> (Potter 1995: 18)

Several other writers have also examined the cultural significance of rap and hip hop as a means by which African Americans can actively unpack and scrutinize the history of race relations in the US. Thus, according to Rose (1994a: 102): 'Rap music, more than any other contemporary form of black cultural expression, articulates the chasm between black urban lived experience and dominant, "legitimate" (e.g., neoliberal) ideology regarding equal opportunity and racial inequality'. Similarly, Dyson makes the following observation:

> As rap expands its vision and influence, its unfavorable origins and its relentless quest to represent black youth are both a consolation and challenge to hip-hoppers. They remind hip hoppers that history is not merely the stuff of imperial dreams from above. It isn't just the sanitizing myths of those with political power. Representing history is within reach of those who seize the opportunity to speak for themselves, to represent their own interests at all costs.
>
> (Dyson 1996: 177–8)

A more extensive exploration of these observed characteristics in African American hip hop culture is made by Decker (1994). According to Decker two distinct but related sensibilities can be identified with African American hip hop – 'nationalism' and **Afrocentricism**. Hip hop nationalists, suggests Decker, are involved in the production of a form of cultural politics which addresses the everyday struggles of working class blacks in the US. **Hip hop nationalism** is modelled on the Black Power movements of the late 1960s (see Chapter 2). Again, Decker draws on the notion of rap as a postmodern discourse using modern technology, notably **sampling** (see Chapter 8) as a means of reframing the 'speeches and TV images of black political leaders of the sixties' for a contemporary audience (Decker 1994: 104). By utilizing sounds and images in this way, 'Hip hop nationalists . . . move beyond romanticizing media images of sixties Black Power . . . recontextualis[ing] and thus mak[ing] black militancy of the 1960s meaningful for the 1990s' (Decker 1994: 104).

The second African American hip hop sensibility identified by Decker, 'Afrocentricism', involves the attempt 'to reverse a history of Western economic dependency and cultural imperialism by placing a distinctly African value system . . . at the centre of the worldview' (Decker 1994: 111). At the heart of this African value system are 'deep [spiritual and psychological] structures' which, according to Decker (1994: 111), can be used by the African American to transcend western oppression. Afrocentric hip hop contests the popular western idea that, prior to its colonization, Africa was a barbaric land. Thus, argues Decker, Afrocentric hip hoppers effectively turn this argument around. Instead of viewing Africa at the lower end of the evolutionary chain, Afrocentric hip hoppers claim that the ancient civilizations of North Africa – Egypt and Nubia – are the origins of Western civilization.

Understandably, perhaps, given the multi-ethnic composition of the Bronx district and other inner-city areas of New York, some writers have questioned the claim that rap and hip hop were exclusively African American innovations. Mitchell (1998), for example, suggests that histories of hip hop overlook the involvement of young white youth in the development of rap and hip hop. Similarly, in his study of Latino Rap, a Puerto Rican variation of rap which developed out of the New York ghettos alongside African American rap, Flores (1994: 92) notes how 'the dominant construction of rap in the media and most narrative accounts has tended systematically, or at least symptomatically, to elide precisely the Puerto Rican role and dimension in staking out this pre-eminent field of contemporary youth sensibility'.

Hip hop and the African diaspora

The dominance of African American perspectives on the origins and significance of rap and hip hop has, to some extent, been countered by work that has attempted to situate hip hop in a more pan-cultural context. Initially such work focused on the role of hip hop as a global discourse that acted to link displaced peoples of African decent throughout the world. Thus, according to Lipsitz:

> [Hip hop] brings a community into being through performance, and it maps out real and imagined relations between people that speak to the realities of displacement, disillusion, and despair created by the austerity economy of post-industrial capitalism.
>
> (Lipsitz 1994a: 36)

The African diasporic association to which Lipsitz alludes here is clearly evident in Cobley and Osgerby's (1995) study of the local hip hop scene in Peckham, London. A dominant frame of reference for the young African Caribbean rappers interviewed was their sense of identification with African American hip hop culture. While such identification highlighted for those who took part in the study both the similarities and differences between themselves and the African American rappers to whom they looked for inspiration, the perceived notion of hip hop as a form of African diasporic discourse linking African Americans with African Caribbeans in Britain was clearly evident. As Cobley and Osgerby observe:

America, for our young people, offered a point of both equivalence and difference. Difference, was manifested in the demand for *authentic* enunciation rather than a home-grown simulacra; our cohort believed that they lived very different lives from their American counterparts. Equivalence was seen in the comparable diversities and points of origin engendered by diasporic identification.

(Cobley and Osgerby 1995: 11)

Speaking more generally about the impact of rap on notions of 'black' identity in Britain and the latter's expression through music, Storry and Childs (1997) suggest that 'the cross-fertilisation of Anglo-American-Caribbean black culture [has created] a new kind of cross-national identity'. Storry and Childs go on to observe that:

The recent popularity of hip-hop culture and rap music from the black American urban ghetto has influenced and been inflected by black British culture such as Soul II Soul's fusion of hip-hop, soul and jazz music and 'jungle' music's recombination of dark raps, the rhythms of techno-dance music and the Caribbean influence of Ragga.

(Storry and Childs 1997: 321)

Clearly, if studies of rap and hip hop's role in linking African diasporic peoples challenge the notion that the former remain African American cultural forms then, at the same time, a concern with the essential 'blackness' of hip hop remains central to such work. In recent years, however, this claim has itself been challenged by a new body of work that has examined the appropriation of rap and hip hop by youth of non-African descent in different parts of the world.

Hip hop as a global resource

As illustrated above, much of the early work on rap and hip hop focuses on how these forms became a voice for a range of issues pertaining to the African American and wider African diasporic populations. At the same time, however, the commercial availability of rap music and hip hop style at a global level has ensured its broadening appeal with the result that it is no longer viable to speak in terms of rap and hip hop as being exclusively 'black' cultural forms.

Taking the basic tenets of the rap style, young people of differing ethnic backgrounds in cities and regions across the globe have reworked the rap text in ways that incorporate local knowledges and sensibilities, thus transforming rap into a means of communication that works in the context of specific localities. A useful model for understanding the cultural mobility of rap is Lull's (1995) concept of *cultural reterritorialization* which recasts cultural forms as malleable resources that can be inscribed with new meanings relating to the particular local context within which such products are appropriated. Thus, argues Lull,

> the foundations of cultural territory – ways of life, artifacts, symbols, and contexts – are all open to new interpretations and understandings . . . Because culture is constructed and mobile, it is also synthetic and multiple.
>
> (Lull 1995: 159–60)

Perhaps because of its street cultural and largely improvised origins, rap appears to be particularly conducive to the process of cultural reterritorialization.

By the same token, however, a common thread running through localised appropriations of rap is a reflexive understanding among rap fans of the music's resonance with the risk and uncertainty (Beck 1992) that increasingly characterizes contemporary social settings and the consequent life chances of individuals in those settings. Thus, as Rose (1994b: 72) argues, rap's 'primary properties of flow, layering and rupture simultaneously reflect and contest the social roles open to inner city youth at the end of the twentieth century'. Central to the localization of rap music then is a process of creative adoption and adaptation, rap's core text being continually re-explored and redefined through the inscription of particular urban narratives.

Hip hop in western Europe

Across western Europe, rap music has become a musicalized forum for a series of locally situated, but thematically linked, discourses concerning issues such as racism, racial exclusion, citizenship, unemployment and poverty (see, for example, Mitchell 1996; Bjurström 1997; Bennett 1999b, 2000). Rappers' engagement with the tension and disruption caused by these related social problems takes a variety of localized forms. Thus, for example, in Italy much rap music embraces a militant, left-wing ideology, a number of Italian rap groups having grown out of the *centri sociali* (social centers) formed during the 1970s by 'left-wing militant students and disaffected young people' (Mitchell 1996: 150). According to Mitchell these rap groups could be collectively regarded as a subcultural movement which discovered a new rhetoric of political militancy of its own, using rap music to criticize political corruption, the mafia, homelessness, unemployment, racism, the mass media, the unions, wage restrictions and a whole range of social and political ills.

(Mitchell 1996: 150–1)

A similar series of observations concerning the localised reworking of rap and hip hop in Italy is offered by Fillipa (1986). Considering the impact of economic decline on different regions of Italy, Fillipa refers to the Sardinian rap group Sa Razza Posse and the way their songs

express the attitude of many young Italians towards the South: an ambivalent feeling compounded of both love and hate, of anger at work denied and yet of pride in having been born there, part of an unbroken tradition . . . of deep attachment to the land, of pride and dignity.

(Filippa 1986: 339)

Primary exponents of much western European rap are second generation immigrants from Africa, the West Indies, Turkey, Morocco and parts of Asia. Originally granted entry into western Europe during the early 1950s to assist with post-war reconstruction (see Foner 1978; Hebdige 1987), such immigrant populations have been forced to deal with constant racial abuse and discrimination, a situation exacerbated during the 1980s and 1990s by the economic downturn in many parts of western Europe, mass unemployment and a concomitant resurgence of Fascism (Fekete 1993). One of the most established European rappers is MC Solaar, born in Dakar, Senegal and raised in Paris (see Huq 1999). Along with several other francophone rappers, notably Soon EMC and IAM, Solaar has become known for a form of intellectualized rap that belies a university education which, according to some critics, results in a form of address which overlooks the essential purpose of the rap text. Thus, as Mitchell observes:

More culturally sophisticated than any of his US counterparts and completely free of expletives, sexism and racism, Solaar is sometimes accused of addressing an educated elite rather than the social, political and cultural concerns of la Goutte d'Or, the Paris suburb and African subculture he comes from.

(Mitchell 1996: 40)

However, as Mitchell then goes on to note, much of the rationale for Solaar's approach to rapping stems from a desire to avoid the stereotypes attached to US rap while simultaneously working within a French literary and cultural tradition deemed to be the foundation for effective socio-political commentary. Indeed, as Huq (1999: 137) argues, in evaluating the impact of MC Solaar on French youth, it is impossible to separate the artist from the 'cultural, economic and social forces that have produced [MC Solaar and allowed him] to function as the first mainstream representative of a music produced by the excluded'. Moreover, according to Huq, French rap music is not only a key form of address for more transparent types of racial exclusion resulting, for example, from structural problems such as ghettoization and unemployment, but also tackles the institutionalized racial exclusion practised by extreme right wing political parties, such as Front National (FN). As Huq explains, the radical cultural policy of the Front National has resulted in a highly negative attitude towards any form of culture linked with ethnic minority groups in France. An aspect of such radical cultural policy has been 'the removal of articles on [rap] from library copies of magazines in FN-governed towns' (Huq 1999: 139).

In Sweden the significance of hip hop as a means of addressing racism and its attendant social problems has also assumed a distinct local resonance as, according to Bjurström (1997: 49), 'hip hop and skinhead styles make up the most conspicuous opposite poles in the ethnic-stylistic warfare of Swedish youth culture'. As Bjurström notes, although both hip hop and skinhead are clearly imported styles, the Swedish skinhead movement has endeavoured to construct 'skinhead' as an authentic expression of Swedishness through the 'incorporation of Viking symbols, Swedish Great Power-kings and the Swedish flag in the skinhead style and anthems' (Bjurström 1997: 50). The response of the Swedish hip hop scene, which largely comprises of immigrant youth, has been to satirize such constructions of identity among white Swedish skinheads. This is most clearly illustrated in rapper Papa Dee's song 'Original Black Viking'. As Bjurström explains:

> the combination of the three words in the title of this song by Papa Dee, who has mixed Swedish-Caribbean origins, challenge traditional borders of race, ethnicity and nationality, and the claims of authenticity that go along with them. At the same time 'Original Black Viking' can be perceived as marking of a new ethnic identity . . . in the struggle for ethnicity it also lays the foundation for a 'conflict of interpretation' (Ricoeur, 1969/1974) of the Viking-symbols used in Viking rock and white noise music.
>
> (Bjurström 1997: 52)

In Germany the problems encountered by second-generation immigrants in relation to racism are compounded by the issue of citizenship, which, unlike many other countries, is not given automatically to any child who is born in Germany. Moreover, those who have acquired German citizenship often find that, in reality, such status does little to enhance their opportunities and general quality of life as they continue to be subject to racial inequality, exclusion and abuse (Bennett 1999b, 2000). Rap group Advanced Chemistry's song 'Fremd im eigenen Land' ('A Foreigner in my own Country'), together with the video made to promote it, was one of the first German rap songs to address the issue of citizenship in Germany. Performed by three rappers, each holding German citizenship, but with respective origins in Haiti, Ghana and Italy, the song documents the struggle of each to be accepted as German and orientates around the phrase 'Ich habe einen grünen Paß, mit einem Goldenen Adler drauf' – 'I have a green passport, with a golden eagle on it' (this being the design of the old German passport). In the video each member of the group is questioned about his nationality. On one occasion group member Frederick Hahn is approached by a white German youth who asks, 'Where do you come from, are you African or American?' When Hahn replies that he is German the youth begins to ridicule him and accuses him of lying, retreating only when Hahn produces his passport and sarcastically retorts, 'Is this the proof you're looking for?' In a further scene, another member of Advanced Chemistry is asked if he is 'going home later?', as in back to his 'home' country, to which he replies 'Always the same stupid questions . . . I've been living in this country for twenty years'. In an interview for British youth magazine *ID*, Advanced Chemistry spoke of their concern to expose the racial exclusion suffered by Germany's ethnic minority groups. Thus, as one of the group explained: 'We rap in German in order to reach our own public, in order that they understand our problem . . . it's a fact of life that if you're not recognised as a full German citizen you face constant harassment and identity checks' (Harpin 1993: 59–60).

A parallel reworking of hip hop as a form of address against localised forms of racial exclusion and more blatantly expressed racist ideologies is evident in Britain. In particular, rap has become a means of critically addressing the discourse of **little Englandism** (Samuel 1988) that continues to inform dominant notions of national identity in Britain. As with the Swedish example noted above, at one level this involves the satirizing of particular icons of Englishness. Thus, as Back (1996: 209) notes: 'Symbols of England, such as the "Royal Family", are used . . . to poke fun at definitions of Englishness that are racially exclusive'. At another level, hip hop is used as a means of marking out of symbolic cultural spaces for the formation of new identities which reject the essentializing notions of Englishness bound up with the discourse of little Englandism. This is evident, for example, in the work of South Asian rap-fusion groups such as Asian Dub Foundation where, according to Sharma (1996: 44), hip hop becomes a means of resisting 'hegemonic culturalist definitions . . . offer[ing] the possibility of simultaneously invoking/affirming/de-centring a politicized category of "Asian" or its particular ethnicities in a racist British social formation'. Similarly, Storey (1997: 91) describes the now defunct Manchester-based rap group 'The Ruthless Rap Assassins' as 'three organic intellectuals articulating their politics with "a funky North Hulme beat" . . . construct[ing] compelling critiques of the everyday racism in British society'. A series of other local issues have also been addressed in British hip hop. Thus, Webb (2000) explains how Bristol-based hip hop act Marxman's debut single was banned from the radio due to its commentary on the political situation in Northern Ireland, while subsequent singles by the group focused on 'slavery, domestic violence, and imperialism' (Webb 2000: 9).

The conflation of hip hop discourses with local knowledges has also resulted in a series of localised debates as to what constitutes authentic hip hop. To refer again to the work of Webb (2000), for example, it is noted that the tendency for some Bristol-based hip hop artists to rap in West Country accents is contested by other local hip hoppers who feel that such experiments distract from the socio-political agenda of hip hop. In my own work on hip hop in Newcastle upon Tyne (Bennett 1999c, 2000), I have encountered similar views expressed by white hip hoppers concerning the attempts by fellow white rappers to incorporate the local Geordie dialect and attendant colloquialisms into the rap text. This is clearly illustrated in the following extract from a discussion I had with local Newcastle hip hoppers in a city centre record shop that specialized in rare US rap imports:

A.B.: There are a lot of white rap fans in Newcastle who are using hip hop to talk about their own experiences.

Jim: There's no such thing as white hip hop.

A.B.: Why is that?

Jim: Because hip hop is a black music. As white people we should still respect it as black music.

Jeff: All the time before, white people were into black music, hip hop's just the same. There's a message in black music which translates for white working class people.

A.B.: What is that?

Dave: It's about being proud of where you come from . . .

Jeff: Yeah and because it [black music] offers a strength and intelligence which no British culture does.

Jim: The trend at the moment is to be real . . . to rap in your own accent and talk about things close to you . . . don't try to be American like. But that's why British hip hop will always be shite . . . I went to New York, well actually to Cleveland near

New York and stayed with a black family. It was brilliant, it changed my life. You can't talk about white hip hop, it doesn't exist.

(Bennett 2000: 155)

The locally situated nature of such collectively held views on notions of authentic hip hop become more apparent when one considers local circumstances of those involved in the above discussion. A central assumption in much sociological work examining white British appropriations of black musical styles is that they take place in settings where a prominent black population serves as a continual point of reference for such appropriations. This can be seen, for example, in Jones's (1988) study of white youth's appropriation of reggae, the ethnographic research for which was carried out in a mixed-race area of Birmingham. Similar assumptions are also evident in the work of Hebdige (1976a, 1976b, 1979) on white British youth and black music. In reality, however, white youth's experimentation with black music also occurs in socio-cultural contexts where there is no established black population. This is certainly the case in Newcastle, where around 95 per cent of the population is white.

Indeed it could be argued that the essential 'whiteness' of Newcastle and, by definition, the local hip hop scene, facilitates a highly particularized series of responses to the 'black' characteristics of the hip hop style which, among certain sections of the local hip hop community, amounts to a celebration of blackness in the absence of blackness. Developing this idea further, it is possible to see how such a celebration becomes a very potent form of local status symbol. Marks (1990) suggests that white appropriations of black musical forms are often symbolically transformed into 'badge[s] of exclusivity', particularly if such conspicuous displays of black taste on the part of young whites enable them to 'manifest their difference from the cultural mainstream' (Marks 1990: 105). It follows that such 'difference' becomes even more strongly articulated if it meets with a negative reaction from other white youth. In his Birmingham-based research on white youth and reggae, Jones (1988: 199) notes how young whites' 'displays of affiliation to black culture' resulted on occasion in them becoming 'the objects of a "deflected" form of racism'. In the social context of Newcastle, perhaps because of the city's predominately white populace, such physical challenges to forms of black association occur more frequently. From the point of view of hip hoppers in Newcastle, however, such challenges become important resources in the marking out of a cultural territory for themselves. The displays of hostility and **deflected racism** experienced by white hip hop fans in Newcastle resulted in them becoming even more forthright in terms of their 'black association'. In effect, this 'black association' became a symbol of 'exclusivity' which was used by hip hoppers as a means of differentiating themselves from the 'towny' youth whose racism, it is argued, went hand in hand with their small-mindedness and conservative tastes in music and fashion (see Bennett 1999c, 2000).

Hip hop in Japan and Oceania

The above examples begin to illustrate how even as rap and hip hop become appropriated and reworked in particular local contexts, new debates about the authenticity of particular groups' and individuals' claims to be hip hoppers arise. A further example of this is provided in Condry's (1999) work on hip hop culture in Japan: 'As American hip hop artists devote themselves to "keeping it real", Japanese rappers and fans debate exactly what "real" means for them in a locale far removed from rap's origins' (Condry 1999: 1). Given the relatively privileged socio-economic life of Japanese youth, little direct identification can be made with the scenarios of hardship and deprivation portrayed in African American rap lyrics. Thus, other means of embracing rap as a form of collective expression are found by Japanese youth. Among many hip hop devotees in Japan, the measure of hip hop's significance as an authentic form of local expression is its use in the articulation of a 'generational protest' against authority figures such as 'parents and teachers' (Condry 1999: 7). In this way, romanticized images of African American street life are used in a form of symbolic rejection of the social and cultural mores which Japanese hip hop devotees feel restrict their lives at all levels from work to leisure. As Condry (1999: 12) explains: 'Drawing images of the U.S. from American hip hop, Japanese fans see their country as peaceful and boring, saturated with meaningless pop icons and lacking the excitement and "reality" of dangerous, inner city streets'.

Research on the local hip hop scene in Sydney, Australia also illustrates quite pointedly the extent to which hip hoppers are actively involved in the 'construction' of particular versions of hip hop culture, 'producing the simulacrum of a culture which they ha[ve] accessed through electronic media' (Maxwell 1994: 14). Using the example of local Sydney rap group Sound Unlimited, Maxwell examines how the group produced a series of strategic discourses through which they claimed to represent the urban experience of young immigrant youth in the western suburbs of Sydney. According to Maxwell (1994), essentialist notions of 'originality' or, conversely, 'imitation' fail to engage with the highly complex syncretisms through which rap is here being recast as a means of addressing and negotiating everyday life in Sydney's western suburbs. Thus as Mitchell, in a further study of Sydney hip hop, explains:

> The Western Suburbs are generally perceived as the main historic centre of hip hop culture in Sydney, partly due to the strong concentration there of non-Anglo migrant communities such as Greeks, Italians, Lebanese and Vietnamese, whose youth were attracted by the racially oppositional features of African–American hip hop and adapted its signs and forms as markers of their own otherness. Muggings, killings and heroin dealing attributed to the Vietnamese street gang the 5Ts in the suburb of Cabramatta have also fuelled the mass media with discourses about ghetto-styled street wars and migrant criminal subcultures which are often highly exaggerated. In their song 'Tales from the Westside', Sound Unlimited reconstructs a history of the Sydney hip-hop scene in the Western Suburbs, locating its origins in the suburb of Burwood in 1983.
>
> (Mitchell 1998: 8)

Mitchell's work also makes important contributions to the study of other localised hip hop cultures in Oceania. Notable in this respect is his research on Maori hip hop in Aotearoa/New Zealand. According to Mitchell, as early as 1983 imported **breakdance** styles had become an important symbol of identity for Maori youth who used breakdancing as a means of gaining the status and recognition denied to them 'through conventional channels such as school, sport and social position' (Mitchell 1996: 244). Similarly, the New Zealand media's failure to engage with Maori culture and history forced Maori youth to seek other ways of articulating their identity, the latter finding expression through the appropriation of African American 'music films, television, programmes and clothes such as baseball caps, baggies, T shirts and jackets' (Mitchell 1996: 245). In this context rap and hip hop 'quickly became an inevitable medium for expressions of Maori militancy, sometimes expressed in Maori language' (Mitchell 1996: 245). One of the first Maori rap groups to achieve commercial success was Upper Hut Posse. A 1990 tour by Upper Hut Posse centred around traditional Maori community centres while in the same year the group supported US rap group public enemy during their tour of Aotearoa/New Zealand. Similarly, the promotional video for the groups 1989 song 'Stormy Weather' featured 'footage of 1977 Maori land rights demonstrations at Bastion point, protests against the 1981 South African rugby tour of Aotearoa/New Zealand and opposition to French nuclear tests in the Pacific' (Mitchell 1996: 247).

Conclusion

During this chapter I have considered the significance of rap and hip hop as central musical and stylistic forms in contemporary youth culture. Having charted the origins of rap and hip hop as street cultural forms emerging from the Bronx district of New York during the early 1970s, I examined the ways in which the socio-cultural significance of rap and hip hop have been represented and analysed in a number of key studies dealing with the latter as African American cultural forms. I then considered how later studies adopted a more pan-cultural perspective in their study of rap and hip hop, such studies suggesting the importance of rap and hip hop as a discourse that helped in the formation of cultural links between globally dispersed peoples of African origin who make up the African diaspora. In the final section of the chapter I examined the appropriation of rap and hip hop by young people at a more ethically diverse level. By drawing on examples of the cultural reterritorialization (Lull 1995) of rap and hip hop across western Europe and in Japan, Australia and Aotearoa/New Zealand, I demonstrated the extent to which rap and hip hop have become culturally mobile. Thus, while certain discourses of African American rap and hip hop, notably those addressing issues of racism, inequality and oppression, remain central to the rap text, at the same time rap and hip hop have become loosened from what was once considered to be an organic connection with the inner-city districts of the US. Rap and hip hop are now reworked in ways that reflect and engage with local issues in different cities and regions around the world.

Further reading

Bennett, A. (2000) *Popular Music and Youth Culture: Music, Identity and Place.* London: Macmillan (Chapter 6).

Bjurström, E. (1997) The struggle for ethnicity: Swedish youth styles and the construction of ethnic identities, *Young: Nordic Journal of Youth Research*, 5 (3): 44–58.

Condry, I. (1999) The social production of difference: imitation and authenticity in Japanese rap music, in H. Fehrenbach and U. Poiger (eds) *Transactions, Transgressions, Transformations: American Culture in Western Europe and Japan.* Providence, RI: Berghahn.

Decker, J.L. (1994) The state of rap: time and place in hip hop nationalism, in A. Ross and T. Rose (eds) *Microphone Fiends: Youth Music and Youth Culture.* London: Routledge.

Dyson, M.E. (1996) *Between God and Gangsta Rap: Bearing Witness to Black Culture.* New York: Oxford University Press.

Flores, J. (1994) Puerto Rican and proud, boyee!: Rap roots and amnesia, in A. Ross and T. Rose (eds) *Microphone Fiends: Youth Music and Youth Culture*. London: Routledge.

Huq, R. (1999) Living in France: the parallel universe of hexagonal pop, in A. Blake (ed.) *Living through Pop*. London: Routledge.

Mitchell, T. (1996) *Popular Music and Local Identity: Rock, Pop and Rap in Europe and Oceania*. London: Leicester University Press (Chapters 1, 3 and 6).

Potter, R. (1995) *Spectacular Vernaculars: Hip Hop and the Politics of Postmodernism*. Albany, NY: State University of New York Press.

Rose, T. (1994) *Black Noise: Rap Music and Black Culture in Contemporary America*. London: Wesleyan University Press.

7 | BHANGRA AND CONTEMPORARY ASIAN DANCE MUSIC

> The emergence of bhangra in the 1980s signalled the development of a self-conscious and distinctively British Asian youth culture. The result was the development of an autonomous alternative public sphere for young Asians that was comparable with the reggae dance-hall.
>
> (Back 1996: 220)

Chapters 5 and 6 have examined the cultural significance of reggae and rap. Significantly, while each of these musics address issues of identity and place for the youth of displaced ethnic minority groups around the world, they are at the same time also highly successful commercial, mainstream musical forms. During the course of this chapter I want to look at bhangra, a style of music which, if its cultural significance is equal to that of reggae and rap, remains relatively unacknowledged outside the communities in which it developed (Baumann 1990: 84). Within Asian neighbourhoods in British cities, bhangra music forms part of the everyday soundscape. Walking through Asian neighbourhoods one hears bhangra music being played on stereo systems in houses, in cars and on **ghetto blasters** carried by young people in the street. And yet, just a few streets away it is highly likely that nobody will have heard of bhangra. Mention the names Alaap or Achanak (two leading bhangra groups) and people will stare at you blankly. As an Asian interviewee pointed out when I conducted my own research into bhangra music in the north-east of England: 'Apart from Asians, not many people . . . know about bhangra and those that do don't understand it' (Bennett 1997: 115; see also Bennett 2000). However, despite bhangra's essential invisibility to the dominant white population in Britain, and its consequent absence from mainstream British popular culture, bhangra, and the forms of Asian dance music that have developed from it, have played a major part in the formation of new Asian youth identities.

This chapter begins by looking at the origins of bhangra as a Punjabi folk music and its subsequent appropriation and modification during the 1970s by young South Asian musicians living in Britain (Baumann 1990). Having considered further modifications to the bhangra sound during the 1980s and 1990s, the chapter then focuses on the significance of bhangra for Asian youth. Drawing on a number of recent studies, this part of the chapter examines the various ways in which bhangra is argued to function as a means for young Asians to construct new identities which both reflect their cultural roots while at the same time articulating new cultural sensibilities based on their experiences growing up in Britain (Back 1996; Sharma *et al.* 1996; Baumann 1997; Bennett 1997, 2000).

The origins and development of bhangra

In its original form, bhangra is a traditional style of folk music performed in the Punjabi provinces of India and Pakistan as part of annual festivals held to mark the end of the sugar cane harvest and also to celebrate the arrival of the Punjabi New Year (Banerji and Baumann 1990: 140). The history of bhangra in Britain dates back to the 1950s when large numbers of Punjabi families began migrating to Britain to meet the post-Second World War demand for unskilled manual labour (Banerji and Baumann 1990: 138). As Baumann (1990: 83) notes: 'The majority of Punjabi families settled in "immigrant" quarters of London and the industrial cities of the English Midlands and remained invisible to the indigenous population's political, social and cultural concerns'. Within such immigrant communities, traditional bhangra music continued to provide an important source of entertainment for Punjabi families. As Baumann observes, there were

> amateur groups performing bhangra at weddings and community celebrations from probably the mid-1960s. These played the traditional repertoire in traditional style, and, with the reconstitution of Punjabi communities in a few suburbs of British cities, most notably Southall in west London, found an increasing demand for live performances at family functions.
>
> (Baumann 1990: 84)

Moreover, following the development of the cassette tape during the early 1970s, cassettes of traditional bhangra music could be bought cheaply from shops in Asian districts (Banerji and Baumann 1990). The experience of listening to traditional bhangra in the family home and at Asian functions provided the inspiration for musical experimentation by Asian musicians that resulted in the creation of two new bhangra styles, bhangra beat, pioneered by Southall-based bands such as Alaap, Heera and Holle Holle, and northern rock bhangra, pioneered by Midlands-based bands such as Achanak and the Safri Boyz (Baumann 1990, 1997).

Each of these bands significantly modified the traditional bhangra style, fusing it with the sounds of western popular music that members of these bands, having grown up in Britain, were also familiar with (Banerji and Baumann 1990: 144). Modern western instruments such as the electric guitar and electric bass, the keyboard synthesizer and the drum kit were combined with traditional bhangra instruments, such as the *dholak* and the *dholki*. The *dholak* is a large double-headed drum which is played with sticks. During bhangra performances the player of the *dholak* carries the instrument on a shoulder strap allowing movement around the stage. The *dholak* is considered to be the central instrument in a bhangra band, and *dholak* player the leader of the traditional dance which often accompanies the performance of bhangra music (Baumann 1990). More than any other instrument, the *dholki* is the one which centrally defines the British bhangra sound. The *dholki* is a smaller version of the *dholak*, which is played by hand. Unlike the *dholak* player, the *dholki* player performs seated (Banerji and Baumann 1990: 140; Baumann 1990: 85).

Bhangra beat and Asian youth

The new bhangra beat style had a significant impact on Asian youth living in Britain. Most importantly, perhaps, it was the first time that young Asians in Britain had had a music which was based around their communities and way of life. Young African Caribbeans living in Britain already had a clearly developed musical tradition and an abundant supply of stylistic resources which they could draw upon as a way of marking out a cultural space from white youth (Hebdige 1976a, 1976b, 1979, 1988; Jones 1988; see also Chapters 5 and 6). Indeed, until the release of the first bhangra beat album, Alaap's 'Teri Chunni De Sitare' (London: Arishma 1984), African Caribbean, and also African American, musics were also a primary form of entertainment for Asian youth (Baumann 1990: 84). Thus, as Baumann points out:

> Throughout the 1970s and early 1980s . . . young people of south Asian backgrounds in Britain continued to favour sound systems playing reggae and, from 1983, fast jazzfunk, hip hop and, particularly among girls, soul.
>
> (Baumann 1990: 84)

During the mid-1980s, however, bhangra beat and northern rock bhangra quickly began to replace hip hop and soul as the preferred music of Asian youth. As Banerji and Baumann (1990: 142) point out: 'The new style [of bhangra] was exactly what the new generation wanted. Young, fresh, lively and modern, it was as genuinely Indian as it was recognisably disco'. Another aspect of the new bhangra style which found an appeal among Asian youth was the **daytimer** disco. Because of parental concern, young Asians were seldom allowed to leave the house at night and had thus been denied access to the pub and club-based leisure enjoyed by white and African Caribbean youth in Britain. The daytimer discos, at which the new bhangra-pop fusion bands were often booked to perform, provided an opportunity for young Asians to participate in club-type events during the day. Problematically, however, daytimer discos took place during school hours, an issue which was quickly picked up on by the British media. According to Banerji and Baumann (1990: 146), although the media interest in daytimers 'helped to give bhangra music the publicity which album releases had denied . . . its pictures of a new generation of Asian youth regularly bunking off school to attend live shows created images that did justice neither to parents' attitudes nor to youngsters' aspirations'. Indeed, as Baumann discovered, Asian parents were deeply concerned that their children were missing school to attend daytime discos. By the same token, however, Asian parents

> did not let their disapproval of [the daytimer] affect their approval of [bhangra] as such, and of its new found attraction to the younger generation. Among younger Punjabis in particular, the newly vibrant *'bhangra scene'* was valued not only because it reinvented a traditional genre, but also because it made the Punjabi, and indeed south Asian, presence in Britain visible and audible for the first time.
>
> (Baumann 1990: 87–8)

Such aspects of the new bhangra music quickly ensured its appeal across a broad spectrum of Asian society in Britain. Consequently, in addition to their appearances at daytimer discos, bhangra bands such as Alaap and Achanak were also booked to appear at 'Punjabi weddings, engagement parties and other family celebrations' (Baumann 1990: 86). Such bands also regularly performed at **Melas** – Asian festivals featuring music, dance and a range of side stalls at which food, literature and Asian clothes are sold.

Addressing the broadening appeal of bhangra during the 1980s, Baumann (1990) argues that, in addition to its significance as an Asian 'youth' music, the genre proved 'remarkably effective in enhancing the cohesion of the Punjabi community across political, moral, aesthetic, and many social divides' (Baumann 1990: 91). While bhangra beat and other forms of bhangra-pop fusion pioneered during the 1980s continue to fulfil this cultural role, much of their appeal as Asian 'youth' musics has now faded. Indeed, even at the height of their popularity, the image of the British bhangra bands did little to endear them to young Asian fans. Thus, as Banerji and Baumann observe, these bands

> tended to consist of a large (ten to fifteen) all-male, all-Punjabi line-up, and their style of self-presentation, moulded as it was on the gaudy tinsel-glamour of Hindi movies, was often reminiscent of the 1970s: flared white trousers and sequinned shirts were the characteristic uni-form of musicians, most of whom tended to be over thirty-five and slightly overweight.
>
> (Banerji and Baumann 1990: 142)

The image problem of the bhangra beat bands became increasingly prob-lematic as the 1980s progressed and the video became an increasingly important means of promoting popular music artists. Again, this is well illustrated by Banerji and Baumann who point out that during 'the video-intensive music scene of the 1980s, enamoured of lean and sullen looking young men' it became increasingly difficult 'to market the glitteringly bright, cheerful, jolly-uncle image of even the most musically competent bhangra bands' (Banerji and Baumann 1990: 144).

Post-bhangra Asian dance music

During the late 1980s and early 1990s, a new variation of bhangra singer emerged whose younger age and 'outward style appeal[ed] more to main-stream expectations, and whose music aim[ed] at a "crossover" into the western field' (Banerji and Baumann 1990: 144). Indeed, the term bhangra became increasingly obsolete. The new generation of Asian musicians and singers, influenced by contemporary dance music, further modified the bhangra sound producing new forms such as **fusion**, which incorporated elements of house and techno, and **ragga**, which blended bhangra with rap and reggae styles (Gilroy 1993: 82). Popular fusion artists include Bally Sagoo, Fun Da Mental and Apache Indian, the latter of these artists becom-ing the most commercially successful.

Apache Indian (aka Steve Kapur) was born of Hindu Punjabi parents and raised in Handsworth, a multi-ethnic district of Birmingham (Back 1996: 220). He chose the name Apache Indian in reference to his Punjabi heritage and also as a tribute to one of his main influences, the Jamaican **raggamuf-fin** star Super Cat, also sometimes referred to as the wild Apache (Lipsitz

1994a: 130). The multi-ethnic nature of Apache Indian's upbringing is also reflected in his music. Thus, as Back states

> [Apache Indian] performs and expresses himself through snatches of Jamaican patois, Punjabi and a unique form of English that is being generated by groups of young people who are growing up alongside each other in Birmingham. His first record, entitled, 'Move Over India', released in 1990, topped the reggae and bhangra charts. The new form was dubbed *bhangramuffin* after its ragga counterpart.
>
> (Back 1996: 220–1)

In discussing this combination of musical styles and influences from the Punjab and Caribbean, Lipsitz (1994a) suggests that Apache Indian's **bhangramuffin** style can be understood at a level which transcends the musical and addresses the cultural experiences which Punjabis and African Caribbeans share due to their common status as displaced peoples. Thus, argues Lipsitz:

> Standing at the crossroads of Punjabi and Jamaican cultures, Apache Indian shows that ... Asian and Afro–Caribbean Britons share more than a common designation as Black people ... Punjabis and Jamaicans both come from regions that contain diverse cultures and beliefs, and they both belong to populations that transnational capital has dispersed all over the globe. From their historical experiences at home no less from what they have learned in order to survive abroad, Punjabis and Jamaicans draw upon longstanding and rich traditions ... The music made by Apache Indian uses performance to call into being a community composed of Punjabis and Jamaicans, South Asians and West Indians.
>
> (Lipsitz 1994a: 130)

Arguably, however, there are problems with Lipsitz's analysis, not least of all because of the differing ways in which Asian and African Caribbean youth in Britain are culturally situated. As pointed out earlier, African Caribbean youth in Britain has a longstanding tradition of cultural innovation dating back to the ska movement of the 1960s (Hebdige 1976b; see also Chapter 5). Moreover, it is widely acknowledged by social theorists that white appropriations, for example in the case of the mods and skinheads, of musical and stylistic innovations (Hebdige 1979; Chambers 1985) and argot (Huq 1996) associated with African Caribbean cultures, have served to some extent to demystify the latter and resulted in a greater degree of tolerance and acceptance of African Caribbeans on the part of white Britons. It is also the case, some suggest, that appropriations by white

British youth of African American music and style have worked to facilitate a wider acceptance of blacks in Britain (see, for example, Chambers 1976). Thus, as Back (1993: 218) argues: 'Young white people may [now] have more in common with Bobby Brown than John Bull, with the result that it is impossible to speak of a black culture in Britain separately from the culture of Britain as a whole'.

In contrast, Asian youth have been much less visible in Britain, largely due to the absence of equivalent Asian cultural influences on mainstream British popular culture. Thus, as Huq observes:

> Despite a short-lived flirtation with, and exoticization of, the Indian subcontinent's supposedly mystical side in the 1960s, Asians have simply never assumed a principal place in the Top of the Pops/MTV youth culture mythology; instead they have perennially been considered unhip. Western popular culture has long been over-endowed with stereotypical images of Asians as submissive, hard-working, passive and conformist.
>
> (Huq 1996: 63)

Such stereotypes undoubtedly contribute in no small part to the high incidence of racism directed against Asians in Britain. In particular, it has been argued that the perceived 'out-and-out alien characteristics' of Asians serve to make them 'the object of a purer hatred' which is not directed at other 'black' ethnic minority groups, who, if not totally accepted by white Britain are, nevertheless, deemed to be *more* acceptable than ethnic minorities of Asian origin (Gilroy and Lawrence 1988: 143). This sentiment is well captured by Pearson in his semi-ethnographic account of 'Paki-bashing' in a Lancashire town:

> The West Indian is 'more like us'. He speaks our language (or so we tell ourselves) and he is of our culture – or so we fool ourselves. 'Pakis' (that is, Indians and Pakistanis) on the other hand are not like us at all, or so the distinction says: they speak a different language, they eat peculiar food which does not smell like our food, and they keep to themselves.
>
> (Pearson 1976: 50)

These perceptions of Asians in Britain remain all too deeply entrenched in the British popular imagination. Despite the affinity of many Asians, especially the young, with the lifestyle orientations and cultural practices of contemporary Britain, Asian communities are still considered by many to exist at the margins of British life. This issue was taken up and discussed at length in an article by Malik (1995) for the *Independent on Sunday* entitled 'What *really* angers young Asians'. Based on a series of interviews with young

Asians in Britain, Malik's article illustrates how attitudes among Asian youth in Britain are moving away from those of their parents:

> There is often a palpable sense of embarrassment among today's young Asians about their parents' attitudes and values. 'I cringe every time I see an old man with a beard who can hardly speak English coming on TV and speaking for a community' says [one of Malik's interviewees].
>
> (Malik 1995: 23)

A similar sentiment is offered by another young Asian interviewed by Malik (1995: 23): 'My parents might . . . still feel attached to Bangladesh . . . But it's different for us. We belong here [in Britain]. We do the same things as anyone else'. As Malik points out, however, despite young Asians' 'sense of ease and familiarity' with many aspects of everyday life in contemporary Britain, conflicts and tensions remain (Malik 1995: 23). This is followed by Malik's subsequent observation that: 'The increased confidence and assertiveness that Asian youth shows today has brought its own problems. To a generation that is so much more integrated into British society, the lash of racism is felt that much more acutely' (Malik 1995: 23).

New Asian youth identities

It is with such issues of identity and place in relation to young Asians in Britain that the most recent work on Asian dance music and youth culture is primarily concerned. Sharma *et al.*'s (1996) edited anthology *Dis-Orienting Rhythms* argues that the significance of contemporary Asian dance music relates not, as Lipsitz (1994a) argues, to its facilitation of new African Asian forms of youth resistance in Britain, nor as a means of allowing young Asians to celebrate their ancestral heritage through the 're-invention of tradition' (Hobsbawm 1983). Rather, it is argued, contemporary Asian dance music acts as a resource in the construction of alternative forms of Asian identity which reflect the everyday experiences of young Asians in contemporary Britain.

This theme is addressed at a number of levels in *Dis-Orienting Rhythms*. In their study 'New Paths for South Asian Identity and Creativity', Kaur and Kalra (1996) introduce the term **Br-Asian** as a way of attempting to culturally situate young Asians in Britain. As the term implies, Kaur and Kalra argue that Br-Asians occupy a new cultural territory, one that has been fashioned out of necessity by young Asian people who no longer feel they have anything in common with the Indian subcontinent and with the culture of their parents. At the same time, however, they feel uncomfortable in Britain and unable to integrate into British society because of the racist stereotypes which are imposed upon them.

A significant property of the Br-Asian youth culture, according to Kaur and Kalra, is the way in which the lines of division which characterize the different Asian parent cultures are crossed. Young Asians whose traditional cultural backgrounds dictate that they should have nothing to do with each other are rejecting what they consider to be antiquated ideas governed by religion and the pre-emigration sensibilities of the parent culture (Baumann 1997). Kaur and Kalra suggest that one of the main motives for the formation of this new Br-Asian youth culture is the realization among young Asians that the internal struggles which they observe in the parent culture do little to resolve the marginalization, exclusion and hostility to which Asians in Britain are subjected. Rather, it is felt, only through unity and solidarity is it possible to effectively counteract such racism and racial exclusion. According to Kaur and Kalra, unity and solidarity are centrally defining features of the Br-Asian youth culture, signifying a form of resistance through which young Asians mark out a new cultural territory for themselves in Britain. Thus, they explain:

> Br-Asian is intended of the centre–margin relationship and to destabilize fixed notions of Asian identities, stressing their contingency on historical and spatial moments. As a hyphenated form of identification, 'Br-Asian' contains possibilities for splintering as it does for other alliances. The question of regional affiliation and the degree of religious and cast consciousness act as breakable joints in this categorization; common subjection to racist oppression and criticisms of mainstream society serve as platforms to align with other marginalized groups.
>
> (Kaur and Kalra 1996: 221)

Kaur and Kalra (1996: 218) further suggest that: 'Music present[s] an accessible and universal forum for articulating this dynamic social flux'.

This view corresponds with that of Lipsitz (1994a), who emphasizes the utility of music 'as a device for building unity between and across aggrieved populations', adding that because of its status 'as a highly visible (and audible) commodity [music] comes to stand for the specificity of social experience in identifiable communities when it captures the attention, and, even allegiance of people from many different social locations' (Lipsitz 1994a: 126–7). In relation to Asian dance music in Britain, such claims date back to the growth in popularity of bhangra beat. Thus, for example, during the mid-1990s, Smith (1994: 12) suggested that 'in Britain Bhangra has, in the course of the past 10 years, become the property of the whole Asian nation'.

In her study 'Asian Kool? Bhangra and beyond', however, Huq (1996) draws attention to the more complex nature of Asian dance music forms in Britain and the ways in which this complexity belies such simplistic representations of bhangra music's function in forging alliances between different factions of Asian youth. Thus, argues Huq:

> Bhangra is a music of very specific derivations, namely Punjabi folk dance, which by definition cannot carry equal appeal to the inhabitants of an entire subcontinent . . . It is something of an over-simplification to see Bhangra as the one force uniting the disparate members of Britain's Asian youth. Indeed, an effort to maintain a distance from (old-style) Bhangra is one of the defining features of those associated with Asian Kool.
>
> (Huq 1996: 64)

Huq's essential point here, that bhangra carries a substantial cultural baggage associated with its Punjabi origins limiting its ability to cross cultural borders between Asians in Britain, can be countered with the argument that bhangra's reinvention (Baumann 1990) in Britain involved 'a merging of traditional Punjabi [bhangra] styles with elements of pop thus erasing forever bhangra's exclusive association with the Punjab' (Bennett 2000: 121). This view is supported by Manuel's observation that many 'aspects of Punjabi culture – and particularly music . . . far from being isolated, have had a prodigious impact beyond the Punjabi's borders, and have been especially receptive to creative syncretism with Western culture' (Manuel 1993: 178).

Indeed, my own research on the significance of bhangra music for young people in Newcastle upon Tyne in the north-east of England (Bennett 1997, 2000) suggested that, if anything, the proclaimed lack of interest among a number of young Asians in 1980s bhangra–pop fusion styles was the product of generational rather than cultural conflict. Thus, as one of my interviewees explained:

> Because it [bhangra] was a traditional music, it had better acceptance among parents. When people started adapting bhangra that got acceptance too. Kids are encouraged to listen to bhangra . . . It's like when an Asian kid takes up cricket instead of football y'know. It's just seen as the right thing to do. The fear of parents is that their kids will slip away . . . they're either going to become a nice young polite boy or girl or a football hooligan y'know. But when you ask kids yourself what kind of music they like bhangra never comes up . . . a lot of 'em will tell you that they like chart music.
>
> (Bennett 2000: 116–17)

The point remains, however, that the more contemporary Asian dance music forms, collectively categorized as Asian Kool (Huq 1996), represent an attempt by Asian 'youth music cultures' (Kaur and Kalra 1996: 218) to progress the Asian dance music scene beyond its bhangra-centredness. In doing so they are attracting a new audience comprising those among the younger generation of Asians for whom 1980s bhangra styles' continuing association with the pre-emigration Asian sensibilities of the parent culture is unacceptable. This in turn has led to new expressions of Asianness in which everyday issues pertaining to young Asians in Britain assume priority over the more traditional lyrical themes explored in 1980s bhangra. As Huq observes:

> The 'political' side of the new wave of Asian-produced second-gener-ation pop [is evident in] its lyrical content, some of whose themes cer-tainly have at least political undertones, tackling old taboos. After all, according to its Web page definition, 'Lyrical content of Bhangra songs relates to celebration, or love, or patriotism or current social issues.' Tracks such as 'Runaway Child' and 'Big Trouble in Little Asia' from Nation Records signings Hustlers HC serve as examples, as do the Voodoo Queens' feminist leanings.
>
> (Huq 1996: 70)

Expanding on this last point, Huq also notes how the contemporary Asian music scene has opened up far more opportunity for Asian women to gain artistic recognition. As Huq points out, even though Asian women have been involved in music-making since the 1980s, when they were 'centrally involved in the [bhangra] scene' they have been largely ignored 'in British popular and academic discourse' (Huq 1996: 71). It is in relation to this observation that Huq makes what is perhaps her most important point regarding the current Asian music scene in Britain.

In noting how many female Asian musicians are resentful of their rep-resentation in the media as 'Asian women' either escaping the confines of traditional Asian life or 'via the cliché of east-meets-west "exoticness"', Huq exposes a broader truism relating to Asian youth. In effect, Huq high-lights the political essentialism which could be argued to encumber terms such as Br-Asian youth (Kaur and Kalra 1996: 76). While there may indeed be sensibilities within contemporary Asian youth formations that corre-spond with the ideology projected through Kaur and Kalra's (1996) coining and application of the term 'Br-Asian', such sensibilities may be far less com-monplace than supposed by Kaur and Kalra. Huq (1996) suggests that, for a growing number of young Asians, issues of race and ethnicity, while clearly retaining an importance, do not assume the political proportions assumed in much academic and journalistic writing. Thus, argues Huq:

Just as the study of youth is often framed in problem-solving terms, Asian youth are forever examined through the prism of race and racism – the recipients, for example, of 'Paki-bashing' (Mungham and Pearson 1976) – constantly caught between two cultures of suffering multiple identity crisis . . . [However y]oung Asians are in a stronger position to assert themselves positively in ways previously unavailable . . . Perhaps the most critical lesson to be drawn from the burgeoning new Asian forms is that they collectively demonstrate that Asian youth are staking out new territories on the (sub)cultural landscape of [contemporary] Britain and claiming them as their own – devoid of the baggage of cross cultural crisis.

(Huq 1996: 78)

Aspects of my own research on Asian youth in Newcastle upon Tyne (Bennett 1997, 2000) go some way towards supporting Huq's observation. Part of this research examined a local Asian radio show entitled *The Bhangra Hustlers* which was broadcast weekly on the Newcastle **community radio station** Kool FM. The show was created to promote contemporary dance music forms, such as rap, jungle and bhangra, which currently receive little airplay on the major radio stations. The young male and female Asian DJs who contributed to *The Bhangra Hustlers* mixed bhangra tracks together with other forms of contemporary music such as rap and house. The aim of those involved with *The Bhangra Hustlers* was effectively to re-invent the bhangra sound and, in doing so, articulate their own localised interpretation of the syncretic quality which they identify with bhangra and other forms of popular music (Bennett 2000: 125). Thus, as one of the programme's organizers explained to me:

on this show we want to appeal to a wide audience. It's a dance music station and we know that in addition to Asians we're gonna have a lot of white people listening to the music too. We want to show that the basis of all music is that it is made up of beats and rhythms and that it can be combined well. So what we do is we mix bhangra with dance music, which is what I like, house music in particular, Afro-Caribbean ragga . . . which is mixing dance with reggae beats . . . and we'll use rap as well. Then within that we might also include something like Peter Gabriel.

(Bennett 2000: 126)

In addressing the deeper political agenda of *The Bhangra Hustlers*, one of the DJs who features in the programme spoke of the need to get away from the archetypal image of the Asian as someone who wishes to remain distanced from British social life and whose own way of life is completely at odds with the rest of Britain (Bennett 2000: 126).

Conclusion

In this chapter I have considered the significance of Asian dance music forms developed in Britain from the 1980s onwards for Asian youth. I have examined the development of bhangra from a traditional Punjabi folk music to a fusion style combining elements of western pop music in westernized variations of the style such as 'bhangra beat' and 'northern rock bhangra'. The performance of these original bhangra-pop fusion bands at 'daytimer' discos, I pointed out, illustrated parallel shifts in the sensibilities of Asian youth. Young Asians' desire for club-type music and dance events indicated their moving away from the pre-emigration values of the parent culture towards a more western lifestyle incorporating the leisure patterns of other western youth cultures. I next considered how further developments in the Asian dance music scene resulted in the decline in popularity of bhangra as Asian dance music artists began to experiment with, and thus popularize, new fusion styles retaining elements of Asian music but mixing these with sounds from contemporary dance music styles such as house and techno. I then examined how such post-bhangra Asian dance music styles have been accompanied by further shifts in the identity politics of young Asians who have used these musics as resources in a series of new Asian youth identities that reflect the day-to-day experience of Asian youth in contemporary Britain. Most significantly, new Asian dance musics have facilitated young Asians' negotiation of cultural spaces in British youth cultural life.

Further reading

Back, L. (1996) *New Ethnicities and Urban Culture: Racisms and Multiculture in Young Lives.* London: UCL Press (Chapter 8).

Banerji, S. and Baumann, G. (1990) Bhangra 1984–8: fusion and professionalization in a genre of South Asian dance music, in P. Oliver (ed.) *Black Music in Britain: Essays on the Afro-Asian Contribution to Popular Music.* Buckingham: Open University Press.

Baumann, G. (1990) The re-invention of Bhangra: social change and aesthetic shifts in a Punjabi music in Britain, *Journal of the International Institute for Comparative Music Studies and Documentation*, 32(2): 81–95.

Baumann, G. (1997) Dominant and demotic discourses of culture: their relevance to multi-ethnic alliances, in P. Werbner and T. Modood (eds) *Debating Cultural*

Hybridity: Multi-Cultural Identities and the Politics of Anti-Racism. London: Zed Books.

Bennett, A. (2000) *Popular Music and Youth Culture: Music, Identity and Place.* London: Macmillan (Chapter 5).

Huq, R. (1996) Asian Kool? Bhangra and beyond, in S. Sharma, J. Hutnyk and A. Sharma (eds) *Dis-Orienting Rhythms: The Politics of the New Asian Dance Music.* London: Zed Books.

Kaur, R. and Kalra, V.S. (1996) New paths for South Asian identity and creativity, in S. Sharma, J. Hutnyk and A. Sharma (eds) *Dis-Orienting Rhythms: The Politics of the New Asian Dance Music.* London: Zed Books.

Lipsitz, G. (1994) *Dangerous Crossroads: Popular Music, Postmodernism and the Poetics of Place.* London: Verso (Chapter 6).

Sharma, S., Hutnyk, J. and Sharma, A. (eds) (1996) *Dis-Orienting Rhythms: The Politics of the New Asian Dance Music.* London: Zed Books.

8 | CONTEMPORARY DANCE MUSIC AND CLUB CULTURES

> The British state has a long history in regulating pleasures associated with parties. A fear seems to exist of the unregulated body that dances and is intoxicated . . . It is therefore not surprising that the acid house parties, that heady mix of house'n'E dance events in 1988, were followed by various moral panics.
>
> (Rietveld 1998: 253–4)

The meaning and significance of 'dance music' has altered substantially since the 1970s when the term was synonymous with discotheque or 'disco'. Disco was generally considered to be the antithesis of more 'serious' 1970s musics such as hard rock, 'progressive' rock and, latterly, punk. Fans of these genres were often heard to mock what they considered to be the centrally defining characteristics of disco: effete melodies, trite lyrics and a commercially driven production ethic. With notable exceptions, such as Dyer (1979) whose work focuses on the significance of disco for gay culture, disco and other forms of dance music were also denied serious academic attention during the 1970s and the early part of the 1980s. This scenario is in extreme contrast to the 1990s, which saw the transformation of dance music into a highly 'serious', often critically acclaimed and academically scrutinized genre. Certainly, contemporary dance music often becomes commercial chart music, much as dance music in the 1970s did. However, a comparison of contemporary dance music acts, such as the Prodigy and the Aphex Twin, with 1970s dance music artists, for example ABBA and the Bee Gees, begins to illustrate how both the fan base for dance music and the sensibilities of the artists themselves have changed.

This chapter considers the significance of contemporary dance music both in terms of the innovative nature of the music itself and its resonance with the cultural sensibilities of young dance club audiences. Beginning with an examination of the origins and development of dance music, I go on to consider the relationship between dance music and technology. This is followed by a look at the role of the dance music DJ. The chapter then examines the relationship between dance music and its audience and considers some of the empirical and theoretical concepts which have been used by sociologists and cultural theorists in their attempts to account for the new youth cultural formations to which, it is argued, dance music has given rise.

The origins of contemporary dance music

The roots of contemporary dance music lie in two distinctive musical innovations – 'house' and 'techno'. House music was developed by DJs in Chicago gay clubs during the late 1970s (see Rietveld 1997) who used a technique known as **blend mixing,** where musical passages from existing recordings pressed on vinyl are 'mixed' together on a twin-turntable record player to produce new sounds and tonal textures, and, in some cases, entirely new songs or pieces of music (see Back 1996: 192). This style of DJing was quickly latched onto by DJs in other parts of the world, many of whom developed distinctive styles of mixing. On the Spanish island of Ibiza, for example, house incorporated a local stylistic inflection that became known as **Balearic Beat** (Saunders 1995: 207). It was via 'Balearic Beat' that young Britons were introduced to the house sound. As Melechi (1993) explains, many young British holiday makers in Ibiza quickly grew tired of the over-anglicized character of the island's main resort, San Antonio; consequently they travelled 'beyond the brochure to Ibiza Town . . . where the tourist could enjoy anonymity whilst settling into the twelve hour cycle of clubbing' in which an 'eclectic mishmash of Peter Gabriel, Public Enemy, Jibaro and the Woodentops [was] fused together' (Melechi 1993: 31).

The second major influence on the development of dance music during the late 1980s and early 1990s was techno. Although the term 'techno' originates from the clubs of Detroit, the roots of the sound can be traced to the city of Düsseldorf in the industrial heartland of Germany. During the early 1970s classical music students Ralf Hutter and Florian Schneider began experimenting with electronic music, the results of which led to the formation of the group Kraftwerk. Frustrated with the long hours of practice that their classical training demanded, Hutter and Schneider began using computers as a means of reproducing complex musical passages which, according to Hutter, allowed more time to be devoted to 'structuring the music' (cited in Gill 1997: 77). A further innovation by Kraftwerk was the use of industrial noise in recorded music. 'Industrial noise' refers to the sounds of urban life such as traffic, factory machinery, shopping mall crowds and so on. According to fellow Kraftwerk member, Schneider, the music of Kraftwerk involved 'making sound-pictures of real environments, what we call tone films' (cited in Gill 1997: 77). During the early 1980s Chicago-based techno DJs such as Derrick May and Carl Graig began using Kraftwerk's music in their club mixes. While Kraftwerk themselves have remained an essentially underground, avant garde group, today they are generally regarded as the founding fathers of techno. As Gill observes:

> In the world of electronic music, Kraftwerk are the Kings across the water. Despite releasing no new material in over a decade, they continue to wield more influence than any of their Anglo-American peers in the arcane business of bleeps and beats. Scratch a techno whizkid or studio engineer, and nine times out of 10 you'll find a Kraftwerk fan (the tenth will be too busy sampling them to respond).
>
> (Gill 1997: 76)

Other 1970s artists whose experiments with electronic music have had a large influence on contemporary dance music are Tangerine Dream (also from Germany), Brian Eno and Giorgio Moroder. In addition to pursuing his own successful music career, Moroder also produced Donna Summer's 1977 hit 'I Feel Love', considered by some to be the first piece of contemporary dance music due to its pioneering use of electronic sequencer devices.

Dance music, technology and the role of the DJ

As the above observation suggests, in addition to the influence of early 'electro-pop' pioneers, contemporary dance music is also very much the product of a series of technological breakthroughs, culminating in the digital revolution of the mid-1980s. Digital technology paved the way for a new era in sound recording, analogue tape machines being replaced with computers. Computers were able both to store and to reproduce sound much more accurately than the old analogue recording machines which produced varying elements of **white noise** or 'tape hiss', partly due to imperfections in the tape itself. Digital technology also facilitated a number of other breakthroughs in the recording process, including sampling, which allows for a recorded sound or short musical passage to be 'triggered' when required using the keyboard of a synthesizer, drum pad or even a human voice in conjunction with a microphone. The triggering of samples is achieved using **MIDI** (Musical Instrument Digital Interface). As Negus (1992: 25) explains, MIDI 'enable[s] various instruments to be connected up together, allowing composition to take place within a computer's memory'.

Sampling enables the manipulation of sound sources on a scale never before possible. Using sampling techniques, musicians and studio producers can effectively take sounds 'out' of their 'original' contexts and rework them into new pieces of music. Early examples of the use of sampling in the construction of 'new music' can be heard in the work of mid-1980s combo the JAMs, who later re-emerged as the KLF. The JAMS created tracks such as 'The Queen and I' that fused snatches of ABBA and the Sex Pistols together with the British National Anthem, and 'Whitney Joins the JAMs' which featured samples from Whitney Houston's 'I Wanna Dance with Somebody (Who Loves Me)', Isaac Hayes' 'Theme from Shaft' and the theme music from the 1970s cult US television series *Mission Impossible* (Beadle 1993: 111–12). During the 1990s, dance music producers and DJs continued to develop the art of working with samples to the extent that whole bass lines, drum patterns, vocal and instrumental passages from widely varying sources could be sampled and seamlessly recombined. While it clearly allows for a new level of innovation and creativity, sampling also raises a series of questions about the ownership of music. Thus, as Frith (1988b: 123) states: 'If a track is sampled from the streets, does its original publisher have any rights in it? Can ABBA or Led Zeppelin still claim to own a harmony riff once it's part of the urban soundscape?'

The creation of contemporary dance music forms has involved a major shift in the role of the DJ from 'passive "record player" to (virtual) musician' (Langlois 1992: 230). Indeed, the apparent blurring of once highly defined roles in music production and performance in the world of contemporary dance music is such that DJs can now legitimately claim to be composer, arranger, producer and performer. In addition to their skills in mixing songs in a 'live' context, many DJs now routinely draw upon the facilities offered by recording studios. Thus, as Langlois notes:

> The most celebrated DJs are often involved in re-mixing other artists' recordings, providing a variety of interpretations of existing material. From the production side of studio work to composing new tracks themselves is a small step which many DJs are able to take.
>
> (Langlois 1992: 230)

As a consequence of this shifting role, a new status has been conferred on the DJ. Melechi (1993) has suggested that one of the major attractions of acid house, for a younger generation tired with the conventions of traditional rock performances, 'was the emergence of a scene without stars, spectacle, gaze and identification' (Melechi 1993: 37). Other writers, however, suggest that, rather than discarding the conventions of rock performance, dance music simply reworks such conventions with the DJ assuming something of the status, prestige and critical acclaim once reserved for rock artists. Thus, as Langlois observes:

> the better known [DJs] enjoy considerable status and sometimes command their own following, who will go to hear *them* rather than to a particular club . . . To a large proportion of the generation now in their teens, it is the DJ rather than the rock and roll guitarist who provides social and musical role models . . . Although House DJs rarely court attention during their performances, some *are* seen and interviewed in the media in their capacity as recording artists.
>
> (Langlois 1992: 234)

Similarly, Laing (1997) points to the large transnational networks which now exist for the production and marketing of dance music, a global flow which also facilitates extensive touring for DJs and their particular brand of club event. Finally, Haslam (1997), a working club DJ from the city of Manchester in north-west England, notes how during 'the last decade DJs have become some of the most highly paid people in the entertainment world . . . with top British DJs attracting [fees] in excess of £2000 (plus VAT) a night' (Haslam 1997: 168). The attachment of such importance to DJs, both in terms of the salaries they demand and the attention they attract in the pop media, is reflected in the commonly expressed feeling among young clubbers that the 'night' can only be as good as the DJ hired to provide the music. Rather than losing sight of the distinction between artist and crowd, clubbers come to regard the DJ as centrally responsible for lifting the mood of the crowd and establishing the 'atmosphere' of the club. This is clearly illustrated in the following quotation from a young clubber I interviewed while researching the local dance music scene in Newcastle upon Tyne in northeast England. She observed:

> You can really tell the difference between the DJ who's checking how they're affecting the crowd and the DJ who's not really bothered and is just going through the motions . . . Even when you just walk into a club, you can sometimes just tell whether a DJ's in touch with the crowd or not.
>
> (cited in Bennett: 2000: 89)

A new moral panic

In Chapter 4, I examined how the British media's response to punk rock resulted in a public outcry with punk becoming the centre of a 'moral panic'

(Cohen 1987). A similar public reaction was prompted by the media with the arrival of house in British clubs during the late 1980s where it quickly acquired the tag 'acid house' due to its associations with a newly available amphetamine based stimulant known as Ecstasy or 'E' (Rietveld 1993: 42). In many ways acid house presented far more opportunities for the media to expose a potential threat to young people than punk had done. Punk, for all the dangers that the media linked with it, had at least been a highly visual form of youth culture, a 'spectacular' form of shock tactic which relied upon public exposure to achieve its desired effect (see Hebdige 1979). Acid house, however, was an altogether different phenomenon. Rather than relying on a stylistic 'intrusion' of public space, acid house made use of abandoned inner-city spaces such as disused warehouses and factories (Hemment 1998). Melechi suggests that such a retreat from public space was linked to acid house's emphasis upon the 'ecstasy of disappearance':

> While subcultural refusals have been traditionally effected through the statement of self-expression and the display of alternative identity, Acid house has relinquished this ground . . . The strategy of resistance to the scene of identity necessitates an escape from the (media) gaze, as, unlike previous subcultures which remain 'hiding in the light' (Hebdige, 1988, p. 35), a whole subculture attempts to vanish.
>
> (Melechi 1993: 38)

The result of acid house's attempts to evade the media gaze was a moral crusade on the part of the tabloid press.

Labelled a 'Killer Cult' (Thornton 1994: 183), acid house was portrayed by the media as something intrinsicly evil that would brainwash young people and lure them away from the safety of the family home to a dark and secretive world of drug taking and immoral behaviour. The fact that acid house was the first youth movement since the 1960s to refer openly to drug use further enhanced the media's ability to portray it in a wholly sinister fashion. Indeed, 'acid house' is itself a media created term inspired by the alleged parallels between house and 1960s psychedelia. The uncanny resonance suggested by the media between acid house and psychedelia was further enhanced by the fact that these two movements occurred exactly 20 years apart. The summer of 1987, it was proclaimed, was the 'Second Summer of Love' (Russell 1993). Significantly, however, the tabloid press was not the only voice heard in the debate regarding acid house. Thornton (1994, 1995) suggests that one of the things which set the house scene apart from previous chapters in youth cultural history was the presence of a 'niche' media, that is, magazines, fanzines and so on catering specifically for young clubbers, which scrutinized the reporting of the mainstream media and offered alternative accounts. Such a reaction on the part of the 'niche' media was seen in the wake of the sensationalized mainstream media reports which compared acid house with psychedelia. Thus, for example, *Face* journalist Peter Nasmyth wrote of the drug Ecstasy:

> It can make you feel very close and empathetic – you might feel like hugging your friends – but the affection it inspires is unlikely to send anyone into the frenzied raptures common in the Haight/Ashbury district in 1967. Ecstasy is a misleading name; the drug is so called more for reasons of promotion than resolution.
>
> (Nasmyth 1985: 75)

Despite such alternative reporting of acid house and its attendant drug culture, however, it was the sensationalism of the tabloid press headlines which gripped the public's imagination during the late 1980s. As a direct consequence of the media attention centred upon it, acid house became a focus of deep concern for the parent culture and other moral guardians (Thornton 1994). Indeed, reactions to acid house were not limited to public outcry but also involved large-scale state intervention. Nightclubs which featured rave events were subject to random spot checks by the police and in some cases had their licences revoked (Redhead 1993a). Similarly, in 1991, former Conservative MP for Luton South Graham Bright's Entertainments (Increased Penalties) Act outlawed the staging of large scale unlicensed raves and warehouse parties. Further restrictions were placed upon the rave scene with the implementation of the Criminal Justice and Public Order Act 1994, particularly section 63 of the Act which gives the police authority 'to remove persons attending or preparing for a rave' (Criminal Justice and Public Order Act 1994: 44). According to the Act, a rave may be classed as any 'gathering on land in the open air of 100 or more persons (whether or not trespassers) at which amplified music is played during the night' (Criminal Justice and Public Order Act 1994: 44). The Act further states that ' "land in the open air" includes a place partly open to the air' while ' "music" includes sounds wholly or predominantly characterised by the emission of a succession of repetitive beats' (Criminal Justice and Public Order Act 1994: 44–5; see also Rietveld 1998: 246).

'Club cultures' and 'neo-tribes'

Despite such authoritative reactions and the legal sanctions placed upon events featuring house and techno, dance music gained in popularity. Indeed, subsequent years saw house and techno diversify into an increasingly complex range of subgenres. Similarly, new forms of dance music, notably 'jungle' (see Noys 1995) emerged. The club-based dance music scene of the 1990s gave rise to a new sociological term 'club cultures'.

A play on the term 'subculture' (see Chapter 1), the concept of club culture was introduced by Thornton (1995) in an attempt both to rethink sub cultural theory and to illustrate something of the stylistic heterogeneity of the British dance club scene of the 1990s. Fundamental shifts in the stylistic sensibilities of those at house events had already been noted by a number of observers who each deduced that the apparent style mixing witnessed on the dance floor signalled the 'end' of the post-war youth subcultural 'tradition'. For example, Redhead notes how

> Music led styles such as heavy metal boys (and girls), goths, new romantics, acid housers or ravers dominated the 80s as cultural critics constantly sought the 'new punk'. Acid House or rave culture was misread in this fashion, when in reality it looked to roots in the club-based Northern soul (all dayers, all nighters) of the 70s and was in fact notorious for mixing all styles on the same dance floor and attracting a range of previously opposed subcultures from football hooligans to New Age hippies.
>
> (Redhead 1993b: 3–4)

In the same year, journalist Tim Willis (1993) wrote an article for the *Sunday Times* entitled 'The lost tribes' in which he offered a similar series of observations to those of Redhead:

> Young men with shaved heads and pigtails, stripped to the waist, are executing vaguely oriental hand movements. Freeze-framed by strobes in clouds of dry ice, revivalist hippies and mods are swaying in the maelstrom. Rastas, ragga girls, ravers there is no stylistic cohesion to the assembly, as there would have been in the (g)olden days of youth culture.
>
> (Willis 1993: 8)

In truth, this extreme merging of visual styles was a short-lived spectacle. It is clear that the visual image of youth is becoming increasingly a matter of individual choice as young people construct and reconstruct their image and identity with reference to what Polhemus (1997) terms 'a supermarket of style'. At the same time, however, the splitting and resplitting of dance music genres has ensured that those who once mixed in the common space of the dance floor are now able to find musics and clubs that cater more specifically for particular 'types' of clubber. It is with such aspects of taste distinction 'within' dance music culture that Thornton (1995) is primarily concerned. Adapting Bourdieu's (1984) concept of 'cultural capital',

Thornton suggests that clubbers use a range of resources – for example, particular knowledges about dance music, personal image, access to certain more 'exclusive' clubs through social networks, access to and expertise in the use of certain drugs to elicit particular forms of club experience – as **subcultural capital**. That is, a means of articulating their status as authentic clubbers in relation to those who are deemed to lack such knowledges and personal clubbing attributes:

> Subcultural capital confers status on its owner in the eyes of the relevant beholder. In many ways it affects the standing of the young like its adult equivalent. Subcultural capital can be *objectified* and *embodied*. Just as books and paintings display cultural capital in the family home, so subcultural capital is objectified in the form of fashionable haircuts and well-assembled record collections . . . Just as cultural capital is personified in 'good' manners, so subcultural capital is embodied in the form of being 'in the know', using (but not over-using) current slang and looking as if you were born to perform the current dance styles.
>
> (Thornton 1995: 11–12, original emphasis)

Despite Thornton's constructive engagement with the politics of taste and the problems this poses for the implicit homogeneity of terms such as 'scene' and 'style', it could be argued that the London-centred concern of Thornton's study fails to take into account how locality impacts upon issues of subcultural capital.

In my own work on dance music in Newcastle, a city where the night-time economy orientates more rigidly around traditional 'club-bars', I note that there is much less scope for the development of the diverse club cultural terrains identified by Thornton. Similarly, the relatively small ethnic minority groups in Newcastle have failed to make their mark on the local club scene in the way that the larger ethnic minorities in London and other major cities, such as Birmingham, have been able to do (see Bennett 1997, 2000). Thus, as one young interviewee explained to me:

> It's a very limited scene here. You get people from the outlying areas coming into the town on a Friday and Saturday as you always have . . . I mean that's exactly what the Bigg Market's all about really isn't it?[1] But away from the Bigg Market and the disco nightclubs, I'll call them 'cause that's what they are really, there's not much of a youth led movement really and certainly there's not much of an alternative scene . . . it's difficult to get that kind of space . . . The dance scene is such a massive church, it's got so many different elements to it and many of those elements just don't seem to get much of an airing in Newcastle.
>
> (cited in Bennett 2000: 86)

The result of this was a very small selection of 'specialist' dance music nights in Newcastle, most of which took place in one venue, the Waterfront. In many respects, on the nights when dance music events were featured this venue became a microcosm of those expressions of subcultural capital identified by Thornton (1995) on a larger scale in London's dance music scene. In Newcastle, the spatial and official pressure placed upon dance music (a number of dance clubs having being closed down by the police, see Hollands 1995) have functioned to reduce local articulations of subcultural capital down to the space of a single venue. The Newcastle example serves as an effective illustration of how local circumstances impact on the provision of club space and other forms of entertainment. As a result, the 'alternative' and 'underground' youth of provincial towns and cities often find themselves faced with a rather more limited set of opportunities for expressions of club cultural solidarity than those which prevail in metropolitan centres. It is in such centres that the majority of research on youth culture and popular music continues to be centred.

As the themes so far examined begin to illustrate, the academic interest in dance music has produced new readings of the relationship between youth and music which invariably challenge the findings and conclusions of existing work, particularly that associated with the subcultural theory of the Birmingham CCCS (see Chapter 1). A further way in which the findings of dance music research differ from earlier work on youth culture and music is its emphasis upon the temporal quality of the club crowd. Such an emphasis acutely problematizes subcultural interpretations of youth and music, the latter being conventionally grounded in a structural framework that stresses the significance of youth culture as tangible expressions of those experiences acquired as a direct result of class, gender and race amongst other social factors. According to the findings of recent research, however, those expressions of 'collective' identity articulated through dance music are largely confined to the temporal setting and atmosphere of the club, the club crowd consisting of individuals whose socio-ethnic origins are often mixed and whose paths rarely cross outside the club setting. Such qualities of contemporary club culture are noted by Rietveld (1997) in her study of the Chicago house scene. As she argues, within the space of the weekend club event,

> new identities could be forged that were not necessarily there to be sustained throughout the rest of the week. The dance, the music, even the club itself were built for that moment in the weekend, to disappear once it had occurred.

> (Rietveld 1997: 127–8)

In my own research on dance music (Bennett 1999a, 2000), I further examine the issue of temporality and club culture using Maffesoli's (1996) concept of *tribus* or **neo-tribes**. Underpinning Maffesoli's concept of tribes is a concern to illustrate the increasingly fluid and unstable nature of social relations in contemporary society. According to Maffesoli (1996: 98), the tribe is 'without the rigidity of the forms of organization with which we are familiar, it refers more to a certain ambience, a state of mind, and is preferably to be expressed through lifestyles that favour appearance and form'. Two readings of Maffesoli's work provide further clarification of this point. Hetherington (1992: 93) suggests that tribalization involves 'the deregulation through modernization and individualization of the modern forms of solidarity and identity based on class occupation, locality and gender . . . and the recomposition into "tribal" identities and forms of sociation'. Similarly Shields (1992) suggests that tribal identities serve to illustrate the temporal nature of collective identities in modern consumer society as individuals continually move between different sites of collective expression and 'reconstruct' themselves accordingly. According to Shields:

> Personas are 'unfurled' and mutually adjusted. The performative orientation toward the Other in these sites of social centrality and sociality draws people together one by one. Tribe-like but temporary groups and circles condense out of the homogeneity of the mass.
>
> (Shields 1992: 108)

Drawing upon such theoretical observations in my own work I argue that the dance club setting provides a vivid example of the tribal associations that Maffesoli, Hetherington and Shields suggest characterize contemporary society. Providing a space for expressions of 'togetherness' based on articulations of fun, relaxation and pleasure, the club setting can be seen as one of many forms of temporal engagement through which such neo-tribal associations are formed. Indeed, in many of the larger clubs which feature urban dance music nights, the desire of the clubber to choose from and engage with a variety of different crowds has been further enhanced through the use of different rooms or floors as a means of staging parallel dance events with club-goers free to move between these events as they please. Consequently, the clubbing experience is becoming increasingly a matter of individual choice, the type of music heard and the setting in which it is heard and danced to being very much the decision of the individual consumer. Significantly, such factors in turn have a marked influence on the way in which clubbers talk about the actual process of music consumption. Thus, for many clubbers, 'clubbing' appears to be regarded less as a singularly definable activity and more as a series of fragmented, temporal experiences as they move between different dance floors and engage with different crowds.

This is clearly illustrated in the following discussion extract in which I asked a group of regular attenders of a particular club event in Newcastle to describe the nature of the event to me:

A.B.:   How would you describe 'Pigbag'? What kind of an event is it?

Diane: Well, I would say um, it's a different experience depending upon . . .

Shelly: Upon what's on . . .

Diane: What music's on and what floor you're on as well.

A.B.:   I know there are different things going on on each floor.

All: Yeah.

Rob: There's three types of thing going on actually. There's like the sort of cafe room which plays hip hop and jazz and then down-stairs there's more singing sort of house music . . . and upstairs there's eh . . . well how could you describe that?

Debbie: Well it's quite sort of eh . . . the more housey end of techno music with sort of like trancey techno . . . the sort of easier, comfortable side of techno.

Diane: Yeah and then you'll get people moving between all three floors and checking out what's going on.

(cited in Bennett 2000: 83–4)

The concept of neo-tribalism is also utilized in a further study of contemporary dance music by Malbon (1999). Malbon makes effective use of neo-tribal imagery together with Maffesoli's (1996) attendant notion of 'sociality' as a means of underscoring the 'tactile . . . forms of communality' which characterize the contemporary club crowd (Malbon 1999: 26). At the same time, however, Malbon is critical of Maffesoli's failure to situate his work empirically, a failure which, according to Malbon, renders Maffesoli's analysis insensitive to hardened discourses of stylistic convention and cultural 'competence' which may persist even as collective associations became more multiple, fluid and transitory. Thus, argues Malbon:

> although provocative and useful in evoking some contemporary forms of temporary community and the sociality through which such belongings are established, Maffesoli's 'neo-tribes' thesis fails to evoke the demanding practical and stylistic requirements and competencies that many of these communities demand, and through which many of them are constituted.
>
> (Malbon 1999: 26)

Relating this observation directly to the club crowd, Malbon notes how the seeming openness of this crowd should not be misread as 'open to all'. Empirical investigation of dance club crowds quickly reveals the shared stock of knowledges, musical stylistic and otherwise, through which members of a crowd communicate with each other – both verbally and non verbally. Through combining Malbon's analysis of contemporary club culture with Thornton's (1995) concept of 'subcultural capital', it is thus possible to see how the former, while exhibiting far less stable and coherent qualities than those attributed to youth cultural groupings by the CCCS subcultural theorists, nevertheless retains a series of cultural practices which are collectively shared and relatively fixed. Association with the club crowd, however transitory it may be, demands that individuals demonstrate a knowledge of those cultural practices.

Dance music and new social movements

Despite the case which can be made for the inherently unstable and fleeting nature of the collective associations between dance club audiences, contemporary dance music, by nature of its attraction for disempowered and disaffected young people, has also played a significant role in inspiring a series of proactive socio-political movements, including **Reclaim the Streets** and the **Anti-Road Protest**. Collectively referred to as the **DiY protest movement** (McKay 1996, 1998; Jordan 1998), such activities have, according to Jordan (1998: 129), broken 'down the barriers between art and protest [using] new forms of creative and poetic resistance'. Jordan examines how 'new creative political methods, using direct action, performance art, sculpture and installation' have been used to mount strategies of resistance to environmental threats from new road-building schemes and mounting air pollution caused through the congestion of city streets (Jordan 1998: 132). According to Jordan, the effectiveness of this form of resistance results from the spectacle that it creates, 'not only [for] the media, but for local passers-by, who are often awestruck by what they see and are thus brought into dialogue about the issues' (Jordan 1998: 133).

Raves and other dance music festivals have also given rise to alternative lifestyles built around self-sufficient communities that closely approximate the commune experiments of the late 1960s (see, for example, Webster 1976). A pertinent example of this is the Exodus Collective. Originally part of the British dance party scene, which organized free raves around Britain during the late 1980s, Exodus occupied disused farm buildings near the town of Luton, in Bedfordshire, and transformed them into a housing cooperative which became known as HAZ (Housing Action Zone). Initially threatened with expulsion by the Department of Transport, which owned the buildings, Exodus was subsequently granted tenancy of the farm after department representatives visited the site and noted the scale and quality of restoration work carried out by Exodus members on the occupied buildings. As Malyon observes:

> extensive renovation was carried out on the farm buildings, as well as a bungalow and house where collective members now live. Almost all the wood was recycled from pallets donated by local businesses. There's a growing herd of animals, including horses, goats, a bullock, sheep, ducks and several love-struck Vietnamese pot-bellied pigs. The plan is to open the farm up to the public, and especially local schools.
>
> (Malyon 1998: 195)

In a TV documentary about Exodus, members of the Collective offered the following accounts of themselves and the circumstances that led to the formation of Exodus:

> [Exodus is] a group of young and old people who are dedicated to doing something for their lives and others.
> . . . we're people who could have been called lazy. Not optionally lazy, not, you know, not wanting to work. But sort of gradually getting used to the idea that there's not a lot about, especially if you're in the excluded group; excluded by colour, style, attitude, criminal records, a whole heap of reasons why people are excluded.
>
> (cited in TV documentary *Exodus* broadcast as part of the Channel 4 'Tribe Time TV' series in November 1994)

In so far as dance music culture can be seen in part as a reaction to the economic and social austerity of contemporary Britain, it is not simply encouraging the discourse of retreatism suggested, for example, in Melechi's (1993) notion of an 'ecstasy of disappearance'. On the contrary, dance music culture can also be seen to be encouraging attitudes among the young which are proactive. The Exodus Collective is illustrative of how dance music's capacity for bringing people together in the common space of the rave has functioned to produce a more concrete series of lifestyle strategies through which individuals engage with the social circumstances that confront them. As McKay states:

> Exodus form[ed] a new movement of the people in the early nineties, one that originat[ed] in something as mundane as a sound system . . . black and white youth pull[ed] their energies together to create their own entertainment, then lifestyle, community, network of campaigns and events.
>
> (McKay 1996: 124–5)

Dance music and gender

Research on contemporary dance music and club cultures also raises issues concerning the shifting nature of gender relations on the dance floor. Early dance music studies suggested that the threat of HIV and AIDS, combined with an Ecstasy induced absorption in the music, produced a widescale rejection among young clubbers of 'the dated 70s notion of the disco as a meat market' (Russell 1993: 98). Merchant and MacDonald add to this picture of the club as a space marked by a new set of gender relations:

> In participating in Raves, in observing the activities of young people taking Ecstasy and in talking to them, it became clear that traditional displays of sexual availability and intent, which are often the raison d'être of conventional nightclubs, were not a central part of the Rave Culture. Unlike most clubs, these are not 'pick-up joints' where young people go to find sexual partners. Indeed, sexual liaisons seemed to give way to more friendly, egalitarian forms of interchange.
>
> (Merchant and MacDonald 1994: 22)

Such apparently progressive attitudes, it has been argued, have considerable implications for the involvement of women in contemporary club culture, giving rise to 'changing modes in femininity' (McRobbie 1994). Thus, it is suggested, women 'feel freed from traditional associations of dancing with sexual invite' and able to engage in 'open displays of physical pleasure and affection' (Pini 1997: 166, 167). According to Pini:

> . . . rave represents the emergence of a particular form of 'jouissance', one which is more centred on the achievement of physical and mental transformation and one which is probably best understood as a non-phallic form of pleasure.
>
> (Pini 1997: 167)

Pini's observations are supported by the findings of my own research on club culture in the city of Newcastle upon Tyne, in the north-east of England. The following extract is taken from an interview with a group of female clubbers during which they discuss their experiences of attending a particular club in Newcastle.

Sandra: I remember when I first came out to Pigbag and sat there and just went 'ahh I've never seen anything like this before in mi' life'. The way people interact together . . . it's so friendly and so open. I'd never been anywhere like that before, I'd only ever been to a normal nightclub where you're . . .

Jane: Where you're worried about some guy coming up and saying 'all right luv!' [*all laugh*].

Sandra: And people are dancing exactly how they want to dance and not self consciously, you know. I really like that about it . . . you don't feel as if you're being watched by other people.

Julie: People aren't going there just to watch a person of the opposite sex and to go over and try and chat them up and stuff . . . it's not for that sort of reason that people come to Pigbag.

Sandra: And it's really lovely at the end of the night when the lights go on and people don't scuffle off into the corners and go and hide and try to fix their make up or whatever . . . people are still dancing to the very last second that the music's on you know.

(cited in Bennett 2000: 93–4)

Other dance music researchers, however, suggest that such interpretations of dance music represent only a 'partial picture' (Malbon 1999). Thornton (1995) discusses this in terms an initial 'blur[ring in club culture] of the boundaries between affective and political freedom', the lyrics of early dance music tracks incorporating key phrases from 'speeches of political figures like Martin Luther King and featur[ing] female vocalists singing "I got the power" and "I feel free" ' (Thornton 1995: 21–2). Similarly, Malbon (1999) notes how the development of club culture and its increasing specialization has given rise to new 'experiences of clubbing in which the practices of sexualisation [are] as – if not more – important as within other social spaces' (Malbon 1999: 43). According to Malbon (1999), a number of the female clubbers he interviewed described their feelings of liberation in a broadly opposite fashion to that described by Pini (1997), 'through what might be termed "*hyper*-sexualisation" ' (Malbon 1999: 44). At the same time, however, Malbon suggests that such sensibilities may still be linked with a liberalizing sensibility rooted in club culture. Thus, he argues:

while this sexualisation infers that being seen as sexy is important to these women, it is less apparent that they are presenting their sexuality in this fashion in order to find a 'partner'. It may well be that these women are constructing *themselves* as 'sexy' for themselves because they cannot or do not express their sexualisation in the same relatively open way in other areas of their lives . . . In this way women may exhibit a confidence and form of self-sufficiency – a disinterest in compulsory and inevitably consummated sexual interaction – which is unlike that which they might exhibit or experience in, say, a pub. The underlying codes of interaction are quite different, and this difference appears to be attractive to women.

(Malbon 1999: 45, original emphasis)

According to Malbon then, rather than functioning as a space in which conventional notions of gender are entirely displaced, the dance clubs allows for the expression of certain conventional gender values, for example an emphasis on the presentation of physical attractiveness and sexuality. At the same time, however, in the contemporary dance club setting, such expressions are not automatically assumed to be linked with the notion of the club as a place where individuals go to find sexual partners.

Conclusion

During the course of this chapter I have focused on contemporary dance music culture. Beginning with a look at the origins of dance music in the respective genres of house and techno, I went on to consider the relationship between dance music and new technology, focusing in particular on the way in which digital sampling allows dance music to draw upon a range of existing musical styles and sounds and repattern them into new soundscapes. I moved on to consider the significance of dance music as a contemporary youth music. I then examined how the composition and inherent temporality of the club crowd has problematized the notion of clear cut and relatively fixed subcultural groupings and given rise to new sociological approaches to understudying the relationship between youth, style and musical taste. This was followed by a consideration of dance music's role in the formation of proactive movements against current social problems such as youth unemployment and homelessness. Finally I examined the claims made in current dance music research that club culture has produced new forms of gender relations due to the non-violent and non-sexist sensibilities which underpin the scene and liberate clubbers, particularly female clubbers, from the more oppressive atmosphere associated with mainstream nightclubs, bars and pubs.

Note

1 The Bigg Market is an area in the centre of Newcastle with a large number of pubs and clubs making it a very popular nightspot for young people (see Lancaster 1992; Hollands 1995).

Further reading

Bennett, A. (1999) 'Subcultures or neo-tribes? Rethinking the relationship between youth, style and musical taste', *Sociology*, 33(3): 599–617.

Bennett, A. (2000) *Popular Music and Youth Culture: Music, Identity and Place*. London: Macmillan (Chapter 4).

McKay, G. (1996) *Senseless Acts of Beauty: Cultures of Resistance since the Sixties*. London: Verso.

McKay, G. (ed.) (1998) *DiY Culture: Party and Protest in Nineties Britain*. London: Verso.

Malbon, B. (1999) *Clubbing: Dancing, Ecstasy and Vitality*. London: Routledge.

Pini, M. (1997) Women and the early British rave scene, in A. McRobbie (ed.) *Back to Reality: Social Experience and Cultural Studies*. Manchester: Manchester University Press.

Redhead, S. (ed.) (1993) *Rave Off: Politics and Deviance in Contemporary Youth Culture*. Aldershot: Avebury.

Redhead, S., Wynne, D. and O'Connor, J. (eds) (1997) *The Clubcultures Reader: Readings in Popular Cultural Studies*. Oxford: Blackwell.

Saunders, N. (1995) *Ecstasy and the Dance Culture*. London: Nicholas Saunders/Turnaround and Knockabout.

Thornton, S. (1995) *Club Cultures: Music, Media and Subcultural Capital*. Cambridge: Polity Press.

9 | YOUTH AND MUSIC-MAKING

> It is true that local music-making in the sense of direct participation in performance is the pursuit of a minority. But this minority turns out to be a more serious and energetic one than is often imagined, whose musical practices not only involve a whole host of other people than just performers, but also have many implications for urban and national culture more generally.
>
> (Finnegan 1989: 6)

As the preceding chapters in this book bear out, for many years the academic study of youth culture and popular music tended towards an emphasis on youth as 'consumers' rather than 'makers' of music. To some extent this was due to a sociological bias which cast the consumption choices of young people in a discourse of resistance. Youth resistance was defined in terms of fashion items and attendant leisure products, including records, becoming key resources in a form of semiotic guerrilla warfare waged by the so-called working class youth subcultures against the dominant middle class society (Hall and Jefferson 1976; Hebdige 1979). Given the fact that the numbers of young people consuming music far outnumbered those who made music (a trend which continues today), sociological studies of youth and music tended to gravitate towards the more socially apparent, and visually 'spectacular', effect of music consumption on young people.

In more recent years, however, the rejection of structuralism as a means of explaining away social processes, combined with an increasing concern with the micro-social, local aspects of everyday life as the focus for critical inquiry, has led to an interest among academic researchers in music-making as an activity via which young people make sense of, negotiate or resist the local circumstances in which they find themselves. Indeed, as much of the research on the issue of young people and music-making illustrates, while this activity may on first appearance seem to be a minority pursuit and thus of relatively little sociological significance, the connections between music-making and the wider processes of social life are such that music-making provides insights into a number of key social issues. These include local identity, self-awareness, gender and ethnic relations and forms of economic life.

Youth, music-making and rock 'n' roll

In Chapter 1 I noted how contemporary youth culture is very much the product of socio-economic changes and technological innovations that occurred during the post-Second World War period. The technological advances that allowed for the development of mass produced goods, such as fashion, make-up, records, record players and transistor radios – which became centrally significant to the post-war youth market (Chambers 1985) – also allowed for the mass production of another item that would play a crucial role in the post-war youth phenomenon, the electric guitar. The primary instrument of the rock 'n' roll music that swept across the western world during the post-war period, the electric guitar had originally been developed during the 1930s in response to the need of guitar players to be heard above the sound of other instruments in jazz and big band ensembles (Middleton 1990: 90). The early electric guitar was basically an acoustic (that is, hollow-bodied) guitar with a small microphone or **pick-up** attached to it. This design was subsequently modified by guitar makers such as Les Paul, Paul Bigsby, Merle Travis, Leo Fender and the Swiss-born Adolf Rickenbacker, who replaced the guitar's traditional hollow body with a solid-body construction (see Bacon 1991).

The emergent rock 'n' roll sound of the post-war era created a surge of interest in music-making among young teenage males who attempted to emulate the guitar-based music of 1950s rock 'n' roll artists such as Buddy Holly, Carl Perkins and Chuck Berry. Demand for electric guitars, the newly developed electric bass guitar (a modified version of the 'stand up' double bass) and the drum kit, the trio of instruments that formed the sonic underpinning of rock 'n' roll, gave rise to the mass production of these instruments. In particular, however, it was the electric guitar that held a particular fascination for young would-be musicians, the increasing popularity of the instrument during the 1950s being illustrated by figures for overall guitar sales in the US which doubled between 1940 and 1959 (Ryan and Peterson 2001). Central to the appeal of the electric guitar was the relative ease with which it could be mastered to the level necessary to reproduce the basic rock 'n' roll sound. Similarly important was the cheapness and portability of the guitar (Chambers 1985: 22).

Indeed, if at one level rock 'n' roll was responsible for reshaping the social profile of youth as a new and distinctive cultural group, at another level it gave rise to a new music-making ethos among those young hopefuls who aspired not just to listen to rock 'n' roll music but to play it. Before the arrival of rock 'n' roll, music-making was something which required a large element of self-discipline and money. Mastering a musical instrument meant long hours of practice and a commitment to studying music theory, often under the experienced eye of a qualified music teacher. Rock 'n' roll functioned to demystify the music-making process, 'the rapidly learned rhythmic possibilities' (Chambers 1985: 22) of the electric guitar removing the need for formal music tuition and 'putt[ing] in question the existing professionalized instrumental skills' (Middleton 1990: 15).

In the 50 years or so since the advent of rock 'n' roll, the scope for young people to become involved in music composition and performance has increased considerably. In particular the development of relatively cheap, high quality home-recording equipment during the 1980s and 1990s, together with digital samplers (see Chapter 8) and various forms of music related computer software, has created new opportunities for young people to make music. Due to computer technology, young people who lack even the basic rudiments of what could be termed 'conventional' musical knowledge, can become involved in the music-making process, using samplers, sequencers and other electronic equipment and effects (see Chapter 8) to make music (see Negus 1992; Smith and Maughan 1997). Indeed, Smith and Maughan (1997) suggest that the digital revolution has led to a new era in music-making among the young which is of equal significance to that inspired by the arrival of rock 'n' roll during the mid-1950s. In effect, argue Smith and Maughan, during the late 1980s popular music-making practices became divided into two distinct categories – those which adhered to a by then established ' "rock" aesthetic' and those which emerged from a new ' "technological", musical aesthetic' (Smith and Maughan 1997: 7). The point remains, however, that if music-making has played an important role in the everyday lives of many young people since the mid-1950s then it has only recently become a focus for the academic study of youth and music. In the rest of this chapter I examine some of the main research to have considered the issue of youth and music-making and discuss the findings that have emerged from this body of work.

Becoming a band

One of the first studies to focus on music-making and young people was H.S. Bennett's (1980) *On Becoming a Rock Musician*. Perhaps the most

significant aspect of Bennett's study is its illustration of the many non-musi-
cal factors which influence the music-making activities of young rock/pop
groups. As Bennett demonstrates, a group is a social unit; whether it suc-
ceeds or fails, even in its initial quest to perform in front of an audience,
depends upon the group agreeing on fixed ground rules relating to collective
codes of conduct, shared beliefs about the importance of music and a
common level of commitment to the group. Among these factors, the most
important rule is agreeing upon a rehearsal schedule. As Bennett points out,
at a very early stage in their playing career, young rock/pop musicians learn
that being a musician is not simply about being able to play a musical instrument but also involves sharing a special commitment to music; a belief that
music should come before everything else. From the point of view of a young
rock/pop group, it is vitally important that each of its members shares this
belief from the outset. As Bennett observes:

> When group members fail to show up for a practice they are doing more
> than breaking commitments to other individuals in the group. Their
> absence demonstrates that something means more than music – that, in
> short, they are not musicians. The ability of an individual to schedule
> everyday activities around the schedule of band practice is the ability of
> a group to exist.
>
> (H.S. Bennett 1980: 132)

A more recent study by Reid *et al.* (1994) notes that such demonstration of
a commitment to music continues to be regarded by young amateur and
semi-professional musicians as a centrally defining characteristic of the
'dedicated' musician. Furthermore, Reid *et al.* advance Bennett's original
thesis by examining the extent to which demonstration of a commitment to
music confers a special status upon the young musician among non-music-
making peers. Thus, they argue:

> The rock musician role . . . is likely to cross a variety of social situations
> and be present within and outside of the context in which the role is
> directly enacted (i.e., rehearsing, recording, or playing for an audience
> versus presentation of self as a rock musician to any others who are not
> present in the role). The musician role is therefore one that gains the
> occupant high status in a wide variety of settings in that it can easily be
> enacted and communicated to others via behavioral and stylistic
> presentations of self.
>
> (Reid *et al.* 1994: 320–1)

Another important aspect of Bennett's work is its insights into the way in
which a young rock/pop group constructs its repertoire of songs. In most

cases a young rock/pop group will aspire to the ultimate goal of writing and performing its own material. However, this is often preceded by a period of perhaps one or two years 'covering', that is copying, the songs of other well-known artists, perhaps supplementing these with an occasional original song. Thus, in addition to the various other organizational issues pertaining to the successful function of a band, the band must also work well as a social unit when attempting to learn songs to include in its on-stage repertoire. Bennett refers to this process of learning songs as 'song getting', because of the way in which a young group typically learns songs. According to Bennett 'song getting' is not achieved by reading from sheet music but by repeated listening to a recorded version of a song in order that different parts of the rhythm and melody can be learned by individual members of a band and subsequently reproduced on their respective instruments. Interesting in this respect is Bennett's illustration of the way in which a recording supplants written sheet music as the 'primary text' (Moore 1993) against which authentic imitation of the piece is continually judged by members of the group:

> The conflict about who was *right* – i.e., whose interpretation of the recorded sound was to be considered legitimate – did not admit a consideration that varying interpretations can be derived from various ways of listening (aesthetics). Throughout it all the recording remained an unquestionable standard to be referred to 'over and over' with expectations of revelation and resolution of doubt.
>
> (H.S. Bennett 1980: 136)

Bennett's concept of 'song getting' offers valuable insights both into the micro-organizational processes of a young rock/pop group and the special significance placed on commodities such as recorded players, tape recorders and CDs, such commodities becoming in effect as centrally important to the young rock/pop musician's craft as musical instruments themselves. At the same time, however, it is important to note that Bennett was writing in 1980 and that, as such, new forms of 'song getting' are now available to young musicians which supplement, or in some respects, replace the collective practices observed by Bennett to begin with. Popular music 'training' is gradually becoming an aspect of school curricula (see Paynter 1982; Green 1988; Blake 1996; Richards 1998), while private institutions such as the Guitar Institute of Technology (**GIT**), founded in Los Angeles but now with branches in most major cities of the world, offers high quality short courses and master classes run by experienced professional musicians (see Walser 1993: 92).

Similarly, since the mid-1980s there has been a steady increase in the amount of self-learning materials available for young aspirant rock/pop musicians. Examples include **play-along CDs** (which allow the learner musician to practise in a simulated band situation), as well as more accurately produced sheet music and guitar **tablature** (a system whereby the notes and basic phrasing of guitar passages are written down on a six line stave, each line representing a string on the guitar) (Müller 1993). Significantly, the increasing use of guitar and bass tablature by young musicians as a means of learning songs, coupled with the growing ease of access to the internet, has led to new forms of 'song getting' based upon a global exchange of ideas and information by young musicians through a series of dedicated **tab websites**. Sometimes these form part of official fan club websites, while in other cases they are created by lone enthusiasts such as 'The U2 Guitar Archive' and the 'Echo & the Bunnymen Guitar Archive' (see p. 187 for website addresses). Such sites are entirely fan generated and rely upon contributions from amateur musicians who transcribe individual guitar and bass parts from records and submit their transcriptions as word processed 'tabulations' for web publication.

Music-making and identity

As the above references to H.S. Bennett (1980) and Reid *et al.*'s (1994) work illustrate, although the micro-organizational processes underpinning the young rock/pop band firmly correspond with shared commitment, or expected commitment, of individual band members to the band and its music, such processes also reflect the way in which 'dedicated' musicians come to perceive themselves in relation to 'significant' others that occupy their lifeworlds. In effect, music-making becomes a shared 'pathway' through which members of young rock/pop bands negotiate the 'impersonal wilderness of urban life' (Finnegan 1989: 306). This is illustrated in Fornäs *et al.*'s (1995) study of local rock and pop bands in Sweden. Fornäs *et al.* show how, through their musical activities, young bands are able to mark themselves off from both the parent culture and the school and the kinds of demands which the latter impose upon young people. Playing in a group gives young people a chance to distance themselves from those aspects of life which they find least appealing and to envisage a different kind of life for themselves, one which is based not around schoolwork and subsequently a job or career, but rather upon musical creativity and artistic expression. Fornäs *et al.* argue that, from the point of view of those young musicians in their study, the negative experience of school was one of the central reasons why they decided to take up music; 'playing rock offer[ed] the possibility of raising themselves out of the rather unattractive future for which school lays the foundations' (Fornäs *et al.* 1995: 203).

Other research on young people and music-making has demonstrated how the collective identities forged by young rock/pop bands may also draw upon and reflect aspects of the local environment from which the group has emerged. A study which pays great detail to the relationship between young people, music-making and locality is Sara Cohen's (1991) *Rock Culture in Liverpool*. Cohen chose Liverpool (in north-west England) as the focus for her study because of the way in which the city's rich musical heritage impacts on contemporary music-making practices in Liverpool and the significance attached to such practices, particularly by younger musicians. Cohen's research illustrates that, due a number of reasons directly related to the depressed socio-economic situation in Liverpool, for many young people music-making has become quite literally a way of life. Since the 1970s, unemployment in Liverpool has dramatically increased. By 1985 it was at 27 per cent, double the national average. In a city which offered very few opportunities, especially for the young, music-making became something which could give young people a purpose in life. As Cohen points out:

> There existed a general feeling that being in a band was a legitimate career to follow ... Thus in a city where the attitude was that you might as well pick up a guitar as take exams, since your chances of finding full-time occupation from each were just the same, being in a band was an accepted way of life and could provide a means of justifying one's existence. 'It's an alternative to walking round town all day', said one band member, while another asked, 'What else is there to do?'
>
> (Cohen 1991: 2)

A further series of insights into the social significance of local music-making is offered by Finnegan (1989) in *The Hidden Musicians*, a study of informal music-making practices in the 'new town' of Milton Keynes in central England. Unlike Cohen, Finnegan does not focus exclusively upon pop and rock music but studies in addition a range of other musical genres including brass bands, choirs, jazz and folk. Within this wide-ranging analysis of local music-making practices, Finnegan offers a number of valuable observations on the role and significance of music-making in the lives of young people. Finnegan begins by suggesting that the existence of local music-making processes exposes inherent flaws in mass cultural theory, especially the latter's extreme view which envisages contemporary individuals as 'a passive and deluded population lulled by the mass media and generating nothing themselves' (Finnegan 1989: 5). To study local music-making processes is, Finnegan argues, to open the door on an important area of creativity in contemporary society. She advances this view through her assertion that

> far from music-making taking a peripheral role for individuals and society – a view propagated in the kind of theoretical stance that marginalises 'leisure' or 'culture' as somehow less real than 'work' or 'society' – music can equally well be seen as playing a central part not just in urban networks but also more generally in the social structure and processes of our life today.
>
> (Finnegan 1989: 5–6)

Finnegan supports this contention with a series of empirical observations on the cultural meaning of music-making at a local level. A particularly important issue emerging from her research on young rock and pop groups in Milton Keynes is the apparent disjuncture between national definitions and categories of musical style and those observed at the local level. For the most part, those local bands studied by Finnegan did not possess a recording contract and, consequently, were not being pressured by a record company to adhere to established stylistic conventions in their songwriting and aim at a particular record buying market. Free of such pressures and considerations, notions of style and musical direction among local bands in Milton Keynes developed in their own particular directions. Thus states Finnegan:

> Several local players had built up informal fan groups who followed *their* band without much interest in the wider typologies. These allegiances were reinforced by stress on locally generated music . . . practically all these bands played a high proportion of their own compositions. What mattered was their style rather than general labels, and though players sometimes like to relate themselves to nationally accepted images their typical interest was to get on with creating and performing their *own* music.
>
> (Finnegan 1989: 105, original emphasis)

Finnegan describes how, when interviewed by her, young rock and pop groups from Milton Keynes would often maintain that stylistic terms such as punk, skinhead and futurist were media generated labels that could not be directly related to the kind of music that the local bands were producing. Many local bands stated that they simply took the bits they liked from a variety of visual and musical styles and mixed them together to produce their own, original style of music.

The apparent opposition on the part of local groups and artists to the national 'mainstream' music industry and its 'packaging' of music and artists is also noted by Street (1993) in his insightful study of the short-lived Norwich music venue, the Waterfront. Thus, according to Street, among the local musicians who campaigned most ardently for a live music venue in Norwich, a city in eastern England, were those who 'saw their musical careers or their musical tastes as existing outside the national network of the mainstream. Indeed, this sense of 'otherness' was crucial to development of a sense of group identity, itself important for the creation of group cohesion' (Street 1993: 50). Clearly, it could be argued that such collective constructions of the local as a space *free* from the pressures and demands of mainstream music-making are inherently fragile as most local bands aspire to 'making it', that is securing recording and management contracts and becoming 'professional'. Thus, as Frith observes:

> As local live performers, musicians remain a part of their community, subject to its values and needs, but as recording artists they experience the pressures of the market; they automatically become 'rock 'n' roll imperialists', pursuing national and international sales. The recording musicians 'community', in short, is defined by purchasing patterns.
>
> (Frith 1983: 51)

The point remains, however, that while young musicians are struggling to 'make it' the local remains their main frame of reference. Moreover, as Cohen's (1991) work on the local music scene in Liverpool effectively illustrates, while 'local' bands and artists may commonly aspire to commercial success and 'star' status, in general terms this is not achieved. It is more often the case that such performers remain tied to their native communities and continue to play to local audiences in local venues.

Women and music-making

While music-making offers young people avenues for expression and creativity through which to negotiate the more restricting features of everyday life, it is at the same time a male dominated activity. Indeed, the male-centredness of music-making effectively functions to exclude or, at best, limit the opportunities for women musicians. Thus, as Frith and McRobbie observe:

> The music business is male-run; popular musicians, writers, creators, technicians, engineers, and producers are mostly men. Female creative roles are limited and mediated through male notions of female ability.
>
> (Frith and McRobbie 1978: 373)

Similarly, in a more recent study of women and the music industry Gottlieb and Wald suggest that

> Women performers go through complicated contortions as they both appropriate and repudiate a traditionally masculine rock performance position which is itself premised on the repression of femininity, while they simultaneously contend with a feminine performance position defined primarily as the erotic object-to-be-looked-at.
>
> (Gottlieb and Wald 1994: 260)

Indeed, the lack of opportunities for aspirant female musicians is not restricted to the sphere of professional music-making but rather permeates music-making at all levels. In her study of the local music scene in Liverpool, Cohen (1991) identified a widespread mistrust among local male musicians towards women actively involved, or with aspirations to become involved, in the Liverpool music scene. During the course of her research Cohen discovered that this mistrust of women was a product of the patriarchal nature of Liverpool's predominantly working class population. Thus, even though many of the musicians who Cohen interviewed were married or had girl-friends, they did not talk very much about this aspect of their lives at rehearsals. Indeed, wives and girlfriends were often barred from attending rehearsals, and if they attended gigs were normally left on their own while their husbands or boyfriends talked to friends and fellow musicians. Bands, it was felt by those involved in them, were social units, built on trust and companionship. Girlfriends and wives threatened the bond between band members, and thus endangered the band itself. Thus, as Cohen observes:

> Many [band members] complained that women were a distraction at rehearsals because they created tension within the band and pressurized the band's members to talk to them or take them home. They were also said to object to their boyfriends spending so much time with the band. One musician described how his girlfriend of four years, fed up with the amount of time he spent with his band, asked him which was more important, her or the band. He replied that band was and she moved out.
>
> (Cohen 1991: 210)

Such mistrust and indifference on the part of male musicians towards female involvement in music-making limits the opportunities for female musicians to join bands and gain experience of playing in a band situation.

In her research on amateur and semi-professional female rock and pop bands in Britain, Bayton (1988) notes how the lack of musical experience possessed by female musicians means that even the initial steps of getting a band together, learning songs and organizing rehearsals are often much more difficult than for male groups. According to Bayton, one of the most typical problems for women wishing to play in a group is deciding what instrument to play. This, suggests Bayton, has much to do with the considerably smaller pool of female musicians as compared with male musicians. It is often the case that a woman musician will turn up for an audition or first rehearsal intending to play a particular instrument and will end up playing something else, or in some cases will actually learn an instrument from scratch because it is required within the band. This kind of scenario is uncommon in male bands because of the much larger number of male musicians both playing and seeking work in bands.

A similar difference is evident in the way in which male and female groups learn songs. I have previously observed in my discussion of H.S. Bennett's (1980) study of amateur male rock groups how 'song getting' was not only about who had learned or 'got' a song, but also about whose interpretation of the song was deemed to be 'correct', that is, closest to the recorded version. Bayton's (1988) study reveals that the 'song getting' process in female groups revolves around a very different process; women musicians will often help each other to learn songs rather than fight over who has interpreted a song in the most authentic fashion. This is evident in the following description, which comes from one of the female musicians which Bayton interviewed for her study:

> [Girls have not had] a whole history of having played guitar in garages and things. What girls have been confronted with . . . is being a girl-band in a male-orientated world. How can we do this? How can we go about this? We were all in the same boat together. None of us could play better than anybody else. So we helped each other. We listened out, on my old record player, for the bass line and all those that could play guitar and bass tried to work it out, until we got it – in the end – and then the bass player played it. We listened to the horns and helped Merle work out the horns. So we helped each other. Right from the word 'Go' there was this working-together atmosphere, each one having an equal say in the matter.
>
> (Bayton 1988: 240)

The relative exclusion of women from music-making, and the strategies which female musicians adopt in order to negotiate the restrictions placed on them by the male-centred nature of music-making activity, is by no means particular to the Anglo American world. This is evidenced, for example, by Fokken's (1993) account of the problems experienced by all-female groups in Germany where, she points out, 'rock music is [still] undoubtedly a male domain' (Fokken 1993: 83). As with Bayton, Fokken notes how the lack of opportunity for female musicians and aspirant musicians results in women adopting a very different approach to music-making from male groups (Fokken 1993: 83–4). For example, they will often spend a long time exploring the different 'sound' possibilities offered by electronic instruments rather than simply opting for maximum, volume – a common aspect of all-male groups. Similarly, female groups often experiment with different instruments, regularly swapping instruments for different songs or pieces of music.

Aside from the technical issues to be addressed when joining a band and becoming involved in the process of music-making, female musicians often share very different ideas about what counts as 'commitment' to a band to those shared by members of male rock/pop bands. As observed above in relation to H.S. Bennett's study, it is an expectation in male bands that each member will view music-making as *the* most important thing which they do and will structure other activities and commitments around their music-making commitments. Similarly, in discussing Cohen's (1991) study, it was shown how male musicians will often sacrifice relationships with girlfriends if it begins to interfere with their band commitments. For female musicians such a form of commitment to a band is often much more difficult, especially if they have babies or young children to care for. As Bayton observes:

> Male musicians do not take their babies along to band practices; indeed they would find the idea unthinkable. Yet some women do have to do this, and clearly, in this situation, their concentration cannot be exclusively riveted on the music; they cannot forget that they are mothers.
>
> (Bayton 1988: 255)

At the same time, Bayton suggests that such extra-musical commitments have the effect of making female musicians much more supportive of each other. Whereas the need to take a child to the doctor, or to stay at home in order to care for a sick child, would not be seen as a legitimate reason for missing a rehearsal session by the majority of male rock and pop groups, in a female band the importance of such extra-musical commitments is both recognized and respected by the other members. Indeed, according to Bayton, female musicians do, on the whole, appear to place as much importance upon the friendship and support which they receive from being in a band as on the music. Friendship seems

> to be important in all women's bands, especially in their early stages. There is usually a lot of getting together apart from practices, lots of

phone calls and general contact and the friendships built up within bands were often as important as the music itself.

(Bayton 1988: 257)

As the above studies illustrate, if music-making does offer important avenues for creativity, expression and the formation of identities, it is at the same time a male-dominated activity. The opportunities for female participation in music-making are still considerably limited.

Music-making and education

The studies considered thus far have variously examined the leisure, artistic and economic functions of music-making for young people. There is, however, a further dimension of music-making's significance for young people which needs to be considered, that of education and personal development. In the context of Britain, recent reports on music education in schools have voiced concern about what is deemed to be the 'inaccurate and monocultural approach' of the school curriculum towards the teaching of music theory and practice which, it is argued, centres almost exclusively around western classical music (Everitt 1997: 71). This observation is supported by Finnegan's (1989) research on local music-making practices in Milton Keynes. Thus

> formal musical education [offered by schools] was mainly within the classical music tradition . . . There were almost no explicit references in teachers' replies to music of the Afro-American tradition – jazz, blues, rock etc. . . . This was a remarkable absence given the huge enthusiasm of so many teenagers and pre-teenagers for rock music in all its many forms'.
>
> (Finnegan 1989: 198, 205)

Such findings are, however, by no means a standard feature of research on music training and education in the school system, a number of researchers pointing to a rather more liberal and progressive approach towards music education in the school in some areas of Britain. For example, in his work on music-making in East London, Blake (1996: 208) notes how music training in local schools 'is provided on the basis of "relevance" and "interest" . . . [p]eripatetic instrumental tuition [being] available in western, African and Asian musics'. Similarly, Paynter (1982) notes the diversity of music education and training in many inner-city schools in Britain where featured styles such as steel band and reggae reflect the ethnic diversity of the localities in which these schools are situated.

Nevertheless, studies continue to suggest that the teaching of popular music lags behind the teaching of classical music in the school curriculum. As Richards (1998) notes, a primary obstacle to the teaching of popular music styles has been a failure on the part of teachers to look beyond 'the orthodox separation and privileging of subject-based (school) knowledge relative to the everyday knowledge acquired by children in everyday contexts' (Richards 1998: 21). Applying a **pedagogical** critique to the issue of popular music education in schools, Comer (1982) suggests that music teachers, due to their classical music backgrounds, tend to bring the theory and technique of classical training to bear on the teaching of popular music through a focus on chord sequences, rhythm and timbre. However, as Comer observes, while it is important to cover such technical aspects of popular music, 'pop is not just a musical style, but a manifestation of a set of meanings, a shorthand reference to larger personal and social values. It [is] wrong to deal with [popular music] simply as "classroom material" providing an alternative route to more traditional goals of music theory' (Comer 1982: 7–8).

Comer's observations illustrate the more informal processes underpinning the acquisition of musical skills by young aspirant pop and rock musicians and also suggest that popular music education consists of far more than a straightforward teaching and learning of theory and technique. On the contrary, the music-making process also functions as an opportunity for young people to have fun, talk meet new people and learn musical skills from each other. Indeed, in addition to musical skills, the music-making process can also be utilized as a means of equipping young people with social and communicative skills which are of use across a broad range of situations and circumstances encountered in everyday life.

Elsewhere, I have developed this analysis of music-making's significance for young people in a study of the Frankfurt **Rockmobil**, a mobile music-making project for young people in Frankfurt, Germany (Bennett 1998). Using facilities and space offered by local youth clubs the Rockmobil travels out to particular areas of Frankfurt to hold weekly music-making workshops. In the early stages of a new project, the Rockmobil will provide all the necessary musical instruments while the youth club is expected to provide a rehearsal space (usually a designated room which the club's staff and users will have soundproofed and decorated with music posters, stickers, original artwork and so on). If the project proves to be a success, then the youth centre will be expected, over a period of time, to buy its own musical instruments.

Throughout the lifetime of a Rockmobil band project, typically two to three years, heavy emphasis is laid on the importance of teamwork. From the early stages of a band's music-making career, the members of the band are continually informed by the 'Teamer' assigned to work with them that success or failure in everything – from successfully playing the first song, to performing the first concert, to recording the first cassette or CD – is down to the combined effort of all the individuals involved in the band. The Rockmobil organizes two to three 'showcase' concerts a year at which bands involved with the project are encouraged to perform. Additionally, bands are invited to spend weekends at the Rockmobil recording studio, a specially converted house in Gießen, a city approximately 30 miles north of Frankfurt. Here the bands gain experience of recording their music in preparation for a more strenuous recording session at a professional studio, the results of which are put onto a compilation CD and given free of charge to band members, family and friends.

At one level the nature of the Rockmobil's work is such that the hopes and expectations of those young people who become involved with the project are, in any case, different from young bands who have invested long hours of practice both in order to master their individual instruments and to create a distinctive group sound. However, a central principle of the Rockmobil's pedagogic strategy is that no one should be excluded from the project's workshops and other music-making activities. Any young person who has an interest in music, irrespective of whether or not they have existing musical ability, is encouraged to become involved with the Rockmobil. Such a policy automatically removes the barriers of expertise and exclusivity which often serve to mark off those involved in music-making from their non-music-making peers.

In a recent pedagogically grounded study of youth-based music projects, German youth researchers Hering *et al.* (1993: 53) suggest that the experience of making music together results in 'a form of "positive feedback" . . . as [young people] learn to co-ordinate their individual performances into an overall group performance and sound'. Herring *et al.* (1993: 53) also noted that: 'The individual band members have to learn to work together, to give their best in group performances and to resolve or "cover up" mistakes which occur during the course of a live performance'. Hering *et al.* further argue that, rather than becoming an end in itself, the experience of collective music-making can have a series of beneficial effects upon the overall personal and social and development of young people. A similar view is expressed by Kratz (1994: 127), who argues that the availability of 'hands-on' music-making experiences to young people opens up new avenues for personal expression and for communication with peers.

Conclusion

During this chapter, I have examined the significance of music-making for young people in contemporary society. Beginning with a consideration of the rock/pop group situation as a social process with its own sets of norms and values – notably shared notions of commitment to the group – I moved on to examine the relationship between membership of a pop/rock group and collective constructions of identity. Such collective identities, I suggested, often result from young people's need to negotiate the more restrictive features of everyday life, such as school or work. Subsequently, I developed this focus on the relationship between music-making and collective identity through an examination of the role played by locality in issues as diverse as authenticating music-making as an acceptable occupation to the preservation of authenticity and artistic integrity. I then examined the issue of women and music-making, noting how the male-dominated nature of music-making activities serves to limit the opportunities for women to join groups and gain experience of playing in a group situation. Finally, I considered the significance of music-making in relation to education and personal development.

Further reading

Bayton, M. (1988) How women become rock musicians, in S. Frith and A. Goodwin (eds) (1990) *On Record: Rock, Pop and the Written Word*. London: Routledge.

Bennett, A. (1998) The Frankfurt Rockmobil: a new insight into the significance of music-making for young people, *Youth and Policy*, 60: 16–29.

Bennett, A. (2000) *Popular Music and Youth Culture: Music, Identity and Place*. London: Macmillan (Chapter 7).

Bennett, H.S. (1980) *On Becoming a Rock Musician*. Amherst, MA: University of Massachusetts Press.

Cohen, S. (1991) *Rock Culture in Liverpool: Popular Music in the Making*. Oxford: Clarendon Press.

Everitt, A. (1997) *Joining In: An Investigation into Participatory Music*. London: Calouste Gulbenkian Foundation (Chapter 3).

Finnegan, R. (1989) *The Hidden Musicians: Music-Making in an English Town*. Cambridge: Cambridge University Press.

Fornäs, J., Lindberg, U. and Sernhade, O. (1995) *In Garageland: Rock, Youth and Modernity*. London: Routledge.

Reid, S.A., Epstein, J.S. and Benson, D.E. (1994) Living on a lighted stage: identity, salience, psychological centrality, authenticity, and role behavior of semi-professional rock musicians, in J.S. Epstein (ed.) *Adolescents and their Music: If It's Too Loud You're Too Old*. New York and London: Garland.

Vulliamy, G. and Lee, E. (eds) (1982) *Pop, Rock and Ethnic Music in School*. Cambridge: Cambridge University Press.

10 WHOSE GENERATION? YOUTH, MUSIC AND NOSTALGIA

> Youth can be a matter of chronology, sociology, ideology, experience, style
> attitude. My argument is that a particular generation was identified with 'youth'
> and invested with a certain power by a broad range of discourses.
>
> (Grossberg 1992: 171)

Throughout each of the chapters in this book it has been taken for granted
that youth is a fixed and easily identifiable social category. In keeping with
those sociologists and cultural theorists whose work I have discussed, it has
been assumed that 'youth' describes a specific age group, typically 15 to 25
year olds. The term youth culture thereby encompassing the collective
responses of individuals within this age range to popular cultural forms such
as music, style and film. The final chapter in this book pursues a different line
of inquiry. That is to say, rather than taking for granted the notion of youth
as a fixed category, as the exclusive domain of the *young*, I will suggest that
youth is a contested term, the site of a struggle between different post-Second
World War generations, each of whom lay claim to a particular knowledge
about youth and what it means to be 'young'. In referring to a 'struggle for
youth', I do not mean a struggle in the physical sense of the word narrowly
understood. Rather, the struggle for youth is an ideological one, albeit with
its own materiality. As different post-war generations invest youth with their
own meanings and significance, the terms 'youth' and 'youth culture' become
ideologically contested. Indeed, this situation is further exacerbated by the
media who also construct particular meanings around the terms 'youth' and
'youth culture' (Thornton 1995). As a consequence, youth has become the
site of a range of conflicting interests. These are both generational, in that
various post-war generations claim the right to 'define' youth, and corporate,
in that, due to a decreasing number of teenagers in the west and high rates of
unemloyment among the young, the 'youth market' increasingly targets the
more affluent 25 to 45 years age bracket.

This chapter first examines how the increasing dominance of the retro market in contemporary popular culture is enabling respective post-war generations effectively to relive their youth and to engage in nostalgic representations of what it means to be young. The chapter then focuses on how such nostalgic representations impact on perceptions of contemporary youth and questions the validity of terms such as 'Generation X', the latter bespeaking the alleged apolitical and disaffected nature of today's young people.

Whose generation?

In his book *We Gotta Get Out of This Place*, Grossberg (1992) suggests that youth

> has become a battlefield on which the current generations of adolescents, baby boomers, parents and corporate media interests are fighting to control its meanings, investments and powers, fighting to articulate and thereby construct its experiences identities, practices, discourses and social differences.
>
> (Grossberg 1992: 183)

Grossberg's observation is telling in terms of its juxtaposition of the intergenerational conflict regarding the ideological definition of the terms *youth* and *youth culture* with the way in which these differing definitions are incorporated and represented by the music, fashion, magazine and advertising industries. While each of these industries plays a significant part in preserving notions of youth for respective post-war generations, popular music, as the sonic underpinning for each successive era in post-war youth cultural history, arguably plays the most significant role in the nostalgic perpetuation of youthful sensibilities from the 1950s onwards.

Without a doubt, one of the single most important events in recent popular music history was the development of the compact disc. The CD was something of a double-edged sword as far as the music industry was concerned. On the one hand, it allowed for a form of musical reproduction more faithful to the sound of the original performance, containing none of the white noise associated with other kinds of recorded product such as vinyl records and analogue cassette tapes (Shuker 1994). At the same time, CD production also legitimized the wholesale reissuing of back catalogue material from a vast array of rock and pop artists stretching back to the 1950s (Burnett 1996). Indeed, in some cases, the releasing of CD reissues could be timed in such a way that they took on an enhanced sense of cultural significance for those who had been around when the album or albums in question were originally released as vinyl product. For example, in 1987 when the first Beatles' music was released on CD, the following EMI Records British press release appeared:

> The big Beatles year of 1987, in which both the twentieth anniversary of the legendary album Sgt. Pepper's Lonely Hearts Club Band and the twenty-fifth anniversary of the group's signing to EMI records and its first single 'Love Me Do' are being celebrated, gets underway in fine style with the first official release of the Beatles' music on compact disc (EMI Records UK press release, February 1987).
>
> (Savage 1988: 163)

As Savage (1988) points out, there is a firm economic rationale behind such marketing strategies. The music industry is now confronted with the dual problem of high youth unemployment and a declining number of teenagers. The result of this situation is that the 'teenage' market, the target for popular culture products from the mid-1950s through to the late 1970s, is now a less lucrative proposition for the music industry and related popular cultural industries who focus increasingly on the more affluent 25 to 45 year age bracket. As Savage notes:

> This age bracket is employed, often 'up-scale', and has already been trained to consume in the period of teenage's greatest outreach. The consumers of those products marked teenage in the commodity market-place are now . . . not teenaged but middle aged.
>
> (Savage 1988: 167)

A similar observation is made by Redhead (1990), who, in attempting to account for the longevity of the appeal of rock artists 'who first built their styles and reputations' during the 1960s and 1970s, suggests that:

> Rock is ageing and maturing with its audience. The massive future potential of rock's global audience is not only in new markets in near-virginal pop territory (China, the Soviet Union, the Eastern bloc, Africa) but in the obvious hold it has over its original generation.
>
> (Redhead 1990: 21)

Redhead's comments regarding the ability of rock, supported by the CD and other recent technological innovations such as video, digital video disc (**DVD**) and mini-disc, to retain its ageing babyboomer audience are given further credence in a review by music journalist Ellen (1996) of a concert in London's Hyde Park during 1996 featuring Bob Dylan, Eric Clapton and The Who. Describing the concert audience, Ellen (1966: 110) noted that, 'for every guitar-toting hippy in an ethnic weave there's a hamper-laden family of four savouring a fresh baguette and a ripe French cheese'. Ellen's description captures perfectly a scenario in which middle aged, middle class professional couples continue to support their generational 'icons', using opportunities such as the Hyde Park concert to share their musical heritage, and the nostalgic moments it inspires, with their own children.

Perhaps the ultimate exercise in rock nostalgia was the release, in November 1995, of 'Free as a Bird'. Advertised as the first new Beatles' song for 25 years, 'Free as a Bird' was originally written by John Lennon in his New York apartment during the late 1970s. Lennon made a rough recording of the song, featuring piano and vocal, and subsequently shelved it along with other private home recordings made during this period. Following Lennon's murder on 8 December 1980, the tapes lay untouched for a number of years. However, in 1994, business and personal disputes settled, Lennon's widow Yoko Ono gave fellow Beatle Paul McCartney a copy of the tape containing 'Free as a Bird'. McCartney and the two other surviving Beatles, George Harrison and Ringo Starr, later transformed the song into a new Beatles' single adding their own instruments and voices to Lennon's vocal and re-recording his original piano track (see Burns 2000: 180). 'Free as a Bird' also became the first Beatles track to use a promotional video, which considerably enhanced the song's power to evoke nostalgic memories among middle aged Beatles fans. Commenting on the 'Free as a Bird' video, Burns (2000: 180–1) notes how it draws on 'nostalgia' and 'contrast' in its 'recapitulati[on] of the Beatles' career'. Burns continues:

the video conveys a strong sense of contrast between present and past. The present is the bird and McCartney's nearby voice. The past is what the bird sees and Lennon's distant voice. Mediating the two tenses is much of the Liverpool footage from the TV series [*The Beatles Anthology*].[1] It appears that all the footage of the Beatles is old. They reappear throughout the video, moving from one location to the next more quickly than is possible, thereby reminding us that they may still be wizards and that the dream is still not over.

(Burns 2000: 181)

A 'golden age' of youth

In his book *Hooligan: A History of Respectable Fears*, Pearson (1983) uses the term **golden age** as a means of describing how social attitudes towards crime are coloured by romantic notions of the past. Pearson (1983: 7) argues that the past 'is lovingly remembered as a time of harmony . . . [as] a "golden age" of order and security'. Partly due to the forms of nostalgic representation noted above, a parallel process can be seen in relation to postwar youth culture, particularly among the 'sixties' generation where there is a tendency to romanticize the extent of the social and political activism deemed to have characterised the decade. This in turn promotes belief in a youth cultural 'golden age' as babyboomer writers and journalists reminisce about their youth, using this as a yardstick by which to compare the youth of the present day. An article by Young (1985) entitled 'The shock of the old' which appeared in the journal *New Society* is a case in point. According to Young:

> The term 'youth culture' is at best, of historical value only, since the customs and mores associated with it have been abandoned by your actual young person . . . The point is that today's teenager is no longer promiscuous, no longer takes drugs, and rarely goes to pop concerts. He leaves all that to the over-25's . . . Whatever the image adopted by teenagers now, it has to have one necessary condition: it must have nothing to do with being a teenager.
>
> (Young 1985: 246)

In many ways, such sentiments lament the 'end of youth culture' (Redhead 1990) by a babyboomer generation who believe themselves to be more youthful than present day youth. As Ross observes:

> an entire parental generation [is] caught up in the fantasy that they are themselves still youthful, or at least more culturally radical, in ways once equated with youth, than the youth of today . . . It is not just Mick Jagger and Tina Turner who imagine themselves to be eighteen years old and steppin' out; a significant mass of baby boomers partially act out this belief in their daily lives.
>
> (Ross 1994: 8)

Generation X

In addition to perpetuating the nostalgic myths which increasingly circulate about youth and music during the 1960s, such sentiments also contribute to what Epstein (1998: 1) describes as the 'narrow ideation' of contemporary youth. This is evidenced, for example, in the appearance of terms such as **Slacker** and 'Generation X' during the 1980s as a means of describing the allegedly apolitical and disaffected youth of that decade. For several years, the British newspaper the *Sunday Times* contained a weekly feature entitled

'Generation X'. In the following extract from the feature, journalist Forrest (1994) criticizes mid-1990s British youth TV programmes such as *Passengers*, *Naked City* and *The Word*:

> Youth TV is so depressing because it keeps on trying to tell us we have some sort of youth culture when we know that Generation X has created nothing of value at all . . . What we have to be proud of, according to Channel 4, are men who eat maggots, dykes on bikes and girls who'll sit naked in a tub of baked beans to get on TV.
>
> (Forrest 1994: 17)

Forrest also refers to the absence of 1990s equivalents of *Oz* magazine[2] and Sid Vicious, the use of such icons being intended to mark out the considered political stance of youth in the 1960s and 1970s in comparison with the allegedly apolitical and generally apathetic youth TV audiences in the 1990s. A similar representation of contemporary youth is evident in a study by Best and Kellner (1998) focusing on the popular US adult cartoon TV series *Beavis and Butthead*, which, they argue, graphically portrays the apathy and disaffectedness of youth in contemporary postindustrial society. Best and Kellner observe that:

> Throughout much of the day, Beavis and Butt-Head sit on their shabby living-room couch watching television, especially music videos, which they criticize in terms of whether the videos are 'cool' or 'suck' . . . Beavis and Butt-Head revel in the absurd, attacking everything but the few fragments of media culture which they find to be cool. They have contempt for everyone, even for each other, as displayed in various episodes when they blithely leave one another to die by choking, drowning, shark attack, or some other painful death.
>
> (Best and Kellner 1998: 74, 75–6)

There are two main problems with such interpretations of contemporary youth. The first relates to the romanticism already noted in accounts which suggest that 'spectacular' and politicized cultures of youth from a previous post-war era, typically the 1960s, have given way to a generation of disaffected 'couch potatoes'. If such spectacular style and radical political sensibilities were evident in former generations of youth, then it was most certainly only a spectacular and radical 'minority' who engaged in such activities.

Indeed, as early as the mid-1970s, Murdock and McCron (1976) argued that subcultural studies of youth, quite apart from the range of theoretical problems which can be associated with the concept of subculture (see Chapter 1), routinely overlooked the 'ordinary' majority of young people who did not become youth stylists. Even in the case of committed youth stylists it has been suggested that subcultural theorists' concept of spectacular 'resistance' (Hall and Jefferson 1976) is overly romantic. As Frith argues:

> The problem is to reconcile adolescence and subculture. Most working-class teenagers pass through groups, change identities, play their leisure roles for fun; other differences between them – sex, occupation, family – are much more significant than distinctions of style. For every youth 'stylist' committed to a cult as a full-time creative task, there are hundreds of working-class kids who grow up in a loose membership of several groups and run with a variety of gangs. There's a distinction here between a vanguard and a mass, between uses of leisure *within* subcultures.
>
> (Frith 1983: 219–20, original emphasis)

The second problem with terms such as Generation X, and the discourses which they set in motion, is their attempt to apply a rhetoric of youthful defiance and revolutionary spirit rooted in the socio-political atmosphere of the middle to late 1960s to conditions in contemporary western society. Such an application blatantly ignores the huge socio-economic upheavals that have taken place in the west since the 1960s. As Lipsitz observes:

> Contemporary discussions of youth culture seem particularly plagued by memories of the 1960s – as if nothing significant has happened over the past twenty years. To be sure, the 1960s deserve recognition as a decade when young people active in the civil rights movement, in student protest groups, in antiwar activity, and in the emergence of the women's liberation took history into their own hands and provoked substantive changes in society at large. But the enduring hold of the 1960s on the imagination of the present has been pernicious.
>
> (Lipsitz 1994b: 17)

Lipsitz goes on to suggest that the preoccupation of contemporary commentators on youth culture with the events of the 1960s is such that it becomes hard not to sympathize with the 'National Association for the Advancement of Time', a Pennsylvania-based protest group founded during the early 1990s in an attempt to end all nostalgia concerning politicized youth movements of the 1960s. Youth culture, argues Lipsitz, is not a static or one-dimensional phenomenon. The character of youth culture is, to a very great extent, moulded and shaped by the social events taking place around it. Contemporary youth culture is faced with different issues and is driven by different needs and desires to those which appeared important during the 1960s, and the way in which we attempt to examine and evaluate contemporary youth culture must take account of this fact. As Lipsitz argues:

If we are to understand, address and redress the conditions facing young people today, we have to acknowledge the new realities that confront them, and we have to reject analyses of youth that rely on outdated and obsolete concepts.

(Lipsitz 1994b: 17)

A further criticism of the way in which contemporary youth are often represented by members of the babyboomer generation is offered by Grossberg (1994). Grossberg is particularly critical of the term 'Generation X' and its labelling of contemporary youth as disaffected and apolitical. According to Grossberg, Generation X

are presented as marking a new generation gap, one defined against the baby boomers. Their identity crisis seems to be defined not within their experience (for within their experience they have no identity crisis) but rather within the experience of the baby boomers, who seem to have a desperate need and a total inability to identify them. Generation X seems to exist in a space of common terror at the ability to name, to understand the next generation. This is the Reagan youth, but it is also the grungers, the rappers and the American punks!

(Grossberg 1994: 53)

In his closing observation, Grossberg makes a fundamentally important point concerning the danger of over-romanticizing past eras of post-war youth cultural history as being more radical and politically active than contemporary youth culture. As previous chapters of this book bear out, there are clear relations between contemporary youth musics and their attendant styles and the socio-economic conditions of late modern, postindustrial society. If the more politically orientated music of the 1960s and 1970s can be seen to resonate with social issues characterizing these eras, then the same can be said for contemporary youth musics such as rap and grunge. Such parallels, however, appear either invisible or irrelevant to the babyboomer generation. Indeed, babyboomer beliefs concerning the apathetic and self-destructive nature of contemporary youth have, in turn, engendered a series of negativizing discourses concerning contemporary youth musics which have resulted in stringent attempts to censor young people's access to particular types of music. This is evidenced, for example, through the founding of organisations such as the Washington DC based Parents Music Resource Center (see Martin and Segrave 1993), which (as noted in Chapters 3 and 6) has campaigned extensively for the censoring of contemporary youth musics such as heavy metal and rap.

Although censorship has been a perennial aspect of post-war popular music from rock 'n' roll to punk (see Chapters 1 and 4), the active involvement of parents in the censorship of popular music is indicative of an increasing concern to block or ban young peoples' access to particular songs or musical styles. Such action centres around the belief that, for example, the violent and misogynistic overtones of rap and metal lyrics put young people at risk (Shuker 1994). Problematically, however, such attitudes towards contemporary youth musics suggest that music can be 'heard' only in prescribed ways and that it is essentially 'pre-programmed' to elicit particular responses from young listeners. Such a view takes no account of youth's ability to interpret musical texts for itself, preferring instead to cast young listeners in the role of cultural dupes. Similarly, and more problematically, this attitude towards contemporary youth music does little to engage with the wider public's indifference to the social circumstances that face today's youth and inform the everyday settings in which they choose for particular styles of music. Young people's appropriations of musical styles and their use of musical and stylistic resources as ways of making sense of everyday life must be seen against a backdrop of postindustrialization and related problems such as rising youth unemployment, the casualization of labour and the resurgence of fascism in countries throughout the world.

Consequently, to return to Grossberg's (1994) observations regarding contemporary US youth, current youth musics such as rap, punk and grunge, together with the youth cultural followings they have generated, are clearly both a product of and response to current socio-economic conditions in the US. Following the domination of the Reagan and Bush administrations' New Right politics during the 1980s and early 1990s, the belief in radical social and political ideology as a key to effecting change, which inspired the counter-cultural movements of the 1960s, has largely disappeared. As Grossberg (1994: 53) points out, among contemporary US youth there is a tendency 'to keep everything at a distance, to treat everything ironically'. Such sentiments are often to be heard in the lyrics of rap and grunge songs and have also manifested themselves in the social practices of slackers and homeboys. Indeed, in relation to rap, hip hop culture as a whole can be seen as a reaction towards the socio-economic circumstances in which young hip hoppers find themselves. As Rose observes:

> Substantial postindustrial shifts in economic conditions, access to housing, demographics and communication networks were crucial to the formation of the conditions which nurtured the cultural hybrids and socio-political tenor of hip hop's lyrics and music.
>
> (Rose 1994b: 73)

Although Rose is focusing here primarily on the US, as illustrated in Chapter 6 parallel scenarios are to be found across western Europe.

Socio-economic austerity, and its particular bearing on the youth of ethnic minorities, has resulted in the development and growth of local hip scenes in countries such as Germany, France and Britain.

Current interpretations of youth as Generation X are often similarly insensitive to the considerable socio-political significance of the British rave and post-rave scenes. The huge gatherings and 'party atmosphere' associated with the early 'illegal' raves can be seen as a direct response on the part of youth to the economic downturn of the late 1980s and early 1990s and its impact on the life chances of young people (Hemment 1998; Rietveld 1998). Moreover (as examined in Chapter 8), the rave and post-rave scenes have also been responsible in part for the formation of 'new social movements', such as the Anti-Road Protest and 'Reclaim the Streets' (Jordan 1998), which engage in proactive campaigns to protect the environment. Other movements associated with the rave and post-rave scenes have attempted to construct alternative lifestyles. For example, New Age hippies promote a back-to-the-land ethos 'shunning much . . . modern technology and materialism and identifying with ancient as opposed to modern freedoms associated with nomadism, the carnival atmosphere of the festival and ancient peasant common land rites' (Hetherington 1998: 334).

Conclusion

During the course of this final chapter, I have sought to examine how the concept of 'youth' has increasingly become the site of conflicting discourses concerning the nature of youth and what it means to be young. In analysing this issue, I have considered how post-war generations are able to hold on to their perceptions of youth and to engage in nostalgic representations with the help of the popular culture industries which continue to market music, styles and various forms of memorabilia to an ageing babyboomer audience. I then considered how such nostalgic notions of youth have also been used as a means of analysing and discussing contemporary youth and have resulted in the coining of terms such as 'Generation X'. In addition to perpetuating romantic myths concerning previous generations of youth, I argued here that such terms overlook the fact that youth culture, and the musics and styles associated with it, cannot be separated from the particular socio-economic circumstances of its time. If contemporary youth is socio-economically contextualized, I have suggested, then, as with previous generations of post-Second World War youth, it can be seen to use musical and stylistic resources to actively engage with, protest against and collectively negotiate the particular socio-economic and political circumstances in which it finds itself.

Notes

1 *The Beatles Anthology* was a six part documentary series first shown on ITV (British Independent TV channel) in early 1996. The series covered the history of the Beatles from their formation during the mid-1950s to their breakup in 1970.
2 *Oz* was a leading magazine of the British underground press during the mid to late 1960s and a regular commentator on socio-political issues (see Fountain 1988).

Further reading

Best, S. and Kellner, D. (1998) Beavis and Butt-Head: no future for postmodern youth, in J.S. Epstein (ed.) *Youth Culture: Identity in a Postmodern World*. Oxford: Blackwell.

Burns, G. (2000) Refab four: Beatles for sale in the age of music video, in I. Inglis (ed.) *The Beatles, Popular Music and Society: A Thousand Voices*. London: Macmillan.

Epstein, J.S. (1998) Introduction: Generation X, youth culture and identity, in J.S. Epstein (ed.) *Youth Culture: Identity in a Postmodern World*. Oxford: Blackwell.

Grossberg, L. (1992) *We Gotta Get Out of This Place: Popular Conservatism and Postmodern Culture*. London: Routledge (Chapter 7).

Grossberg, L. (1994) Is anybody listening? Does anybody care? On talking about 'The State of Rock', in A. Ross and T. Rose (eds) *Microphone Fiends: Youth Music and Youth Culture*. London: Routledge.

Lipsitz, G. (1994) We know what time it is: race, class and youth culture in the nineties, in A. Ross and T. Rose (eds) *Microphone Fiends: Youth Music and Youth Culture*. London: Routledge.

Martin, L. and Segrave, K. (1993) *Anti-Rock: The Opposition to Rock 'n' Roll*. New York: Da Capo.

Redhead, S. (1990) *The End-of-the-Century Party: Youth and Pop towards 2000*. Manchester: Manchester University Press (Chapter 1).

Ross, A. (1994) Introduction, in *Microphone Fiends: Youth Music and Youth Culture*. London: Routledge.

Savage, J. (1988) The enemy within: sex, rock and identity, in S. Frith (ed.) (1990) *Facing the Music: Essays on Pop, Rock and Culture*, 2nd edn. London: Mandarin.

GLOSSARY

Acid house: the term given by the media to the explosion of house music in British clubs during the late 1980s and the association of house with **Ecstasy**, a newly available amphetamine-based stimulant.

Acid rock: the term given to the music of 1960s groups such as the Grateful Dead and the Jefferson Airplane, whose long improvised performances and unusual musical sounds and rhythms were believed to have been created under the influence of **LSD**.

Afrocentricism: the ideology underpinning the 'back to Africa' beliefs of Rastafarianism and subsequently appropriated by other black cultural forms, notably elements of hip hop. Afrocentricism rejects western notions of history and evolution, arguing that the real origins of western civilization are to be found in the ancient civilizations of North Africa – Egypt and Nubia.

Androgyny: the act of blurring gender divisions through cross-dressing, the feminization of the male body or the masculinization of the female body.

Anti-Road Protest: a movement which developed in part from the early British illegal dance party scene. Protesters occupy land designated for redevelopment as roads and bypasses, digging intricate systems of tunnels and building tree houses (see McKay 1996; Jordan 1998).

Babyboomer: a person born during the period immediately following the end of the Second World War in 1945.

Back-masking: technique whereby messages are recorded onto a master-track played backwards in the recording studio. When the tape is played forwards again, and the music transferred to disk, the messages are heard backwards thus disguising their content. During the 1980s, it was popularly believed that **heavy metal** bands, notably Judas Priest, had recorded subliminal messages on their records which, in the most extreme cases, had caused teenager listeners to commit suicide.

Balearic Beat: the local variation of house music played in Ibiza clubs during the 1980s.

Berlin Hausbesetzer-Szene: the politicized squatting scene in West Berlin during the 1980s.

Bhangra: originally a Punjabi folk music form, bhangra was modified by Asian musicians in Britain who combined it with aspects of western pop music to produce bhangra beat.

Bhangramuffin: combination of **bhangra** and **raggamuffin** styles, made popular by UK post-bhangra artist Apache Indian.

Black pride: ideology promoted by the US Black Power Movement of the mid to late 1960s which held that, following decades of oppression by white society, African Americans should take pride in their race, colour and heritage.

Blend mixing: style of DJing originally pioneered by US **house** music DJs where sections of existing vinyl records are seamlessly mixed together to produce musical pieces and ambient tonal textures.

Br-Asian: term introduced by Kaur and Kalra (1996) to describe new cultural sensibilities of Asian youth in Britain. According to Kaur and Kalra, these sensibilities are neither British nor Asian but signal a new cultural identity and a cultural space between British and Asian society.

Breakbeat: the technique employed by rap DJs of mixing two copies of a vinyl record on a twin-turntable record deck (see Back 1996).

Breakdance: an element of hip hop culture involving such 'street dance' techniques as 'body popping' and 'head spinning'.

Bricolage: originally associated with the Dadaist painters of the early 1900s, describes the way in which familiar everyday objects are used in unusual contexts in which they acquire surrealistic meanings. The term adopted by Hebdige (1979) in his analysis of punk rock style.

CBGBs: name of famous nightclub (now closed down) in New York where many of the 1970s New York punk/underground groups, such as the Talking Heads, the Ramones, Blondie, the Patti Smith Group and Television, played their early gigs.

Centri sociali: left wing youth centres established in Italy during the 1970s. In the 1980s a number of left-wing Italian hip hop groups emerged from *centri sociali*.

CD: compact disc.

CCCS: Centre for Contemporary Cultural Studies in Birmingham, England. The CCCS adapted the concept of **subculture** from the Chicago School to explain the meaning of style for post-war working class youth in Britain. According to the CCCS, working class youth appropriated style in strategies of resistance to both the ruling class ideology and to structural changes taking place in British society during the 1960s.

Chaos Tage: (translation chaos days). Annual punk gathering in Hannover, Germany during August.

Chicago School: a group of sociologists based at the University of Chicago during the 1920s and 1930s. The Chicago School were interested in formulating sociological theories of deviance, in opposition to the dominant psychological theories of the time, and are credited with the coining and introduction of the term **subculture**.

Club culture: a term introduced by Thornton (1995) to describe the stylistic sensibilities of contemporary dance club crowds.

Cock rock: term used to describe **heavy metal** artists whose lyrics, image and stage performance display machoistic and/or misogynistic traits.

Commune: shared or 'communal' living arrangement which characterised hippie culture of the mid to late 1960s. Communes could take the form of a shared household or a bigger concern, such as a farm. Most communes had relatively short lifespans though a few were successful and continue to this day, for example in North Wales (see Webster 1976).

Community discourse: a term introduced by Back (1996) to describe the way in which racial difference becomes less important between members of a 'community', for whom common experience of that community is centrally important. Significantly, argues Back, inasmuch as community discourse leads to racial tolerance, this is experienced only at a community level. In their judgements of racial groups outside of the community residents generally rely on conventional stereotypes and media reports.

Community radio station: a radio station established and run by amateur enthusiasts with a licence to broadcast over a short range, generally within the city or town where the station is based.

Counter-culture: term used to describe the hippie movement of the mid to late 1960s. According to sociologists and cultural theorists, the main differences between the counter-culture and **subcultures** were class and ideology. Subcultures were working class and their subversion amounted to spontaneous acts of deviance. The counter-culture was middle class and comprised middle class students whose understanding of political systems led to planned and sustained counter-hegemonic attacks on the power structures of society.

Country rock: a blend of country and rock music styles made popular during the 1970s by groups such as the Eagles and the Allman Brothers.

Cultural imperialism: the process by which global capitalism allows developed western nations to dominate the world, politically, economically and culturally (see Tomlinson 1991).

Cultural reterritorialization: a term introduced by Lull (1995) to describe the way in which aspects of global popular culture are appropriated in particular everyday contexts where they take on locally specific meanings.

Daytimer: daytime discos organised for young Asians in Britain during the 1980s. Due to restrictions placed on their leisure time by parents, young Asians were generally forbidden to leave the family home in the evening in order to go to nightclubs.

Dead Heads: name given to fans of the US psychedelic rock group the Grateful Dead (see Sardiello 1994).

Deflected racism: a term introduced by Jones (1988) to describe the way in which white youth who appropriate black style are sometimes subjected to racist remarks and attacks by other white youth.

Diaspora: a term originally used to describe the geographical dispersion of the Jews after their exile from Babylon. The term has since gained a much wider application and is now used to describe any race or peoples who, because of a whole range of circumstances such as exile or slavery or, more recently, economically motivated emigration, have become globally dispersed across a range of geographical locations (see Gilroy 1993).

DiY protest movement: protest movements which develop at the grassroots level, often by disempowered groups (see McKay 1998).

Dreadlocks: characteristic hairstyle of Rastafarians where individual strands of hair are bound together into thicker, knotted lengths referred to as 'dreads'.

DVD: digital video disc.

Ecstasy: an amphetamine based stimulant introduced in Britain during the late 1980s where it was typically consumed by young house and techno fans as a means of building up their physical stamina for all night **raves** and dance parties (see Saunders 1995).

Extreme metal: covers the range of heavy metal subgenres that have emerged since the mid-1980s, including 'thrash', 'speed', 'black' and 'doom' metal.

Feedback: humming or whining sound created when part of the electronic signal produced by an electric guitar played at high volume is fed back to the guitar through the amplifier. Many electric guitarists incorporate controlled feeback sounds into their playing style.

Female exscription: a term introduced by Walser (1993) to describe the way in which heavy metal bands exclude the 'threat' of women to notions of masculinity by creating in their songs, videos and on album covers fantasy science fiction worlds from which women are absent and where survival depends upon male camaraderie.

Fetishization: a form of obsession, in this case with expensive items of fashion clothing, in which the object is held in esteem by the group because of the special meaning which it is collectively deemed to have.

Folk devil: a person or 'type' of person stigmatized by society as deviant and, thus, to be feared and avoided. In pre-industrial times folk devils were created by communities. In industrialized societies folk devils are created by the mass media (see Cohen 1987).

Fusion: term used to refer to the combining or fusing together of different musical styles. In this case, refers to fusing of **bhangra** with contemporary forms of western dance music, for example, **house** and **techno**.

Garage band: synonymous with the US garage band scene of the mid-1960s. Garage bands were comprised of young, inexperienced musicians with rudimentary musical skills. Most garage bands performed at local High School dances, usually recording one or two singles before disbanding.

Generation X: the term applied to the post-**babyboomer** US youth of the 1980s. Denotes the apolitical, disaffected attitude often associated with the youth of this period. See also **Slacker**.

Ghetto blaster: originally a custom built music playback system comprising a cassette recorder connected to more powerful speakers and a battery supply. The ghetto blaster was designed to be carried on the shoulder, allowing for the owner to take on the role of neighbourhood DJ. Ghetto blasters were also used to provide music for **breakdancing**. As ghetto blasters increased in popularity, commercially produced versions became available.

GIT: Guitar Institute of Technology. The GIT specializes in the teaching of contemporary rock, pop and fusion guitar styles. Founded in Los Angeles, the GIT is now a global concern.

Glam: short for 'glam rock', a phenomenon of the early 1970s. Glam rock artists wore heavy make-up, jewellery and stage costumes designed to blur or confuse their gender identity. In the mid-1980s, glam was periodically revived by 'glam metal' artists such as Mötley Crüe and Poison (see Walser 1993).

Globalization: the process by which globally exported information, capital, resources, images and goods, generally from the west, are said to result in a flattening out process as indigenous local cultures are subsumed by a unified global culture.

Golden age: nostalgic references to the past as a time of harmony and order.

Graffiti: the use of spray paint to write or paint pictures in public spaces or on public transport. An element of hip hop culture.

Gramophone: an early form of disc sound recording.

Haight-Ashbury: a bohemian district of San Francisco which became famous during the mid-1960s due to its associations with hippie culture.

Happenings: multimedia events of the hippie era featuring light shows, avant garde films, live music, **tape loops** and lurid posters. Happenings were made popular by Ken Kesey who used these events as a means of bringing young people together and handing out free **LSD** during his infamous mid-1960s acid tests (see Wolfe 1968).

Heavy metal: a guitar-based music incorporating repeated sequences of notes ('riffs') inspired by blues and heavily amplified.

Hegemony: a term introduced by Italian Marxist Antonio Gramsci. According to Gramsci the ruling class possessed not only the means of production but also the ruling ideas, that is to say, the ruling hegemony.

Hip hop: the wider street-cultural form of which **rap** is one aspect, the other aspects being **graffiti** and **breakdance**.

Hip hop nationalism: a term introduced by Decker (1994) to describe the appropriation by elements of African American hip hop culture of the political ideology expressed by the 1960s Black Power Movement.

Hippies: a youth cultural group of the mid-late 1960s whose preference for psychedelic music and hallucinogenic drugs, such as LSD, was linked with a desire to achieve a higher level of consciousness and transcend the material world.

Homology: a term used by Willis (1978) to explain the meaning and significance of youth cultural style. According to Willis, meanings were homologically precoded in items of fashion particular to certain youth cultural groups.

House: a style of contemporary dance music, which involved the mixing of sound textures from different sources. House was pioneered in the gay clubs of Chicago, notably the Warehouse, and quickly became the preferred music at 'house parties' in the Chicago area.

Indobands: groups comprising Indonesian immigrants in Holland playing a style of music based on 'rock 'n' roll'. Indobands were hugely popular, both in Holland and Germany, from the mid-1950s through to the early 1960s when their appeal began to fade and **Merseybeat** took over.

Lifestyle: originally developed by Weber to describe the aesthetic meaning of leisure commodities as symbols of status, lifestyle subsequently became a term associated with market research. It has recently re-emerged in social and cultural theory as a means of studying power and meaning in contemporary patterns of consumption.

Little Englandism: a discourse of English national identity which rejects issues of multiculturalism and harks back to an idealized, 'white' past.

LSD: Lysergic Acid Diethylamide, a synthetic hallucinogenic drug invented during the 1930s by Swiss chemist Dr Albert Hoffman. Popularized during the 1960s by Timothy Leary (a former Harvard professor sacked because of his promotion of LSD) and Ken Kesey who toured the US in the 'magic bus' conducting 'acid tests' (see Wolfe 1968).

Mela: a traditional Asian festival featuring music and dance. Melas are held annually in British cities with Asian populations.

Merseybeat: a term given to the sound and songwriting style of Liverpool groups such as the Searchers and Gerry and the Pacemakers.

MIDI: Musical Instrument Digital Interface, a technique which allows for a number of electronic instruments, typically keyboards, to be linked together and triggered by the playing of one instrument.

Misogyny: hatred of women. Often expressed in rap and heavy metal music through accounts of violence or cruelty towards women.

Moral panic: situation of public unrest generated by the mass media's concentration upon and representation of a particular social group or action as a problem.

Neo-Greenism: recent revival of interest in the protection of the natural environment.

Neo-tribe: a term introduced by Maffesoli (1996) to explain the character of contemporary social crowds and gatherings as inherently fragile, temporal and fluid.

New Age Traveller: a person who rejects the dominant institutions of late modern society and opts for a rural, nomadic lifestyle. Often associated with **neo-Greenism** and eco-politics.

New social movement: recent forms of mass protest which exist outside the sphere of institutionalized politics. Examples of new social movements in Britain include **Reclaim the Streets** and the **Anti-Road Protest**.

Pedagogical: teaching/training which, in addition to the imparting of practical skills, also stresses the importance of social and personal skills development.

Phonograph: an early form of sound recording using cylinders.

Pick-up: a small magnetic device positioned under the strings of an electric guitar and electric bass guitar. The pick-up transforms the acoustic sound of the strings into an electronic signal which is then boosted in volume by an amplifier. Developments in technology during the 1980s and 1990s led to the developments of pick-ups for acoustic guitars, brass, woodwind and most other musical instruments.

Play-along CDs: compact discs produced to enable musicians to practise in a simulated band situation.

PMRC: Parents Music Resource Center, founded in Washington DC in 1985 to monitor the lyrics of rap and rock music.

Polysemy: a term originally associated with works of art, used by Hebdige (1979) to describe the plurality of meanings which could be attached to aspects of the punk rock style.

Popular music: as used in this book, popular music refers to youth-orientated music, from the 1950s to the present day, which rely on technologies first developed during the post-Second World War period, notably tape recording, mass production and television, for their production and distribution.

Pork pie hat: short brimmed hat worn by black **rude boys** in Britain and subsequently appropriated by the white British mod culture.

Post-punk: name given to the period in British popular music between 1978 and 1981 which saw the emergence of new wave artists such as the Police, Elvis Costello and the Attractions and Squeeze.

Prague Spring: term given to the attempt in Spring 1968 by members of the Czechoslovak Communist Party, with considerable public support, to gain more control over domestic affairs without abandoning membership of the Warsaw Pact. This led to intervention of the Soviet Union and the invasion of Czechoslovakia by Soviet armed forces.

Progressive rock: a style of music made popular in the early 1970s by British groups such as Yes, Genesis and Emerson, Lake and Palmer. Progressive rock was characterised by its classical overtones, with emphasis upon shows of individual musicianship and reliance on technological effects.

Pub rock: a music scene centred around London pubs during the early 1970s. Pub rock groups rejected the musical and technological excesses of progressive rock, opting instead for short songs, uncomplicated musical arrangements and small venues allowing musicians to remain 'in touch' with their audiences. Many pub rock musicians were later to join or form punk bands.

Punk: a harmonically basic, guitar-driven style which emerged during the mid-1970s as a reaction to the increasingly complex and self-indulgent music of progressive rock groups such as Yes, Genesis and Emerson Lake and Palmer. Stylistically, punk employed visual shock tactics such as the wearing of dog collars, cheeks and noses pierced with safety pins and T-shirts with swastikas.

Ragga: short for **raggamuffin**.

Raggamuffin: Jamaican variation of **rap**, combining rap and **reggae** sounds.

Rap: a spoken lyric which uses the natural rhythmic qualities of the voice. Lyrics are 'rapped' over a **breakbeat,** produced by mixing two copies of a vinyl record together on a twin-turntable record player.

Rave: an event featuring 'house', 'techno' or other new dance music styles.

Reclaim the Streets: a form of environmental protest initiated during the 1990s where crowds of people occupy city streets, often turning them into spontaneous dance parties, in order to prevent their use by traffic.

Reggae: a bass-heavy style of music which originated from Jamaica. Reggae is characterized most distinctively by the guitar style, which features sharp, staccato downstrokes on the second and the fourth beat of the bar.

Retro-marketing: the marketing of popular cultural commodities, notably music and fashion and associated memorabilia, from previous decades.

Risk society: a term introduced by Beck (1992) to describe the uncertainty associated with contemporary everyday life as a result of, for example, unemployment, environmental hazards, rising crime rates and the threat to health from HIV and AIDS.

Rock Against Racism: a movement begun in the late 1970s by musicians concerned about rising levels of racism and racist violence in Britain.

Rock gegen Rechts: (translation: Rock Against the [far] 'Right'). German equivalent of Rock Against Racism.

Rockmobil: a mobile music-making project for young people based in various German cities in the state of Hessen (see Bennett 1998).

Rude boys: term given to youth gangs in Jamaica during the 1960s and the ska influenced music preferred by these gangs. Rude boy music and style was subsequently appropriated by young African Caribbeans living in Britain.

Sampling: the recording of sounds (musical, natural, industrial and so on) in a computer's memory for use in music composition and performance.

Ska: a quick tempo, Rhythm and Blues inspired musical style originating from Jamaica in which a driving horn section is juxtaposed with a high treble electric guitar featuring staccato chords played on the off-beat.

Slacker: a US term to describe the allegedly apolitical, disaffected youth of the 1980s (same meaning as **Generation X**).

Soft metal: a more melodic style of heavy metal, made popular during the mid-1980s by groups such as Bon Jovi. Soft metal combined a guitar-based sound of earlier heavy metal styles with rich harmonies, strings and keyboard sounds associated with mainstream pop.

Sound system: a large public address system, generally custom built to its owner's specifications, for the playing of music at dance events. Sound systems were originally associated with African Caribbean reggae parties (see Back 1996) although the term and concept were appropriated by white dance party organizers with the emergence of **rave** in the late 1980s.

Stadium rock: term given to music of 1970s groups such as Led Zeppelin, Emerson, Lake and Palmer and the Eagles. Despite the different styles of these groups, a common feature of each was that their live performances were large-scale, and sometimes theatrical, productions, which took place in sports stadiums capable of holding audiences of between 70,000 and 100,000 people.

Stagediving: the act of leaping off the stage into the arms of the audience below. Popular among male fans at heavy metal concerts.

Subcultural capital: a term introduced by Thornton (1995). Adapted from Bourdieu's (1984) concept of cultural capital, subcultural capital describes the way in which style of dress, knowledge of a particular genre of music, dancing ability and so on are used by young people as a means of demonstrating their membership of and 'status' within subcultural groups.

Subculture: term originally introduced by the **Chicago School,** and subsequently appropriated by the Birmingham CCCS, to describe a social group distinguished from the dominant society by its own normative structures, rules and, in the case of youth subcultures, style of dress and musical taste. See also **counter-culture.**

Swing Jugend: (translation: Swing Kids). Groups of young people in Germany and across occupied wartime Europe who gathered at illegal events featuring the music of American jazz artists such as Duke Ellington, Benny Goodman, Glenn Miller and Artie Shaw (see Willett 1989).

Tablature: a simplified system of notation for guitarists and bassists.

Tab websites: websites established by enthusiasts for the sharing of self-tabbed guitar and bass music.

Tam: a woven, loose fitting hat worn by Rastafarians.

Tape loop: a piece of tape with the ends joined (or spliced) together to form a loop. When the loop is played back on a tape machine the music or sounds contained on it are repeated in a continuous cycle. One of the early commercial uses of tape loops was on the Beatles' track 'Tomorrow Never Knows' (from the group's 1966 *Revolver* album). In more recent years the tape loop effect has been recreated using electronic sampling devices.

Techno: apart from **house,** probably the most well known style of contemporary dance music. Techno has its roots in the German band Kraftwerk's experiments with electronic music during the early 1970s. Sounds and musical sections from Kraftwerk recordings were subsequently used in club mixes by African American DJs in Detroit, the latter introducing the term 'techno'.

Technocracy: a term introduced by Roszak (1969) to describe contemporary society's increasing reliance on science and technology.

Tin Pan Alley: professional songwriting teams who composed many popular music hits of the 1950s and 1960s (see Shepherd 1982).

Top of the Pops: British popular music television show broadcast weekly since its inception in 1967.

White noise: the background hissing and/or humming sounds which accumulate on analogue multi-track recording tape from sources such as electronic instruments, microphones and sound processing effects.

Woodstock: officially titled the 'Woodstock Music and Art Fair', this was a three day festival held on farmland near the town of Woodstock in upstate New York during August 1969. Artists appearing at the festival included The Who, Janis Joplin, Santana and Jimi Hendrix. At the height of the festival there were said to be 500,000 people in attendance (see Young and Lang 1979).

Youth culture: term used to describe the musical, stylistic and broader leisure sensibilities of young people. Youth culture has conventionally been used in relation to people between the ages of 15 and 25 although the term youth is becoming increasingly problematic due to the increasing reach of **retro-marketing** and the desire of successive post-war generations to remain young.

REFERENCES

Andes, L. (1998) Growing up punk: meaning and commitment careers in a contemporary youth subculture, in J.S. Epstein (ed.) *Youth Culture: Identity in a Postmodern World*. Oxford: Blackwell.

Arnett, J. (1991) Heavy metal music and reckless behavior among adolescents, *Journal of Youth and Adolescence*, 20(6): 573–91.

Arnett, J.J. (1996) *Metal Heads: Heavy Metal Music and Adolescent Alienation*. Oxford: Westview.

Back, L. (1993) Race, identity and nation within an adolescent community in South London, *New Community*, 19(2): 217–33.

Back, L. (1996) *New Ethnicities and Urban Culture: Racisms and Multiculture in Young Lives*. London: UCL Press.

Bacon, T. (1991) *The Ultimate Guitar Book*. London: Dorling Kindersley.

Banerji, S. and Baumann, G. (1990) Bhangra 1984–8: fusion and professionalization in a genre of South Asian dance music, in P. Oliver (ed.) *Black Music in Britain: Essays on the Afro-Asian Contribution to Popular Music*. Buckingham: Open University Press.

Baumann, G. (1990) The re-invention of Bhangra: social change and aesthetic shifts in a Punjabi music in Britain, *Journal of the International Institute for Comparative Music Studies and Documentation*, 32(2): 81–95.

Baumann, G. (1997) Dominant and demotic discourses of culture: their relevance to multi-ethnic alliances, in P. Werbner and T. Modood (eds) *Debating Cultural Hybridity: Multi-Cultural Identities and the Politics of Anti-Racism*. London: Zed Books.

Bayton, M. (1988) How women become rock musicians, in S. Frith and A. Goodwin (eds) (1990) *On Record: Rock, Pop and the Written Word*. London: Routledge.

Beadle, J.J. (1993) *Will Pop Eat Itself? Pop Music in the Sound Bite Era*. London: Faber and Faber.

Beattie, G. (1990) *England After Dark*. London: Weidenfeld and Nicolson.

Beck, U. (1992) *The Risk Society*. London: Sage.

Bennett, A. (1997) Bhangra in Newcastle: music, ethnic identity and the role of local knowledge, *Innovation: European Journal of the Social Sciences*, 10(1): 107–16.

Bennett, A. (1998) The Frankfurt Rockmobil: a new insight into the significance of music-making for young people, *Youth and Policy*, 60: 16–29.

Bennett, A. (1999a) Subcultures or neo-tribes? Rethinking the relationship between youth, style and musical taste, *Sociology*, 33(3): 599–617.

Bennett, A. (1999b) Hip hop am Main: the localisation of rap music and hip hop culture, *Media, Culture and Society*, 21(1): 77–91.

Bennett, A. (1999c) Rappin' on the Tyne: white hip hop culture in Northeast England – an ethnographic study, *Sociological Review*, 47(1): 1–24.

Bennett, A. (2000) *Popular Music and Youth Culture: Music, Identity and Place*. London: Macmillan.

Bennett, H.S. (1980) *On Becoming a Rock Musician*. Amherst, MA: University of Massachusetts Press.

Berger, H.M. (1999) *Metal, Rock and Jazz: Perception and the Phenomenology of Musical Experience*. Hanover, NH: Wesleyan University Press.

Best, S. and Kellner, D. (1998) Beavis and Butt-Head: no future for postmodern youth, in J.S. Epstein (ed.) *Youth Culture: Identity in a Postmodern World*. Oxford: Blackwell.

Billig, M. (2000) *Rock 'n' Roll Jews*. Nottingham: Five Leaves.

Bjurström, E. (1997) The struggle for ethnicity: Swedish youth styles and the construction of ethnic identities, *Young: Nordic Journal of Youth Research*, 5(3): 44–58.

Black, J. (1998) The trial of Judas Priest, *Q Magazine*, 138, March: 60–1.

Blake, A. (1996) The echoing corridor: music in the postmodern East End, in T. Butler and M. Rustin (eds) *Rising in the East? The Regeneration of East London*. London: Lawrence and Wishart.

Bocock, R. (1993) *Consumption*. London: Routledge.

Bourdieu, P. (1984) *Distinction: A Social Critique of the Judgement of Taste* (trans. R. Nice). Cambridge, MA: Harvard University Press.

Bradley, D. (1992) *Understanding Rock 'n' Roll: Popular Music in Britain 1955–1964*. Buckingham: Open University Press.

Brake, M. (1985) *Comparative Youth Culture: The Sociology of Youth Cultures and Youth Subcultures in America, Britain and Canada*. London: Routledge and Kegan Paul.

Breen, M. (1991) A stairway to Heaven or a highway to Hell?: heavy metal rock music in the 1990s, *Cultural Studies*, 5(2): 191–203.

Bright, T. (1986) Pop music in the USSR, *Media, Culture and Society*, 8: 357–69.

Buckman, P. (1970) *The Limits of Protest*. London: Victor Gollancz.

Burnett, R. (1996) *The Global Jukebox: The International Music Industry*. London: Routledge.

Burns, G. (2000) Refab four: Beatles for sale in the age of music video, in I. Inglis (ed.) *The Beatles, Popular Music and Society: A Thousand Voices.* London: Macmillan.

Butler, D.E. and Rose, R. (1960) *The British General Election of 1959,* London: Frank Cass.

Byron, M. (1998) Migration, work and gender: the case of post-war Labour migration from the Caribbean to Britain, in M. Chamberlain (ed.) *Caribbean Migration: Globalised Identities.* London: Routledge.

Cagle, V.M. (1995) *Reconstructing Pop/Subculture: Art, Rock and Andy Warhol.* London: Sage.

Carlson, S., Luce, G., O'Sullivan, G. *et al.* (1989) *Satanism in America: How the Devil Got More than his Due.* El Cerrito, CA: Gaia Press.

Cashmore, E. (1983) *Rastaman: The Rastafarian Movement in England.* London: George Allen and Unwin.

Chambers, I. (1976) A strategy for living: black music and white subcultures, in S. Hall and T. Jefferson (eds) *Resistance through Rituals: Youth Subcultures in Post-War Britain.* London: Hutchinson.

Chambers, I. (1985) *Urban Rhythms: Pop Music and Popular Culture.* London: Macmillan.

Chaney, D. (1996) *Lifestyles.* London: Routledge.

Christgau, R. (1981) *Christgau's Record Guide.* New Haven, CT: Tickner and Fields.

Clarke, G. (1981) Defending ski-jumpers: a critique of theories of youth subcultures, in S. Frith and A. Goodwin (eds) (1990) *On Record: Rock, Pop and the Written Word.* London: Routledge.

Clarke, J. (1976) The Skinheads and the magical recovery of community, in S. Hall and T. Jefferson (eds) *Resistance through Rituals: Youth Subcultures in Post-War Britain.* London: Hutchinson.

Clarke, J., Hall, S., Jefferson, T. and Roberts, B. (1976) Subcultures, cultures and class: a theoretical overview, in S. Hall and T. Jefferson (eds) *Resistance through Rituals: Youth Subcultures in Post-War Britain.* London: Hutchinson.

Clecak, P. (1983) *America's Quest for the Ideal Self: Dissent and Fulfilment in the 60s and 70s.* Oxford: Oxford University Press.

Cobley, P. and Osgerby, W. (1995) 'Peckham Clan ain't nothin' to fuck with': urban rap style in Britain. Paper presented to conference, 'Youth 2000', University of Teesside, 19–23 July.

Cohen, P. (1972) *Subcultural Conflict and Working Class Community,* working papers in Cultural Studies 2. Birmingham: University of Birmingham.

Cohen, Stanley (1987) *Folk Devils and Moral Panics: The Creation of the Mods and Rockers,* 3rd edn. Oxford: Basil Blackwell.

Cohen, Sara (1991) *Rock Culture in Liverpool: Popular Music in the Making.* Oxford: Clarendon Press.

Comer, J. (1982) How can I use the Top Ten?, in G. Vulliamy and E. Lee (eds) *Pop, Rock and Ethnic Music in School.* Cambridge: Cambridge University Press.

Condry, I. (1999) The social production of difference: imitation and authenticity in Japanese rap music, in H. Fehrenbach and U. Poiger (eds) *Transactions, Transgressions, Transformations: American Culture in Western Europe and Japan.* Providence, RI: Berghahn.

Criminal Justice and Public Order Act 1994, Chapter 33. London: HMSO.

Crocker, C. (1993) *Metallica: The Frayed Ends of Metal.* London: Boxtree.

Davies, C.L. (1993) Aboriginal rock music: space and place, in T. Bennett, S. Frith, L. Grossberg, J. Shepherd and G. Turner (eds) *Rock and Popular Music: Politics, Policies, Institutions.* London: Routledge.

Decker, J.L. (1994) The state of rap: time and place in hip hop nationalism, in A. Ross and T. Rose (eds) *Microphone Fiends: Youth Music and Youth Culture.* London: Routledge.

Denisoff, R.S. (1972) Folk music and the American Left, in R.S. Denisoff and R.A. Peterson (eds) *The Sounds of Social Change.* Chicago: Rand McNally.

Denisoff, R.S. and Romanowski, W.D. (1991) *Risky Business: Rock in Film.* New Brunswick, NJ: Transaction.

Denski, S. and Scholle, D. (1992) Metal men and glamour boys: gender performance in heavy metal, in S. Craig (ed.) *Men, Masculinity and the Media.* Newbury Park, CA: Sage.

Dyer, R. (1979) In defense of disco, in S. Frith and A. Goodwin (eds) (1990) *On Record: Rock, Pop and the Written Word.* London: Routledge.

Dyson, M.E. (1996) *Between God and Gangsta Rap: Bearing Witness to Black Culture.* New York: Oxford University Press.

Easton, P. (1989) The rock music community, in J. Riordan (ed.) *Soviet Youth Culture.* Bloomington, IN: Indiana University Press.

Edelstein, A.J. (1985) *The Pop Sixties.* New York: World Almanac.

Ehrenreich, B., Hess, E. and Jacobs, G. (1992) Beatlemania: girls just want to have fun, in L.A. Lewis (ed.) *The Adoring Audience: Fan Culture and Popular Media.* London: Routledge.

Ellen, M. (1996) 1996 Hyde Park concert review, *Mojo*, August: 110–11.

Epstein, J.S. (1998) Introduction: Generation X, youth culture and identity, in J.S. Epstein (ed.) *Youth Culture: Identity in a Postmodern World.* Oxford: Blackwell.

Epstein, J.S., Pratto, D.J. and Skipper Jr, J.K. (1990) Teenagers, behavioral problems, and preferences for heavy metal and rap music: a case study of a southern middle school, *Deviant Behavior*, 11: 381–94.

Everitt, A. (1997) *Joining In: An Investigation into Participatory Music.* London: Calouste Gulbenkian Foundation.

Eyerman, R. and Jamison, A. (1998) *Music and Social Movements: Mobilizing Traditions in the Twentieth Century.* Cambridge: Cambridge University Press.

Fekete, L. (1993) Inside racist Europe, in T. Bunyan (ed.) *Statewatching the New Europe: A Handbook on the European State.* London: Statewatch.

Filippa, M. (1986) Popular song and musical cultures, in D. Forgacs and R. Lumley (eds) *Italian Cultural Studies: An Introduction.* Oxford: Oxford University Press.

Finnegan, R. (1989) *The Hidden Musicians: Music-Making in an English Town.* Cambridge: Cambridge University Press.

Flores, J. (1994) Puerto Rican and proud, boyee! Rap roots and amnesia, in A. Ross and T. Rose (eds) *Microphone Fiends: Youth Music and Youth Culture.* London: Routledge.

Fokken, H. (1993) Beobachtung aus der Arbeit einer Mädchenband, in W. Hering, B. Hill and G. Pleiner (eds) *Praxishandbuch Rockmusik in der Jugendarbeit.* Opladen: Leske und Budrich.

Foner, N. (1978) *Jamaica Farewell: Jamaican Migrants in London.* London: Routledge and Kegan Paul.

Fornäs, J., Lindberg, U. and Sernhade, O. (1995) *In Garageland: Rock, Youth and Modernity.* London: Routledge.

Forrest, E. (1994) Generation X, *Sunday Times*, 10 July: 17.

Fountain, N. (1988) *Underground: The London Alternative Press 1966–74.* London: Comedia/Routledge.

Fowler, D. (1992) Teenage consumers? Young wage-earners and leisure in Manchester, 1919–1939, in A. Davies and S. Fielding (eds) *Workers' Worlds: Cultures and Communities in Manchester and Salford, 1880–1939.* Manchester: Manchester University Press.

Friedlander, P. (1996) *Rock and Roll: A Social History.* Boulder, CO: Westview.

Friesen, B.K. and Epstein, J.S. (1994) Rock 'n' roll ain't noise pollution: artistic conventions and tensions in the major subgenres of heavy metal, *Popular Music and Society*, 18: 1–18.

Frith, S. (1980) Formalism, realism and leisure: the case of punk, in K. Gelder and S. Thornton (eds) (1997) *The Subcultures Reader.* London: Routledge.

Frith, S. (1981) The magic that can set you free: the ideology of folk and the myth of rock, *Popular Music*, 1: 159–68.

Frith, S. (1983) *Sound Effects: Youth, Leisure and the Politics of Rock.* London: Constable.

Frith, S. (1987) Towards an aesthetic of popular music, in R. Leppert and S. McClary (eds) *Music and Society: The Politics of Composition, Performance and Reception.* Cambridge: Cambridge University Press.

Frith, S. (1988a) *Music for Pleasure: Essays in the Sociology of Pop.* Oxford: Polity Press.

Frith, S. (1988b) Video pop: picking up the pieces, in S. Frith (ed.) (1990) *Facing the Music: Essays on Pop, Rock and Culture*, 2nd edn. London: Mandarin.

Frith, S. and McRobbie, A. (1978) Rock and sexuality, in S. Frith and A. Goodwin (eds) (1990) *On Record: Rock, Pop and the Written Word.* London: Routledge.

Frith, S. and Street, J. (1992) Rock against racism and red wedge: from music to politics, from politics to music, in R. Garofalo (ed.) *Rockin' the Boat: Mass Music and Mass Movements.* Boston, MA: South End Press.

Furlong, A. and Cartmel, F. (1997) *Young People and Social Change: Individualization and Risk in Late Modernity.* Buckingham: Open University Press.

Gaines, D. (1991) *Teenage Wasteland: Suburbia's Dead End Kids.* New York: HarperCollins.

Garofalo, R. (1992a) Understanding mega-events: if we are the world, then how do we change it?, in R. Garofalo (ed.) *Rockin' the Boat: Mass Music and Mass Movements*. Boston, MA: South End Press.

Garofalo, R. (ed.) (1992b) *Rockin' the Boat: Mass Music and Mass Movements*. Boston, MA: South End Press.

Geiling, H. (1995) 'Chaos-Tage' in Hannover: Vom Ereignis zum Mythos, *Vorgänge: Zeitschrift für Bürgerrechte und Gesellschaftspolitik*, 4: 1–6.

Geiling, H. (1996) *Das andere Hannover: Jugendkultur zwischen Rebellion und Integration in der Großstadt, Hannover*. Hannover: Offizin Verlag.

Gill, A. (1997) We can be heroes, *Mojo*, 41, April: 54–80.

Gillett, C. (1983) *The Sound of the City: The Rise of Rock and Roll*, 2nd edn, London: Souvenir Press.

Gilroy, P. (1993) *The Black Atlantic: Modernity and Double Consciousness*. London: Verso.

Gilroy, P. and Lawrence, E. (1988) *Two-tone Britain: white and black youth and the politics of anti-racism*, in P. Cohen and H.S. Bains (eds) *Multi-racist Britain*. Basingstoke: Macmillan.

Gleason, R.J. (1972) A cultural revolution, in R.S. Denisoff and R.A. Peterson (eds) *The Sounds of Social Change*. Chicago: Rand McNally.

Glock, C.Y. and Bellah, R.N. (1976) *The New Religious Consciousness*. London: University of California Press.

Gold, J. (1995) Why rap doesn't cut it live, in A. Sexton (ed.) *Rap on Rap: Straight-Up Talk on Hip-Hop Culture*. New York: Delta.

Gottlieb, J. and Wald, G. (1994) Smells like teen spirit: riot girls, revolution and women, in independent rock, in A. Ross and T. Rose (eds) *Microphone Fiends. Youth Music and Youth Culture*. London: Routledge.

Green, L. (1988) *Music on Deaf Ears: Musical Meaning, Ideology, Education*. Manchester: Manchester University Press.

Gross, R.L. (1990) Heavy metal music: a new subculture in American society, *Journal of Popular Culture*, 24(1): 119–29.

Grossberg, L. (1992) *We Gotta Get Out of This Place: Popular Conservatism and Postmodern Culture*. London: Routledge.

Grossberg, L. (1994) Is anybody listening? Does anybody care? On talking about 'The state of rock', in A. Ross and T. Rose (eds) *Microphone Fiends: Youth Music and Youth Culture*. London: Routledge.

Hafeneger, B., Stüwe, G. and Weigel, G. (1993) *Punks in der Großstadt Punks in der Provinz: Projektberichte aus der Jugendarbeit*. Opladen: Leske und Budrich.

Hall, S. (1968) *The Hippies: An American 'Moment'*. Birmingham: Centre for Contemporary Cultural Studies, University of Birmingham.

Hall, S. and Jefferson, T. (eds) (1976) *Resistance through Rituals: Youth Subcultures in Post-War Britain*. London: Hutchinson.

Halliday, F. (1969) Students of the world unite, in A. Cockburn and R. Blackburn (eds) *Student Power: Problems, Diagnosis, Action*. Harmondsworth: Penguin.

Harker, D. (1992) Still crazy after all these years: what *was* popular music in the 1960s?, in B. Moore-Gilbert and J. Seed (eds) *Cultural Revolution? The Challenge of the Arts in the 1960s*. London: Routledge.

Harpin, L. (1993) One continent under a groove, *ID: The Europe Issue*, 16 May: 58–60.

Harrell, J. (1994) The poetics of destruction: death metal rock, *Popular Music and Society*, 18(1): 91–107.

Harris, K. (2000) 'Roots?' The relationship between the global and the local within the extreme metal scene, *Popular Music*, 19(1): 13–30.

Harron, M. (1988) McRock: pop as a commodity, in S. Frith (ed.) (1990) *Facing the Music: Essays on Pop, Rock and Culture*, 2nd edn. London: Mandarin.

Haslam, D. (1997) DJ culture, in S. Redhead, D. Wynne and J. O'Connor (eds) *The Clubcultures Reader: Readings in Popular Cultural Studies*. Oxford: Blackwell.

Hebdige, D. (1976a) The meaning of Mod, in S. Hall and T. Jefferson (eds) *Resistance through Rituals: Youth Subcultures in Post-War Britain*. London: Hutchinson.

Hebdige, D. (1976b) Reggae, Rastas and Rudies, in S. Hall and T. Jefferson (eds) *Resistance through Rituals: Youth Subcultures in Post-War Britain*. London: Hutchinson.

Hebdige, D. (1979) *Subculture: The Meaning of Style*. London: Routledge.

Hebdige, D. (1987) *Cut 'n' Mix: Culture, Identity and Caribbean Music*. London: Routledge.

Hebdige, D. (1988) *Hiding in the Light: On Images and Things*. London: Routledge.

Hemment, D. (1998) 'Dangerous dancing and disco riots: the northern warehouse parties, in G. McKay (ed.) *DiY Culture: Party and Protest in Nineties Britain*. London: Verso.

Hering, W., Hill, B. and Pleiner, G. (1993) Rockmusik in der Jugendarbeit – eine Einführung, in W. Hering, B. Hill and G. Pleiner (eds) *Praxishandbuch Rockmusik in der Jugendarbeit*. Opladen: Leske und Budrich.

Hetherington, K. (1992) Stonehenge and its festival: spaces of consumption, in R. Shields (ed.) *Lifestyle Shopping: The Subject of Consumption*. London: Routledge.

Hetherington, K. (1998) Vanloads of uproarious humanity: New Age travellers and the utopics of the countryside', in T. Skelton and G. Valentine (eds) *Cool Places: Geographies of Youth Culture*. London: Routledge.

Hinds, E.J.W. (1992) The Devil sings the blues: heavy metal, gothic fiction and 'postmodern' discourse, *Journal of Popular Culture*, 26(3): 151–64.

Hobsbawm, E. (1983) Introduction: inventing traditions, in E. Hobsbawm and T. Ranger (eds) *The Invention of Tradition*. Cambridge: Cambridge University Press.

Hollands, R. (1995) *Friday Night, Saturday Night: Youth Cultural Identification in the Post-Industrial City*, working paper no. 2. Newcastle upon Tyne: Department of Social Policy, University of Newcastle.

Hosokawa, S. (1984) The Walkman effect, *Popular Music*, 4(4): 165–80.

Huq, R. (1996) Asian Kool? Bhangra and beyond, in S. Sharma, J. Hutnyk and A. Sharma (eds) *Dis-Orienting Rhythms: The Politics of the New Asian Dance Music*. London: Zed Books.

Huq, R. (1999) Living in France: the parallel universe of hexagonal pop, in A. Blake (ed.) *Living through Pop*. London: Routledge.

Jefferson, T. (1976) Cultural responses of the Teds: the defence of space and status, in S. Hall and T. Jefferson (eds) *Resistance through Rituals: Youth Subcultures in Post-War Britain*. London: Hutchinson.

Jenkins, R. (1983) *Lads, Citizens and Ordinary Kids: Working Class Youth Lifestyles in Belfast*. London: Routledge and Kegan Paul.

Jones, S. (1988) *Black Culture, White Youth: The Reggae Tradition from JA to UK*. London: Macmillan.

Jordan, J. (1998) The art of necessity: the subversive imagination of anti-road protest and reclaim the streets, in G. McKay (ed.) *DiY Culture: Party and Protest in Nineties Britain*. London: Verso.

Kaplan, E.A. (1987) *Rocking around the Clock: Music Television, Postmodernism and Consumer Culture*. London: Methuen.

Kaur, R. and Kalra, V.S. (1996) New paths for South Asian identity and creativity, in S. Sharma, J. Hutnyk and A. Sharma (eds) *Dis-Orienting Rhythms: The Politics of the New Asian Dance Music*. London: Zed Books.

Keith, M. and Pile, S. (1993) The politics of place, in M. Keith and S. Pile (eds) *Place and the Politics of Identity*. London: Routledge.

Keyes, C.L. (1991) Rappin' to the beat: rap music as street culture among African Americans. Doctoral thesis, Ann Arbor, MI: University Microfilms International.

Kotarba, J.A. (1994) The postmodernization of rock 'n' roll music: the case of metallica, in J.S. Epstein (ed.) *Adolescents and their Music: If It's Too Loud You're Too Old*. New York and London: Garland.

Kratz, U. (1994) Musikangebote in der Jugendarbeit – Konzeptionelle Ansätze, Problemstellungen und Praxisbeispiele, in J. Terhag (ed.) *Populäre Musik und Pädagogik: Grundlagen und Praxismaterialien*. Oldershausen: Institut für Didaktik populärer Musik.

Krüger, H.H. (1983) Sprachlose Rebellen? Zur Subkultur der 'Halbstarken' in den Fünfziger Jahren, in W. Breyvogel (ed.) *Autonomie und Widerstand: Zur Theorie und Geschichte des Jugendprotestes*. Essen: Rigidon.

Laing, D. (1985) *One Chord Wonders: Power and Meaning in Punk Rock*. Milton Keynes: Open University Press.

Laing, D. (1997) Rock anxieties and new music networks, in A. McRobbie (ed.) *Back to Reality: Social Experience and Cultural Studies*. Manchester: Manchester University Press.

Lancaster, B. (1992) Newcastle – capital of what?', in R. Colls and B. Lancaster (eds) *Geordies: Roots of Regionalism*. Edinburgh: Edinburgh University Press.

Langlois, T. (1992) Can you feel it? DJs and house music culture in the UK, *Popular Music*, 11(2): 229–38.

Lévi-Strauss, C. (1976) *The Savage Mind*. London: Weidenfeld and Nicolson.

Lewis, J. (1992) *The Road to Romance and Ruin: Teen Film and Youth Culture*. London: Routledge.

Lewis, W.F. (1993) *Soul Rebels: The Rastafari*. Prospect Heights, IL: Waveland Press.

Leys, C. (1983) *Politics in Britain: An Introduction*. London: Verso.

Lipsitz, G. (1994a) *Dangerous Crossroads: Popular Music, Postmodernism and the Poetics of Place*. London: Verso.

Lipsitz, G. (1994b) We know what time it is: race, class and youth culture in the nineties, in A. Ross and T. Rose (eds) *Microphone Fiends: Youth Music and Youth Culture*. London: Routledge.

Locher, D.A. (1998) The industrial identity crisis: the failure of newly forming subculture to identify itself, in J.S. Epstein (ed.) *Youth Culture: Identity in a Postmodern World*. Oxford: Blackwell.

Logan, N. and Woffinden, B. (eds) (1976) *The NME Book of Rock 2*. London: Wyndham.

Lull, J. (1992) Popular music and communication: an introduction, in J. Lull (ed.) *Popular Music and Communication*, 2nd edn. London: Sage.

Lull, J. (1995) *Media, Communication, Culture: A Global Approach*. Cambridge: Polity Press.

Macan, E. (1997) *Rocking the Classics: English Progressive Rock and the Counterculture*. Oxford: Oxford University Press.

McKay, G. (1996) *Senseless Acts of Beauty: Cultures of Resistance since the Sixties*. London: Verso.

McKay, G. (ed.) (1998) *DiY Culture: Party and Protest in Nineties Britain*. London: Verso.

McRobbie, A. (1980) Settling accounts with subcultures: a feminist critique, in S. Frith and A. Goodwin (eds) (1990) *On Record: Rock Pop and the Written Word*. London: Routledge.

McRobbie, A. (1994) *Postmodernism and Popular Culture*. London: Routledge.

McRobbie, A. and Garber, J. (1976) Girls and subcultures: an exploration, in S. Hall and T. Jefferson (eds) *Resistance through Rituals: Youth Subcultures in Post-War Britain*. London: Hutchinson.

Maffesoli, M. (1996) *The Time of the Tribes: The Decline of Individualism in Mass Society* (trans. D. Smith). London: Sage.

Malbon, B. (1999) *Clubbing: Dancing, Ecstasy and Vitality*. London: Routledge.

Malik, K. (1995) What *really* angers young Asians, *Independent on Sunday*, 25 June: 23.

Malyon, T. (1998) Tossed in the fire and they never got burned: the Exodus Collective, in G. McKay (ed.) *DiY Culture: Party and Protest in Nineties Britain*. London: Verso.

Manuel, P. (1993) *Cassette Culture: Popular Music and Technology in North India*. London: University of Chicago Press.

Marcus, G. (1972) A new awakening, in R.S. Denisoff and R.A. Peterson (eds) *The Sounds of Social Change*. Chicago: Rand McNally.

Marcus, G. (1977) *Mystery Train*. London: Omnibus Press.

Marks, A. (1990) Young, gifted and black: Afro-American and Afro-Caribbean music in Britain 1963–88, in P. Oliver (ed.) *Black Music in Britain: Essays on the Afro-Asian Contribution to Popular Music.* Buckingham: Open University Press.

Martin, B. (1998) *Listening to the Future: The Time of Progressive Rock.* Chicago: Open Court.

Martin, L. and Segrave, K. (1993) *Anti-Rock: The Opposition to Rock 'n' Roll.* New York: Da Capo.

Maxwell, I. (with Bambrick, N.) (1994) Discourses of culture and nationalism in contemporary Sydney hip hop, *Perfect Beat*, 2(1): 1–19.

Melechi, A. (1993) The ecstasy of disappearance, in S. Redhead (ed.) *Rave Off: Politics and Deviance in Contemporary Youth Culture.* Aldershot: Avebury.

Mercer, K. (1987) Black hair/style politics, in K. Gelder and S. Thornton (eds) (1997) *The Subcultures Reader.* London: Routledge.

Merchant, J. and MacDonald, R. (1994) Youth and the rave culture, ecstasy and health, *Youth and Policy*, 45: 16–38.

Middleton, R. (1990) *Studying Popular Music.* Buckingham: Open University Press.

Mitchell, T. (1996) *Popular Music and Local Identity: Rock, Pop and Rap in Europe and Oceania.* London: Leicester University Press.

Mitchell, T. (1998) Australian hip hop as a 'glocal' subculture. Paper presented to 'Ultimo Series' Seminar, University of Sydney, 18 March.

Moore, A.F. (1993) *Rock: The Primary Text – Developing a Musicology of Rock.* Buckingham: Open University Press.

Müller, T. (1993) 'Musikschulen' – Lehrmaterialien (nicht nur) für die Jugendarbeit: Gitarre, Baß, Tasteninstrumente, Schlagzeug/percussion, Songbücher/arrangement, in W. Hering, B. Hill and G. Pleiner (eds) *Praxishandbuch Rockmusik in der Jugendarbeit.* Opladen: Leske und Budrich.

Müller-Wiegand, I. (1990) Jugendliche als Punks in einer osthessischen Stadt: Untersuchung zu ihrer Selbstdefinition und Lebenslage. Unpublished diploma thesis (Educational Science), University of Frankfurt, Frankfurt/Main.

Mungham, G. and Pearson, G. (eds) (1976) *Working Class Youth Culture.* London: Routledge and Kegan Paul.

Murdock, G. and McCron, R. (1976) Youth and class: the career of a confusion, in G. Mungham and G. Pearson (eds) *Working-Class Youth Culture.* London: Routledge and Kegan Paul.

Mutsaers, L. (1990) Indorock: an early Eurorock style, *Popular Music*, 9(3): 307–20.

Nadelson, R. (1991) *Comrade Rockstar: The Search for Dean Reed.* London: Chatto and Windus.

Nasmyth, P. (1985) MDMA we're all crazy now, in R. Benson (ed.) (1997) *Nightfever: Club Writing in the Face 1980–1997.* London: Boxtree.

Negus, K. (1992) *Producing Pop: Culture and Conflict in the Popular Music Industry.* London: Edward Arnold.

Noys, B. (1995) Into the 'Jungle', *Popular Music*, 14(3): 321–32.

O'Sullivan, D. (1974) *Youth Culture.* London: Methuen.

Palmer, T. (1976) *All You Need is Love: The Story of Popular Music.* London: Futura.

Paynter, J. (1982) *Music in the Secondary School Curriculum: Trends and Developments in Class Music Teaching.* Cambridge: Cambridge University Press.

Pearson, G. (1976) Paki-bashing in a North-East Lancashire cotton town: a case study and its history, in G. Mungham and G. Pearson (eds) *Working Class Youth Culture.* London: Routledge and Kegan Paul.

Pearson, G. (1983) *Hooligan: A History of Respectable Fears.* London: Macmillan.

Peterson, R. (1990) Why 1955? Explaining the advent of rock music, *Popular Music,* 9(1): 97–116.

Pilkington, H. (1994) *Russia's Youth and its Culture: A Nation's Constructors and Constructed.* London: Routledge.

Pini, M. (1997) Women and the early British rave scene, in A. McRobbie (ed.) *Back to Reality: Social Experience and Cultural Studies.* Manchester: Manchester University Press.

Polhemus, T. (1997) In the supermarket of style, in S. Redhead, D. Wynne and J. O'Connor (eds) *The Clubcultures Reader: Readings in Popular Cultural Studies.* Oxford: Blackwell.

Pond, I. (1987) Features of Soviet Pop. Paper presented to UNESCO, conference, Delhi, July.

Potter, R. (1995) *Spectacular Vernaculars: Hip Hop and the Politics of Postmodernism.* Albany, NY: State University of New York Press.

Price, K. (1981) Black identity and the role of reggae, in D. Potter (ed.) *Society and the Social Sciences: An Introduction.* London: Routledge and The Open University.

Redhead, S. (1990) *The End-of-the-Century Party: Youth and Pop towards 2000.* Manchester: Manchester University Press.

Redhead, S. (ed.) (1993a) The politics of ecstasy, in S. Redhead (ed.) *Rave Off: Politics and Deviance in Contemporary Youth Culture.* Aldershot: Avebury.

Redhead, S. (1993b) The end of the end-of-the-century party, in S. Redhead (ed.) *Rave Off: Politics and Deviance in Contemporary Youth Culture.* Aldershot: Avebury.

Reich, C.A. (1971) *The Greening of America.* London: Allen Lane.

Reid, S.A., Epstein, J.S. and Benson, D.E. (1994) Living on a lighted stage: identity, salience, psychological centrality, authenticity, and role behavior of semi-professional rock musicians, in J.S. Epstein (ed.) *Adolescents and their Music: If It's Too Loud You're Too Old.* New York and London: Garland.

Reimer, B. (1995) Youth and modern lifestyles, in J. Fornäs and G. Bolin (eds) *Youth Culture in Late Modernity.* London: Sage.

Richards, C. (1998) *Teen Spirits: Music and Identity in Media Education.* London: UCL Press.

Richardson, J.T. (1991) Satanism in the courts: from murder to heavy metal, in J.T. Richardson, J. Best and D.G. Bromley (eds) *The Satanism Scare.* New York: Aldine de Gruyter.

Ricoeur, P. (1967/74) *The Conflict of Interpretations: Essays in Hermeneutics.* Evanston, IL: Northwestern University Press.

Rietveld, H. (1993) Living the dream, in S. Redhead (ed.) *Rave Off: Politics and Deviance in Contemporary Youth Culture*. Aldershot: Avebury.

Rietveld, H. (1997) The house sound of Chicago, in S. Redhead, D. Wynne and J. O'Connor (eds) *The Clubcultures Reader: Readings in Popular Cultural Studies*. Oxford: Blackwell.

Rietveld, H. (1998) Repetitive beats: free parties and the politics of contemporary DiY dance culture in Britain, in G. McKay (ed.) *DiY Culture: Party and Protest in Nineties Britain*. London: Verso.

Rimmer, D. (1985) *Like Punk Never Happened: Culture Club and the New Pop*. London: Faber and Faber.

Rose, T. (1994a) *Black Noise: Rap Music and Black Culture in Contemporary America*. London: Wesleyan University Press.

Rose, T. (1994b) A style nobody can deal with: politics, style and the postindustrial city in hip hop, in A. Ross and T. Rose (eds) *Microphone Fiends: Youth Music and Youth Culture*. London: Routledge.

Ross, A. (1994) Introduction, in A. Ross and T. Rose (eds) *Microphone Fiends: Youth Music and Youth Culture*. London: Routledge.

Roszak, T. (1969) *The Making of a Counter Culture: Reflections on the Technocratic Society and its Youthful Opposition*. London: Faber and Faber.

Ruddick, S. (1998) How 'homeless' youth sub-cultures make a difference, in T. Skelton and G. Valentine (eds) *Cool Places: Geographies of Youth Culture*. London: Routledge.

Russell, K. (1993) Lysergia suburbia, in S. Redhead (ed.) *Rave Off: Politics and Deviance in Contemporary Youth Culture*. Aldershot: Avebury.

Ryan, J. and Peterson, R.A. (2001) The guitar as artifact and icon: identity formation in the babyboom generation, in A. Bennett and K. Dawe (eds) *Guitar Cultures*. Oxford: Berg.

Samuel, R. (1988) Little Englandism today, *New Statesman and Society*, 1(20): 27–30.

Santiago-Lucerna, J. (1998) 'Frances Farmer will have her revenge on Seattle:' pan-capitalism and alternative rock, in J.S. Epstein (ed.) *Youth Culture: Identity in a Postmodern World*. Oxford: Blackwell.

Sapsford, R.J. (1981) Individual deviance: the search for the criminal personality, in M. Fitzgerald, G. McLennan and J. Pawson (eds) *Crime and Society: Readings in History and Theory*. London: Routledge and Kegan Paul.

Sardiello, R. (1994) Secular rituals in popular culture: a case study for Grateful Dead concerts and dead head identity, in J.S. Epstein (ed.) *Adolescents and their Music: If It's Too Loud, You're Too Old*. New York and London: Garland.

Saunders, N. (1995) *Ecstasy and the Dance Culture*. London: Nicholas Saunders/Turnaround and Knockabout.

Savage, J. (1988) The enemy within: sex, rock and identity, in S. Frith (ed.) (1990) *Facing the Music: Essays on Pop, Rock and Culture*, 2nd edn. London: Mandarin.

Savage, J. (1992) *England's Dreaming: Sex Pistols and Punk Rock*. London: Faber and Faber.

Shank, B. (1994) *Dissonant Identities: The Rock 'n' Roll Scene in Austin, Texas.* London: Wesleyan University Press.

Sharma, S. (1996) Noisy Asians or 'Asian noise'?, in S. Sharma, J. Hutnyk and A. Sharma (eds) *Dis-Orienting Rhythms: The Politics of the New Asian Dance Music.* London: Zed Books.

Sharma, S., Hutnyk, J. and Sharma, A. (eds) (1996) *Dis-Orienting Rhythms: The Politics of the New Asian Dance Music.* London: Zed Books.

Shearman, C. (1983) The inner light?, *The History of Rock*, 6(70): 1396–400.

Shepherd, J. (1982) *Tin Pan Alley.* London: Routledge and Kegan Paul.

Shields, R. (1992) The individual, consumption cultures and the fate of community, in R. Shields (ed.) *Lifestyle Shopping: The Subject of Consumption.* London: Routledge.

Shuker, R. (1994) *Understanding Popular Music.* London: Routledge.

Shumway, D. (1992) Rock and roll as a cultural practice, in A. DeCurtis (ed.) *Present Tense: Rock and Roll and Culture.* Durham, NC: Duke University Press.

Sion, P.A. (1998) Voices of resistance: Geraint Jarman and the roots of reggae in Welsh popular music, in T. Hautamäki and H. Järviluoma (eds) *Music on Show: Issues of Performance.* Tampere, Finland: Department of Folk Tradition, University of Tampere. Conference Proceedings of Eighth International Association for the Study of Popular Music International Conference, University of Strathclyde, 1–6 July 1995.

Skelton, T. and Valentine, G. (eds) (1998) *Cool Places: Geographies of Youth Culture.* London: Routledge.

Sloat, L.J. (1998) Incubus: male songwriters' portrayal of women's sexuality in pop metal music, in J.S. Epstein (ed.) *Youth Culture: Identity in a Postmodern World.* Oxford: Blackwell.

Smith, A. (1994) Some like it kool, *Sunday Times*, 10 July: 12–13.

Smith, R. and Maughan, T. (1997) *Youth Culture and the Making of the Post-Fordist Economy: Dance Music in Contemporary Britain*, Occasional Paper. London: Department of Social Policy and Social Science, Royal Holloway, University of London.

Snowman, D. (1968) *USA: The Twenties to Vietnam.* London: B.T. Batsford.

Snowman, D. (1984) *America since 1920.* London: Heinemann.

Spencer, J.M. (1997) A revolutionary sexual persona: Elvis Presley and the white acquiescence of black rhythms, in V. Chadwick (ed.) *In Search of Elvis: Music, Race, Art, Religion.* Boulder, CO: Westview.

Storey, J. (1997) *An Introduction to Cultural Theory and Popular Culture*, 2nd edn. Hemel Hempstead: Prentice Hall.

Storry, M. and Childs, P. (eds) (1997) *British Cultural Identities.* London: Routledge.

Straw, W. (1983) Characterizing rock music culture: the case of heavy metal, in S. Frith and A. Goodwin (eds) (1990) *On Record: Rock Pop and the Written Word.* London: Routledge.

Street, J. (1992) Shock waves: the authoritative response to popular music, in

D. Strinati and S. Wagg (eds) *Come on Down? Popular Media Culture in Post-War Britain*. London: Routledge.

Street, J. (1993) Local differences? Popular music and the local state, *Popular Music*, 12(1): 43–54.

Szemere, A. (1992) The politics of marginality: a rock musical subculture in socialist Hungary in the early 1980s, in R. Garofalo (ed.) *Rockin' the Boat: Mass Music and Mass Movements*. Boston, MA: South End Press.

Thompson, H.S. (1993) *Fear and Loathing in Las Vegas*. London: Flamingo.

Thornton, S. (1994) Moral panic, the media and British rave culture, in A. Ross and T. Rose (eds) *Microphone Fiends: Youth Music and Youth Culture*. London: Routledge.

Thornton, S. (1995) *Club Cultures: Music, Media and Subcultural Capital*. Cambridge: Polity Press.

Tomlinson, J. (1991) *Cultural Imperialism: A Critical Introduction*. London: Pinter.

Vestal, V. (1999) Breakdance, red eyed penguins, Vikings, grunge and straight rock 'n' roll: the construction of place in musical discourse in Rudenga, East Side Oslo, *Young: Nordic Journal of Youth Research*, 7(2): 4–24.

Vulliamy, G. and Lee, E. (eds) (1982) *Pop, Rock and Ethnic Music in School*. Cambridge: Cambridge University Press.

Waksman, S. (1999) *Instruments of Desire*. Cambridge, MA: Harvard University Press.

Walser, R. (1993) *Running with the Devil: Power, Gender and Madness in Heavy Metal Music*. London: Wesleyan University Press.

Webb, P. (2000) Hip hop as a global cultural phenomenon: the export of contradiction, complexity and dialogue. Paper presented to conference, 'Globalization, Culture and Everyday Life', Manchester Metropolitan University, 5–7 July.

Webster, C. (1976) Communes: a thematic typology, in S. Hall and T. Jefferson (eds) *Resistance through Rituals: Youth Subcultures in Post-War Britain*. London: Hutchinson.

Weinstein, D. (1991) *Heavy Metal: A Cultural Sociology*. New York: Lexington.

Weinstein, D. (1994) Expendable youth: the rise and fall of youth culture, in J.S. Epstein (ed.) *Adolescents and their Music: If It's Too Loud You're Too Old*. New York and London: Garland.

Whiteley, S. (1992) *The Space between the Notes: Rock and the Counter-Culture*. London: Routledge.

Whiteley, S. (2000) *Women and Popular Music: Sexuality, Identity and Subjectivity*. London: Routledge.

Willett, R. (1989) Hot swing and the dissolute life: youth, style and popular music in Europe 1939–49, *Popular Music*, 8(2): 157–63.

Willis, P. (1976) The cultural meaning of drug use, in S. Hall and T. Jefferson (eds) *Resistance through Rituals: Youth Subcultures in Post-War Britain*, London: Hutchinson.

Willis, P. (1978) *Profane Culture*. London: Routledge and Kegan Paul.

Willis, T. (1993) The lost tribes: rave culture, *Sunday Times*, 18 July: 8–9.

Wilmer, V. (1998) Skanking ahoy!, *Mojo*, 56, July: 55–7.

Wolfe, T. (1968) *The Electric Kool-Aid Acid Test*. New York: Bantam.

Young, J. and Lang, M. (1979) *Woodstock Festival Remembered*. New York: Ballantine.

Young, T. (1985) The shock of the old, *New Society*, 14 February: 246.

Zanetta, T. and Edwards, H. (1986) *Stardust: The Life and Times of David Bowie*. London: Michael Joseph.

Zolov, E. (1999) *Refried Elvis: The Rise of the Mexican Counterculture*. London: University of California Press.

Website references

Echo and the Bunnymen Guitar Archive
http://cu.comp-unltd.com/~noneal/echo/echo.html
The U2 Guitar Archive
http://cu.comp-unltd.com/~noneal/right.html

INDEX